TOP 20

Great Grammar for Great Writing

Second Edition

Irene belyakov

TOP 20

Great Grammar for Great Writing

Second Edition

Keith S. Folse

Elena Vestri Solomon

Barbara Smith-Palinkas

HEINLE
CENGAGE Learning™

Detroit • New York • San Francisco • New Haven, Conn • Waterville, Maine • London

HEINLE
CENGAGE Learning™

Top 20, Second Edition

Folse/Solomon/Smith-Palinkas

Publisher: Sherrise Roehr

Acquisitions Editor, Academic ESL: Tom Jefferies

Director of Content Development: Anita Raducanu

Director of Product Marketing: Amy Mabley

International Marketing Manager: Ian Martin

Executive Marketing Manager: Jim McDonough

Senior Field Marketing Manager: Donna Lee Kennedy

Assistant Marketing Manager: Stephanie Blanchard

Development Editor: Kathleen Smith

Content Project Manager: Tan Jin Hock

Print Buyer: Susan Carroll

Production Management: Matrix Productions, Inc.

Compositor: Integra

Cover Designer: Dammora Inc.

Printer: Thomson West

Library of Congress Control Number: 2007926467

ISBN-13: 978-0-618-78967-2
ISBN-10: 0-618-78967-7

ISE ISBN-13: 978-1-4240-1748-5
ISE ISBN-10: 1-4240-1748-3

Heinle
25 Thomson Place
Boston, MA 02210
USA

Cengage Learning is a leading provider of customized learning solutions with office locations around the globe, including Singapore, the United Kingdom, Australia, Mexico, Brazil and Japan. Locate our local office at: **international.cengage.com/region**

Cengage Learning products are represented in Canada by Nelson Education, Ltd.

Visit Heinle online at **elt.heinle.com**
Visit our corporate website at **cengage.com**

Photo Credits
p. 10 © Peter Arnold/IndexOpen; p. 19, 29, 30 © Photos.com; p. 35 © photolibrary.com pty. ltd./Index Open; p. 45 © Index Open; p. 60 © Stewart Cohen/IndexOpen; p. 62 © Photos.com; p. 65 © FogStock LLC/IndexOpen; p. 72 © Photos.com; p. 79 © Franky De Meyer/iStockphoto; p. 105 © Photos.com; p. 107 © LLC, VStock/IndexOpen; p. 137 © LLC, VStock/IndexOpen; p. 151 © Bettmann/CORBIS; p. 154 © Pamela Moor/iStockphoto; p. 169 © Photos.com; p. 193 © Underwood Archive/IndexOpen; p. 208 © FogStock LLC/IndexOpen; p. 236 © IndexOpen; p. 240 © VStock LLC/IndexOpen; p. 249 (left) © Barry Winiken/IndexOpen, (right) © Cay-Uwe Kulzer/iStockphoto; p. 276 © VStock LLC/IndexOpen; p. 286 © Stewart Cohen/IndexOpen; p. 288 © Image DJ/IndexOpen; p. 291 © IndexOpen.

Printed in the United States of America
2 3 4 5 6 7 8 9 10 11 10 09 08

Contents

Overview

Top 20 reviews twenty grammar areas that are essential for good English writing at the intermediate to advanced level. In the review in *Top 20*, however, emphasis is placed on helping students to notice the gap between their own language and correct English. Therefore, the focus of *Top 20* is for students to produce and edit original pieces of writing as they learn how to find and correct common grammatical errors.

New to this Edition

Based on user feedback, the second edition of *Top 20* has been modified in the following ways:

- Inclusion of new chapters on conditionals and on editing essays.

- Revision and reordering of chapters to reflect a progression from nouns to pronouns to verbs.

- Streamlined chapter on confusing words to deal with the most commonly mistaken word pairs.

- Clearer grammar explanations.

- Inclusion of authentic grammar examples from actual academic textbooks. These examples represent seven academic disciplines most common to our students: law, history, psychology, humanities, communication, study skills, and physical science.

Course and Students

Depending on the class level and the amount of writing and work that is done outside of class, there is enough material in *Top 20* for seventy to ninety classroom hours. However, if time limitations exist, the material could be covered in as few as forty-five hours with an advanced-level group, provided that many of the exercises are done as homework.

This book is designed for intermediate to advanced students. However, the passages in many of the exercises are from real textbooks that were written for native speakers. Thus, students will have to understand the grammar points well to be able to apply them in the exercises.

For many students, a major obstacle to future educational plans is not being able to write effectively and easily in English, so the quality of any written work they do is very important. Poor grammar is often what keeps students from producing a solid piece of original writing. Because grammar is such an integral part of good student writing, the exercises in *Top 20* focus exclusively on grammar problems.

The title *Top 20* refers to the twenty chapters in the book. Each chapter focuses on a common area of difficulty in English grammar, including verb tenses, articles, gerunds and infinitives, noun clauses, modals, pronouns, subject-verb agreement, word forms, and parallel structure. We selected the topics in the chapters of *Top 20* after surveying many experienced teachers, student writers, textbooks, and course curricula.

You, the teacher, are always the best judge of which chapters should be covered and in which order and to what extent. No one knows the language needs of your students better than you do. It is up to you to gauge the needs of your students and then match those needs with the material presented in the chapters of *Top 20*.

Text Organization

As we have said, each of the twenty chapters focuses on one grammatical question that affects the quality of student writing. To facilitate customized instruction, each chapter is independent of all other chapters and can be taught in any order. In addition to the twenty chapters, with their specific grammatical focus, at the back of the book are four appendixes: Appendix 1 reviews the parts of speech; Appendix 2 briefly reviews how to construct comparative and superlative forms of adjectives and adverbs; Appendix 3 lists irregular verb forms; and Appendix 4 lists conjunctions and transitions and their functions.

Contents of a Chapter

Following is a description of the common features of each chapter and the types of exercises found in them.

Opening Discussion: Check Your Grammar

Each chapter opens with a Check Your Grammar exercise designed to test students' knowledge of the grammar point to be examined, using subject matter drawn from one of seven academic areas familiar to the majority of students. After the students have done the exercise and discussed their findings with a partner, it is up to the teacher to go over the exercise with the students to help them understand the nature of the grammar problem they will be studying.

Grammar Reviews and Explanations

The grammar reviews and explanations cover problems that characterize student *writing*, not speaking. *Top 20* is not meant to be a complete grammar book; instead, it reviews common problem areas and helps students focus their attention on the gap between what they are writing and what they should be writing. For this reason, certain grammar points have been given special emphasis, others very little. For example, we have not focused much on the future perfect tense because our analysis of student writing needs indicates that attention to other areas such as the present perfect and consistent verb tense usage is the more prudent approach.

Exercise Types

Second-language acquisition (SLA) research shows the importance of awareness in the second-language learning process. Students using this text have had basic grammar instruction, but many continue to make errors. The exercises in *Top 20* are designed to raise students' consciousness of the types of errors they make in their writing. Studies have also demonstrated that the number of exercises— frequency of practice—is as important as the nature of the exercises themselves (Folse 2006, Fotos 2002, and Laufer and Hulstijn 1998).

Original Sentences   Some exercises ask students to write original sentences to illustrate a very specific aspect of a given grammar point. We recommend that you have students discuss their answers in groups and possibly write some of their sentences on the board for general class discussion about what is correct, what is not correct, and why a gap between the two exists.

Selecting the Correct Form   Some exercises present students with two to three answer options, and students must underline or circle the correct answer. The incorrect answer options are almost always forms that students with various first languages would use. Thus, this kind of exercise is harder than it might appear.

Editing
▲ Exercise

Editing of Sentences   Because a paragraph is only as good as the sentences in it, the exercises on editing sentences present students with sentences one at a time. The sentences are often about a single topic and are related to each other. Students are asked to focus on one specific grammar issue—for example, verb tenses—and check for that specific grammar point in each of the sentences.

Editing of Paragraphs   In the exercises on editing paragraphs, students are given a paragraph written for native speakers. Common sources for the exercise text are business books, history books, education texts, speech books, sociology texts, the Internet, and newspapers. Students are not told where the errors are, but they are always told how many errors to look for or what type of errors there are.

These two points are important in helping students practice looking for, finding, and correcting *specific* errors that they are likely to be making. Since the teaching goal is to enable students to edit for specific kinds of errors, it makes sense to tell them what errors to look for. For example, if we want students to check for subject-verb agreement and word endings, then teachers and materials should train students to look for these particular mistakes. Instead of the more typical directions that ask students to find "the errors" in a given piece of writing, the most effective exercises direct students to find, for example, five errors: two subject-verb errors and three pronoun errors. In this way, student writers are actually editing for the types of errors that teachers want them to focus on.

Multiple Choice   Multiple-choice exercises follow the traditional format. Four choices are usually offered with only one choice being correct. The Chapter Quiz in each chapter follows this format as well.

Locating the Error   In error identification exercises, students read single sentences in which four words or phrases have been underlined. Students must circle the letter labeling the word or phrase that contains a grammatical error and then write their edited answer above the error. Error identification exercises are helpful in the overall SLA process because they can raise learners' consciousness of a linguistic feature by requiring learners to focus their attention on the difference, or gap, between the incorrect form and the correct form (Schmidt, 2001).

Original Writing   To achieve the goal of connecting grammar instruction and focused review, each chapter of *Top 20* ends with an exercise called Original Writing. Students are given a prompt to which they are asked to respond by writing a paragraph, two paragraphs, or an essay. (It is up to each teacher to establish the writing length parameters of any exercise.) We believe that students should not be writing extensively but rather intensively when the goal is to improve writing accuracy. Thus, this activity asks students to write a short piece, but the demands on grammar proficiency are high. Students are told to practice certain aspects of the grammar covered in the chapter, to underline their original examples, and to check their correctness with a partner. Underlining key linguistic features has been shown to enhance noticing and learning of new material.

More About the Exercises in Top 20

Teachers have long noticed that students may do well in a grammar class where the focus is on one grammatical form in one type of exercise, but these same students may experience writing problems when trying to transfer or apply this knowledge to original writing. For some reason, students do not transfer the material they have just been taught to their writing. As a result, the majority of the exercises in *Top 20* deal with language in context—that is, language in a series of related sentences, in a whole paragraph, or in a short essay. Our experience has shown that students can improve their editing for a specific kind of grammatical error when they review the grammar issue and then practice their editing skills in written exercises of various lengths (sentences, paragraphs, or essays). The 239 exercises in *Top 20* and the additional web activities offer more than enough material to satisfy most students' written-grammar needs.

Though a wide array of exercise types is included (see the previous section, Contents of a Chapter), the three exercises most commonly used are fill-in-the-blank, error correction (editing), and original student writing of paragraphs. The most important objectives of *Top 20* are to enable students to feel more comfortable with ESL grammar and to improve their writing by honing their editing skills. Consequently, the number and variety of exercises that students tackle are crucial to the success of *Top 20*.

References

Ferris, D. *Treatment of error in second language writing.* Ann Arbor: University of Michigan Press, 2002.

Folse, K. (2006). *The effect of type of written exercise on second language vocabulary retention.* TESOL *Quarterly 40*, 273–293.

Fotos, S. "Structure-based interactive tasks for the EFL grammar learner." In *New Perspectives on Grammar Teaching in Second Language Classrooms*, edited by E. Hinkel and S. Fotos, 135–154. Mahwah, New Jersey: Lawrence Erlbaum Associates, 2002.

Laufer, B., and J. Hulstijn. "What leads to better incidental vocabulary learning: Comprehensible input or comprehensible output?" Paper presented at the Pacific Second Language Research Forum (PacSLRF), Tokyo, March 1998.

Jourdenais, R., et al. "Does textual enhancement promote noticing: A think-aloud protocol analysis." In *Attention and awareness in foreign language learning*, edited by R. Schmidt, 183–216. University of Hawaii at Manoa, Second Language Teaching and Curriculum Center: Technical Report #9, 1995.

Schmidt, R. "Attention." In *Cognition and second language instruction*, edited by P. Robinson, 3–32. Cambridge: Cambridge University Press, 2001.

Acknowledgments

Top 20 is the result of the planning, input, and encouragement of a great many people. We are especially grateful to our editorial team at Houghton Mifflin, including Susan Maguire, Joann Koyzrev, and Kathy Sands-Boehmer, as well as our new team at Thomson Heinle, including Tom Jefferies. This second edition is truly a conglomerate work produced by many minds.

We wish to express our immense gratitude to Kathy Smith, our developmental editor, who so diligently helped us implement reviewers' and teachers' suggestions into the first and now this second edition. Without her contributions, *Top 20* would most certainly not be *Top 20*.

Thanks to the members of TESL-L, an invaluable means of communicating with ESL and EFL professionals all over the globe, who offered their ideas on the use of context in practicing grammar through writing, and to the hundreds of students and teachers who have given us feedback and ideas on our writing and grammar materials.

Finally, we thank these reviewers, whose comments were instrumental in the development of *Top 20*: Mary Burdick, Northern Essex CC; Lee Culver, Miami Dade College; Kathy Flynn, Glendale CC; Janet Harclerode, Santa Monica College; Mary Hill, North Shore CC; Nick Hilmers, DePaul University; Nancy Megarity, Collin County CC; Maria Spelleri, Manatee CC; Mo-Shuet Tam, City College of San Francisco; and Kent Trickel, Westchester CC.

Keith S. Folse
Elena Vestri Solomon
Barbara Smith-Palinkas

Nouns

In this chapter, you will review the forms and characteristics of nouns and the words that go with them. Two important categories of nouns are <u>count nouns</u> and <u>noncount nouns</u>. Briefly, count nouns name things that can be counted, such as *car* and *computer*. Noncount nouns name things that cannot be counted, such as *freedom* and *happiness*.

✓ CHECK YOUR GRAMMAR

Three of the five underlined words contain an error related to nouns. Can you explain why each of these underlined words is (or is not) wrong? Discuss with a partner.

The Environmental Protection Agency

The Environmental Protection <u>Agent</u> (EPA) was created by <u>Congress</u> in 1970 to replace the fifteen federal agencies that previously were <u>responsibility</u> for enforcing the <u>legals</u> that regulate environmental <u>pollution</u>.

From: Frank A. Schubert (2004). *Introduction to Law and the Legal System*. Boston: Houghton Mifflin, p. 665.

1.1   Count Nouns

Nouns that can be counted are called count nouns. They can be singular or plural in form.

Singular:	one subject	a problem	one reason	a child
Plural:	five subjects	two problems	three reasons	eight children

1.1.1   *Singular Count Nouns*

Singular count nouns, together with any descriptive adjectives, have an article (*a, an, the*) or another determiner before them (*my, your, this, one, every, each*).

an exam, a long exam, my brother, my oldest brother,

each chapter, each new chapter

Don't use a singular count noun without an article or other determiner.

Incorrect:	~~house~~	~~new house~~	~~car~~	~~old car~~
Correct:	a house	their new house	my car	our old car

However, in a few idiomatic expressions, no article is used:

have dinner   in school   at home   at work

by bus (*by* + transportation)   by phone (*by* + communication)

Exercise 1   Underline the fifteen singular count nouns that have articles or determiners. Circle the articles and determiners. The first one has been done for you.

Modern Households

By (the) end of the twentieth century, almost every person in the country owned at least one telephone and one television set. Most homes also had a washing machine, and many possessed a microwave oven. Since the beginning of the new millennium, the cellular phone has become commonplace, and most households now have a computer. The times have certainly changed. They have changed so much that most people cannot even imagine an evening at home without a computer or some other appliance.

1.1.2   *Plural Count Nouns*

Plural count nouns are sometimes preceded by the definite article *the* or by another determiner, or they may appear alone. Plural count nouns are NOT preceded by *a* or *an*.

Incorrect:	~~a houses~~	~~an expensive houses~~		
Correct:	the houses	some houses	big houses	some big houses

Regular Plurals

Most count nouns form their plural by adding *-s* to the singular noun.

cat / cats   tree / trees   taxi / taxis   sweater / sweaters

schedule / schedules   course / courses   professor / professors

Irregular Plurals

A few common count nouns have an irregular plural form.

man / men	woman / women	child / children	mouse / mice
fish / fish	tooth / teeth	foot / feet	person / people or persons
knife / knives	thesis / theses	criterion / criteria	fungus / fungi
self / selves	analysis / analyses	datum / data	focus / foci
life / lives	alumnus / alumni	medium / media	hypothesis / hypotheses
half / halves	sheep / sheep	hero / heroes	species / species

A few plural nouns do not have a singular form:

glasses   pants   jeans   scissors   tongs   clothes

Special Spellings of Plurals

A few types of count nouns form their plurals in a slightly different manner. Nouns ending in a CONSONANT + *y* form their plurals by changing the -*y* to -*i* and adding -*es*.

library / libraries   lady / ladies   copy / copies   theory / theories

This rule does *not* apply to nouns that end in a VOWEL + *y*.

tray / trays   monkey / monkeys   survey / surveys   boy / boys

Nouns ending in -*s*, -*ss*, -*sh*, -*ch*, -*x, and* -*z* add -*es* to form the plural.

class / classes   bush / bushes   bench / benches   box / boxes   quiz / quizzes

Editing
△ Exercise 2
Six of the ten underlined words and phrases in this paragraph contain an error. Circle the errors and write the corrections above.

Current Economic Indicators

All economic indicators are up. People are building <u>new houses</u> at a very high rate.
1

They are also buying <u>a new cars</u>. Among consumer products that are selling well are
2

cellular telephones, <u>computer</u>, and big-screen <u>TV sets</u>. Unemployment is low—<u>jobs</u>
3   **4**   **5**

are not difficult to find, but <u>a good employees</u> are. <u>Some firms</u> are offering bonuses
6   **7**

or stock options to attract <u>capable person</u>. <u>Interest rate</u> are at a comfortable level,
8   **9**

resulting in heavy sales of <u>consumer item</u>.
10

Exercise 3   Read the paragraph and underline the twenty-one plural nouns. Do not include possessive forms. Then circle the seven irregular plural nouns. The first one has been done for you.

Current Stress Research

Research has shown that everyone, even (children,) is subject to stress. In addition, statistics indicate that stress affects people's physical health, causing headaches and heart problems. After conducting surveys and collecting a large amount of data, some psychologists are now trying to determine the best methods for coping with stress. They are also testing various hypotheses to determine why some workers seem less affected by stress than their counterparts. Preliminary analyses seem to support the theory that people with adaptive skills and optimistic attitudes suffer fewer physical problems associated with stress. Finally, new research to measure the physical effects on health of both positive and negative stress in people's lives is under way. The results of this research will guide physicians in treating their patients who suffer from chronic stress.

1.2   Noncount Nouns

Nouns that cannot be counted are called noncount or mass nouns. They are used with singular verbs.

- Noncount nouns are often liquids or gases.

    water   air   oil   oxygen

- Noncount nouns often refer to a whole or a mass made up of small particles or items.

    sugar   salt   white sand
    new furniture   homework   good news
    equipment   money   expensive clothing

- Noncount nouns are often weather phenomena, fields of study, raw materials, abstractions, or sports and pastimes.

    rain   economics   gold   happiness   respect   soccer
    hot weather   psychology   hard coal   luck   satisfaction   cards

Note: *Cards* can be a noncount noun meaning a game of cards, or it can be a count noun meaning individual cards.

The following noncount nouns are often mistakenly used as plural count nouns:

Incorrect:	furnitures	advices	homeworks	equipments	informations
Correct:	furniture	advice	homework	equipment	information

Exercise 4 Read the paragraph and underline the seventeen count nouns. Draw a circle around the twelve noncount nouns. The first two have been done for you.

Protein

It is a commonly known <u>fact</u> that dairy products such as (milk,) yogurt, and cheese are rich sources of calcium, but how many people know that these food products are also loaded with protein? This is the reason that dietitians recommend that people consume two to four servings of this group each day. A glass of milk or a cup of yogurt has high-quality protein that is equivalent to an ounce of meat or cheese or to one egg. These food items are certainly good for your health. Whenever possible, however, you should opt for items that are not so high in fat.

1.2.1   *Comparing Noncount and Count Nouns*

Noncount nouns are like count nouns in certain ways.

1. Noncount nouns act like singular and plural count nouns.

   - Like singular and plural count nouns, noncount nouns may have certain determiners in front of them, such as the definite article *the* or the possessive adjectives *my* and *your.*

   - Possessive adjectives have the same forms in front of all three types of nouns: singular count nouns, plural count nouns, and noncount nouns.

   - You can use *this* and *that* with singular count nouns and noncount nouns; *these* and *those* can appear in front of plural count nouns only.

Singular Count Nouns		Plural Count Nouns		Noncount Nouns	
Determiner	**Example of noun**	**Determiner**	**Example of noun**	**Determiner**	**Example of noun**
the	car	**the**	cars	**the**	traffic
an	apple	**Ø**	apples	**Ø**	fruit
my, your	vegetable	**my, your**	vegetables	**my, your**	rice
his, her, its	job	**his, her, its**	jobs	**his, her, its**	work
our, their	job	**our, their**	jobs	**our, their**	work
this, that	cat	**these, those**	cats		

2. Noncount nouns act like plural count nouns. Like plural count nouns, noncount nouns may be preceded by determiners and certain expressions of quantity, or they may appear alone.

In the chart below, the determiners before plural count nouns and noncount nouns are the same.

Singular Count Nouns		Plural Count Nouns		Noncount Nouns	
Determiner	Example of noun	Determiner	Example of noun	Determiner	Example of noun
a	taxi	Ø	taxis	Ø	traffic
the	taxi	the	taxis	the	traffic
one	taxi	some	taxis	some	traffic
		a lot of	taxis	a lot of	traffic
		enough	taxis	enough	traffic
		plenty of	taxis	plenty of	traffic

Incorrect: Let's get taxi.
Correct: Let's get **a taxi.**

Remember that singular count nouns must have an article or determiner.

Some taxis have air conditioning.

There aren't **enough taxis** in this city.

Taxis are more comfortable than buses.

There will be **some traffic** on the highway tonight.

There is **plenty of traffic** on that narrow road.

Traffic is always heavy on weekends.

In the following chart, the determiners—certain expressions of quantity—before plural count nouns and noncount nouns are different.

Singular Count Nouns		Plural Count Nouns		Noncount Nouns	
Determiner	Example of noun	Determiner	Example of noun	Determiner	Example of noun
		many	taxis	much	traffic
		a few	taxis	a little	traffic
a/the/one	taxi	few	taxis	little	traffic
		several	taxis	a great deal of	traffic
		four	taxis		

Exercise 5 Underline the correct noun form(s) or determiner in each sentence. The first one has been done for you.

1. Dr. Rachel Lindstrom is studying a special aspect of (a biology / biology).

2. She is doing (research / a research) on (a certain plant / certain plants) and their products that countries export.

3. For example, Dr. Lindstrom has found that (some plants / a plants) contain substances that can fight (a diseases / a lot of diseases).

4. She and her colleagues now have (an information / enough information) to write (book / a book) about their investigations.

5. Specifically, this new volume will examine the consequences that can result from a country's (export / exports).

6. For example, does the fact that Colombia exports (several / a great deal of) coffee have any negative impact on Colombia?

7. In Ecuador, (many / much) types of bananas can be found all over. They are harvested and sent worldwide.

8. In the United States, bananas grow in only (a few / a little) places, so the fact that Ecuador exports its bananas is good for the United States. However, is there any negative effect of this exportation on Ecuador? Only time will tell.

Exercise 6   Read each sentence and underline the correct choice(s) in parentheses. The first one has been done for you.

Studying for the Law

Henry is studying at Harvard University; he's going to become (lawyer / <u>a lawyer</u>).
1
(A law / Law) is a difficult subject. It requires (a concentration / a lot of
2   **3**
concentration). (A lawyer / Lawyers) study in law school for three years. After law
4
school, the graduates have to take (a difficult examination / difficult examination).
5
(Some graduates / Some graduate) pass this examination, but others don't.
6
(A little graduates / A few graduates) take the examination a second or even a third
7
time. (Some people / A people) say that there aren't (enough good lawyer / enough
8   **9**
good lawyers). Others say that there aren't (many good lawyers / many good
10
lawyer). (Some lawyers / A lawyers) feel satisfied with (a work / their work).
11   **12**
(This lawyers / These lawyers) have clearly chosen the right profession. At the end
13
of each day, (satisfaction / satisfactions) with one's work is extremely important.
14

Exercise 7 Put a check mark (✔) beside each of the expressions that could be used correctly before each noun. The first one has been done for you.

_____ new student in our class didn't pass the test.

_____ students failed the test.

The students said that they had _____ information, but it was not enough.

__✔__ A	_____ A	_____ an
_____ Ø	_____ Ø	_____ Ø
_____ The	_____ Some	_____ some
_____ That	_____ Much	_____ the
_____ These	_____ A lot of	_____ enough
_____ Some	_____ A few	_____ a lot of
_____ Many	_____ A little	_____ many
_____ Much	_____ Enough	_____ a few
_____ Enough	_____ Several	_____ a little
_____ A few	_____ Four	_____ one
_____ Two	_____ That	_____ those
_____ Plenty of	_____ Plenty of	_____ plenty of
_____ A great deal of	_____ A great deal of	_____ a great deal of

Editing
▲ **Exercise 8** Read the following article from a business publication. If the underlined noun phrase is incorrect, write your corrected edit on the line. If it is correct, write *correct* on the line.

1. _____   6. _____

2. _____   7. _____

3. _____   8. _____

4. _____   9. _____

5. _____   10. _____

Small Business Success

In today's world, what does it take to make a business succeed? <u>A study</u> of
$\underset{1}{}$
hundreds of successful small businesses found they had <u>much characteristics</u> in
$\underset{2}{}$
common. It found that the owners of successful businesses:

- have <u>enough time</u> to devote to the business, typically 60+ hours each week;
  $\underset{3}{}$
- have <u>many capital</u> to cover costs for six months;
  $\underset{4}{}$
- provide <u>an adequate training</u> to each employee;
  $\underset{5}{}$
- provide close supervision of new employees;

- treat both customers and employees with <u>a great deal of respect</u>
  $\underset{6}{}$
- request feedback from customers.

Second, the employees of successful businesses:

- have sufficient education to handle the job;

- understand <u>the importance</u> of customer service;
  $\underset{7}{}$
- earn <u>good salary</u> and have access to health insurance;
  $\underset{8}{}$
- receive <u>a little weeks of vacation</u> every year;
  $\underset{9}{}$
- have some flexibility in work hours;

- receive <u>a regular feedback</u> on their performance from their supervisor.
  $\underset{10}{}$

Editing

⚠ Exercise 9   In eleven of the underlined noun phrases, the quantifiers are used incorrectly. Find the errors and make the corrections. More than one option may be correct. Use Ø to indicate that no article or other quantifier is needed.

Rainforest Island

Rainforest Island has been treated extremely well by <u>nature</u>. It has <u>much dense forests</u>, which produce <u>beautiful wood</u>. On the north side of the island it has <u>mountains</u> where <u>a coffee</u> is grown. In the southern area, there are thousands of acres of <u>bananas</u> and <u>one sugar</u> there as well. The island exports <u>a lot of wood, coffee, bananas, and sugar</u>. There are other resources to be developed, too. The eastern shore has <u>a beautiful beaches</u> and would be ideal for tourism; so far, however, tourism has not brought <u>many money</u>. There are only <u>a little hotels</u> on the island, and these are not in good condition. There is <u>a good news</u>, though; the Islands Hotel Investment Group is planning to invest heavily in the area. This will result in <u>much excellent facilities</u> and will provide <u>many work</u> for the inhabitants of the island. Even more important, at the end of the twentieth century, <u>a few oil</u> was discovered just off the northern shore. Since then, scientists have found that there is <u>many oil</u> underneath the island. Until now, Rainforest Island has had to depend on agriculture, but in the future—with <u>oil and tourism</u> about to be developed—it is likely that there will be <u>some changes</u> in the character of the island.

Exercise 10 Circle the letter of the correct answer. Be prepared to explain your answers.

1. We need to buy _____ for the living room.

   A. a new furniture   C. new furnitures

   B. new furniture   D. a few new furnitures

2. I got _____ wonderful news today! I'm getting a 10% raise.

   A. a   C. a few

   B. some   D. those

3. Before we decide where to go on vacation, we have to get _____ information about

   hotel costs.

   A. an   C. some

   B. a few   D. one

4. My son spends too _____ watching television.

   A. much time   C. many time

   B. much times   D. many times

5. David, can you give me _____ about asking for a promotion at work?

   A. an advice   C. some advices

   B. some advice   D. advices

6. Since we moved into this neighborhood, the kids have made _____ new friends and

   have spent _____ time with them, so I think they're adjusting OK.

   A. a little ... a few   C. a little ... a little

   B. a few ... a little   D. a few ... a few

7. Carol: What time do you want to _____?

   David: Not too late. Jan is giving us a ride to the restaurant, but we have to come home

   _____, remember?

   A. have dinner ... by a bus   C. have dinner ... by bus

   B. have a dinner ... by bus   D. have a dinner ... by a bus

8. We need to help the kids with their _____ tonight. That's _____ important part of

   our family routine.

   A. homeworks ... a very   C. homeworks ... very

   B. homework ... very   D. homework ... a very

Exercise 11   Write a paragraph about a field of study or a job you are interested in. Include at least five items about the field or job that you like. Include the following expressions in your essay: *a, some, several, many, a lot of, much, a little, little, a few, few, a great deal of, plenty of,* and *enough.* Then underline all the count and noncount nouns and have a partner check to see if the articles and determiners are correct.

_____

_____

_____

_____

_____

_____

_____

_____

_____

_____

_____

_____

_____

_____

_____

_____

_____

_____

_____

_____

_____

2 Articles: *a, an, the*

Articles—those little words that can be so difficult to use correctly—introduce and identify nouns. There are two kinds of articles in English: indefinite (a, an) and definite (the). Articles occur before nouns (the book) and before adjective + noun combinations (a big book).

✔ CHECK YOUR GRAMMAR

Five of the eight underlined words or phrases contain an error related to articles. Can you explain why each of these underlined areas is (or is not) wrong? Discuss with a partner.

> ### Architecture—More Than Solving Problems
>
> In <u>the architecture</u>, as in any art, it is never enough to solve <u>a problem</u>. Building forms have <u>the profound</u> effect on <u>the quality</u> of life; <u>the painting</u> and <u>the sculpture</u> reflect, comment on, and affect <u>future</u> of the arts and of <u>humanity</u>.

From: M. Witt, Brown, C., Dunbar, R., Tirro, F., and Witt, R. (2005). *The Humanities: Cultural Roots and Continuities*, 7th ed., Vol. 1. Boston: Houghton Mifflin, p. 304.

2.1 Article Basics

This chart gives you the basic uses of articles in English. (For a review of count and noncount nouns, see Chapter 1.)

Articles			
	Count Nouns		**Noncount Nouns**
Indefinite articles (a, an)	a cat	cats	money
	an ugly cat	ugly cats	
	an answer	answers	
Definite article (the)	the cat	the cats	the money

2.1.1 Three Rules for Avoiding Common Article Mistakes

The following three rules, repeated later in the chapter, are grouped here because they are the main rules that will help you avoid the most common mistakes with articles.

1. Use *a, an,* or *the* (or another word such as *my* or *this*) with singular count nouns.

Incorrect:	Most university students own computer.
Correct:	Most university students own **a** computer.

2. Use *the* with specific noun references, either singular or plural. Specific noun references are definite.

Incorrect:	Title of this course sounds interesting.
Correct:	**The** title of this course sounds interesting.
Incorrect:	Questions on yesterday's grammar test were difficult.
Correct:	**The** questions on yesterday's grammar test were difficult.

3. Do not use *the* with general noun references, either singular or plural. General noun references are indefinite.

Incorrect:	Our government should spend more money on ~~the~~ education.
Correct:	Our government should spend more money on education.
Incorrect:	~~The~~ successful presentations require planning and practice.
Correct:	Successful presentations require planning and practice.

Exercise 1 As you read the paragraph, fill in each blank with *a, an, the,* or Ø. Be prepared to explain your answer choice using information from one of the three rules discussed in Section 2.1.1. The first one has been done for you.

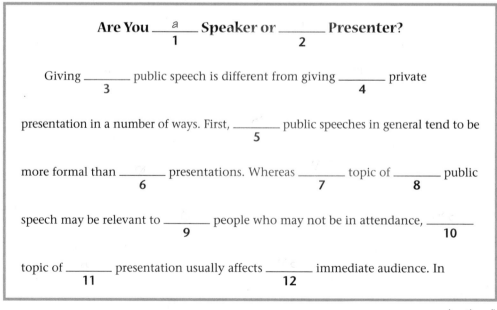

Are You __*a*__ Speaker or _____ Presenter?
      1   2

Giving _____ public speech is different from giving _____ private
          3   4

presentation in a number of ways. First, _____ public speeches in general tend to be
                                              5

more formal than _____ presentations. Whereas _____ topic of _____ public
                      6   7   8

speech may be relevant to _____ people who may not be in attendance, _____
                              9   10

topic of _____ presentation usually affects _____ immediate audience. In
             11   12

(continued)

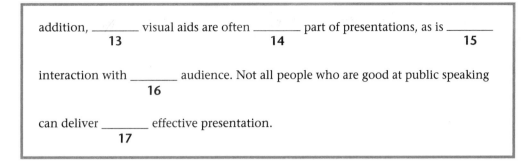

addition, _____ visual aids are often _____ part of presentations, as is _____
             13   **14**   **15**

interaction with _____ audience. Not all people who are good at public speaking
                         16

can deliver _____ effective presentation.
                 17

2.2   Indefinite Articles

The indefinite articles are *a* and *an*. Use *a* and *an* with indefinite singular count nouns. Here are the main rules for indefinite articles.

2.2.1   *Uses*

1. Use *a* and *an* to introduce a singular count noun.

   Let's take **a** speech class this semester.

   There is **an** excellent show on TV tonight.

2. Use *a* and *an* to define or classify something.

   Jambalaya is **a** rice dish that is native to south Louisiana.

   My brother is **an** investigator for the city health department.

3. Use *a* and *an* to show that you are talking about one (of the item).

   Excuse me. Do you have **a** pencil that I could borrow?

   I need **an** eraser, as well.

Do not use *one* interchangeably to mean *a*. "Do you have one pencil?" emphasizes the *number,* not the *pencil.*

Special time expressions: One is used before *day, week, month,* and so forth, to refer to a particular time when something occurred, as in "One day I visited the new museum in town."

4. Use *a* and *an* for a general truth about a singular count noun. Reference is to all or most of the members in the group. (Note that a plural count noun without any article expresses the same idea.)

   A piano has 96 keys. (= Pianos have 96 keys.)

   A teacher should plan lessons. (= Teachers should plan lessons.)

We do not usually use an article with a noncount noun. Articles *can* be used with abstract nouns that are derived from verbs.

   Time is money. (no article)

   Hospitals saw **a** demand for better care. (abstract noun)

Exercise 2   Read the sentences and determine which of the four rules applies to the underlined noun or noun phrase. Put the rule number(s) in the blank. The first one has been done for you.

1. ___3___ Georgia O'Keeffe was <u>an American painter</u> born in 1887 near Sun Prairie, Wisconsin.

2. _____ O'Keeffe grew up on <u>a dairy farm</u> and knew at <u>an early age</u> that she wanted to be <u>an artist</u>.

3. _____ She held jobs as <u>a commercial artist</u> and as <u>a teacher</u> before moving to New York in 1918.

4. _____ In New York, O'Keeffe found <u>a new life</u> with Alfred Stieglitz, a photographer and owner of the 291 gallery.

5. _____ In 1928, she took <u>a vacation</u> and went to Taos, New Mexico.

6. _____ The trip had <u>an impact</u> of such enormity that it changed her life forever. She referred to northern New Mexico as "the faraway."

7. _____ New Mexico was <u>a place</u> with wide vistas and far-reaching horizons. O'Keeffe bought <u>a Model A Ford</u> with which to explore the back roads of her new home.

8. _____ O'Keeffe's large-flower paintings have been referred to as <u>a woman's art style</u>, as though art created by <u>a woman</u> differed from that made by <u>a man</u>.

9. _____ Today O'Keeffe remains <u>an important contributor</u> to American art of the twentieth century.

2.3	**Definite Article *the***

The definite article is *the*. Use *the* with definite singular, plural, and noncount nouns. Use *the* to indicate that you are referring to something specific. Here are the main rules for definite articles.

2.3.1	*Uses*

1. Use *the* to refer to a specific thing or person. This includes nouns made specific by prepositional phrases or adjective clauses.

   Specific: **The** window in the kitchen has been closed all day.

   General: **A** window is usually rectangular in shape. (= Windows are usually rectangular in shape.)

Specific: **The** pilots who work for that airline will go on strike at midnight.

General: **A** pilot wears a uniform. (= Pilots wear a uniform.)

2. Use *the* for the second and all subsequent references to the same item. Note that sometimes different nouns are used to refer to the same thing. Using a variety of vocabulary items with the article *the* is an excellent device for coherence in your writing.

> **A *deadly car crash*** (noun A—first reference) involving ***three vehicles*** (noun B—first reference) occurred on Highway 62 last night. Police said that **the *wreck*** (noun A—second reference) happened just after midnight. Though damage to **the *three cars*** (noun B—second reference) appeared to be minimal, **the *accident*** (noun A—third reference) claimed two lives.

Crash → *wreck* → *accident:* Notice how *crash* becomes *wreck* and then becomes *accident.* *Vehicles* → *cars: Vehicles* becomes *cars.* These different words still refer to the same original thing, and the article changes from indefinite (*a*) to definite (*the*).

3. Use *the* with a superlative, with a ranking, or with a comparison between amounts.

> Many sports offer good exercise, but tennis is **the** best sport for people of all ages.

> **The** third part of any joke is usually the punch line.

> **The** more time you spend editing, **the** more corrections you'll make.

4. Use *the* with the parts of something or members of a group.

> I like this watch. **The** minute hand is blue, and **the** hour hand is red.

> Today **the** small-business owner finds it hard to compete against superstores.

The is used to talk about a body part in a more formal way, for example, in science or health discussion.

> **The** stomach contains special liquids to help with digestion.

However, when we are referring to our own bodies, we use possessive adjectives, not *the.*

> **My** stomach hurts because I ate all the chocolates.

5. Use *the* when the item is known to both the writer and the reader (or to the speaker and the listener), when the context makes it clear, or when there is only one possible item.

> Rick: Where's your phone?

> Cara: It's next to **the** refrigerator.

6. Use *the* in general statements about a whole species (kind), class, or category.

> **The** Apple computer was not developed by Bill Gates.

> **The** green sea turtle is on the threatened and endangered list.

> More medicine is needed for **the** sick. (*the sick* = sick people)

The use of *the* + SINGULAR NOUN is more formal than the more conversational style of using **plural** + no article.

> **The tiger** is native to India. (formal) **Tigers** are native to India. (less formal)

7. Use *the* with unique, one-of-a-kind items (especially when talking about nature).

> **The** sun is shining directly overhead.
>
> Take a look at **the** sky! **The** clouds are moving fast today.
>
> There's nothing you can do to change **the** past, so plan for **the** future.

8. Use *the* with certain proper nouns: oceans; seas; rivers; groups of islands, lakes, mountains; deserts; plural names of countries; areas identified by direction words; buildings; schools with *of / for*; and sports teams.

the Atlantic Ocean	**the** Hawaiian Islands	**the** United States
the Sears Tower	**the** University of Texas	**the** Academy for the Arts
the Boston Red Sox	**the** North	

Exercise 3   As you read the paragraph, fill in each blank with *a* or *the.* The first one has been done for you.

<u>The</u> **Wainwright and Reliance Buildings**
                     1

_____ Wainwright Building in St. Louis, Missouri, has all _____ elements
          2   3
of _____ modern skyscraper: _____ entire building is carried on _____
        4   5   6
fireproofed steel frame, and its three sections are connected in relation to their

functions: ground-floor shops and entry, midsection offices, and topmost floors

where mechanical systems were placed. It should be compared with _____
                                                                          7
Reliance Building, designed by Burnham and Root. Built in _____ summer of
                                                                  8
1891, it is also _____ self-supporting metal cage with glass infill. It was simple to
                  9
erect and maintain. _____ walls were great expanses of glass, some fixed, some
                       10
movable panels, providing light and ventilation for _____ offices lining each side
                                                          11
of its central corridor. Visually, _____ building is _____ very clear expression
                                      12   13
of its function, which is to be tall, economical, and useful. Chicagoans pointed with

pride to _____ development of _____ "Commercial Style," but some critics felt
            14   15
its simple expression of function through form was too commercial. It would not be

until after World War I that _____ tradition would be completely broken.
                                16

Adapted from Witt et al., *The Humanities,* 7th ed., Vol. 1, p. 304.

2.4 No Article (ø)

In English, articles are not always necessary with nouns. Here are the main rules indicating when no article is needed before a noun.

2.4.1 *Uses*

1. No article is needed when you are referring to the whole group, class, or category.

   Most people agree that more **tax money** should be spent on **education.**

   We need to buy **furniture** for the new house.

   Tigers are native to India.

2. No article is needed when you are referring to a thing in general, rather than to a specific member of a group.

   The most popular subjects are **English, math,** and **world history.**

   Love is easier for some people to express than for others.

   I've never been interested in studying **nature.**

   Beaches offer a place to play or to relax.

Exception: Use an article when you refer to a specific kind within a general thing.

   I understand English well, but I sometimes have difficulty understanding **the English spoken by young children.**

   The love he felt for his children couldn't be measured in words.

   He developed a sudden interest in **the nature of rainforests.**

   The beach he runs on is pure white sand.

3. No article is needed with names of cities, states, countries, and continents. Exceptions include place names with the words *united, union,* or *republic of,* as well as plural names. (See Section 2.3, Rule 8.)

   New York   **Florida**   **France**   **Argentina**   **Asia**   **North America**

4. No article is needed with a (single) lake, but use *the* with all other bodies of water. (See Section 2.3, Rule 8.)

(Exception: the Great Salt Lake)

   Lake Michigan   **Lake Tikal**   **Lake Okeechobee**   **Lake Victoria**

5. No article is needed with directions, but use *the* with areas identified by direction words.

   Go **north** on the highway. I live **south** of the city.

   He lives in **the South.** (the southern part of the U.S.)

6. No article is needed with diseases:

> **HIV**   **AIDS**   **cancer**   **cholera**   **heart disease**   **diabetes**

Some exceptions to this rule include the following:

> **the flu**   **the measles**   **the mumps**   **the chicken pox**

Use *a* with injuries, symptoms, and other nondiseases:

> **a cold**   **a headache**   **a heart attack**   **a broken leg**

7. No article is needed with the names of people, businesses, and most magazines.

> **Dr. Jenk's** office is next to **Brenda's** office.
>
> **Microsoft** has its head office in the state of Washington.
>
> I just bought a subscription to **Newsweek.**

Exception: With a person's title that has no proper name, use the article.

> This is **the President.**

8. No article is needed with months, dates, days, holidays, or seasons.

> Christmas is **December** 25th.   My birthday is **January 23rd.**
>
> Classes start on **Tuesday.**   **Valentine's Day** is next week.
>
> We travel to California every **winter.**

Exception: Use *the* with dates in a phrase using the preposition *of*:

> **the 12th of August**

9. No article is needed with chapters, numbers, highways, and interstates.

> Please read **Chapter 8** for tomorrow and answer question **number 15.**
>
> Can you tell me whether **Highway 60** will take me to **Interstate 95?**

10. No article is needed with commonplace words in certain idiomatic expressions. No article implies that an activity is taking place at that location; **the** refers to the place of the activity.

> He is **at home** now. (NOT at *the* home)
>
> He's **at work.** (NOT at *the* work)
>
> Marguerite is still **in bed.** (NOT in *the* bed)
>
> They're **on vacation.** (NOT on *the* vacation)

Exercise 4 As you read the paragraph, fill in each blank with *the* or Ø. The first one has been done for you.

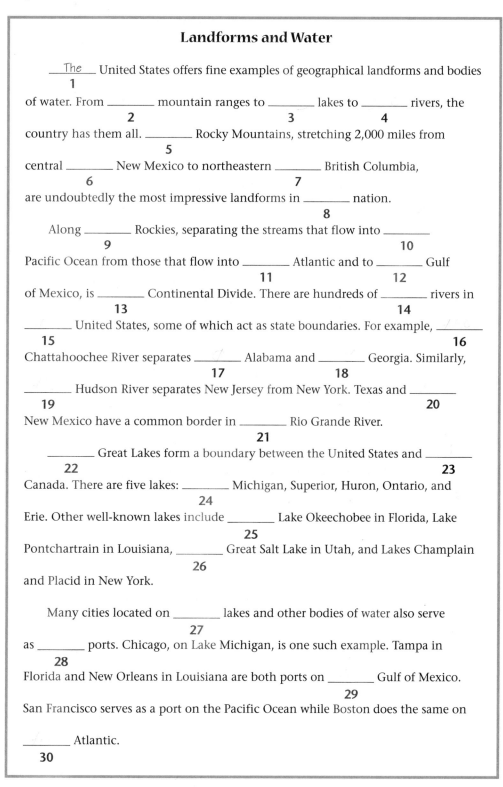

Landforms and Water

___The___ United States offers fine examples of geographical landforms and bodies
    1
of water. From _____ mountain ranges to _____ lakes to _____ rivers, the
        2   **3**   **4**
country has them all. _____ Rocky Mountains, stretching 2,000 miles from
          5
central _____ New Mexico to northeastern _____ British Columbia,
      6   **7**
are undoubtedly the most impressive landforms in _____ nation.
         8

Along _____ Rockies, separating the streams that flow into _____
    9   **10**
Pacific Ocean from those that flow into _____ Atlantic and to _____ Gulf
        11   **12**
of Mexico, is _____ Continental Divide. There are hundreds of _____ rivers in
      13   **14**
_____ United States, some of which act as state boundaries. For example, _____
  15   **16**
Chattahoochee River separates _____ Alabama and _____ Georgia. Similarly,
                17   **18**
_____ Hudson River separates New Jersey from New York. Texas and _____
  19   **20**
New Mexico have a common border in _____ Rio Grande River.
                 21
_____ Great Lakes form a boundary between the United States and _____
  22   **23**
Canada. There are five lakes: _____ Michigan, Superior, Huron, Ontario, and
              24
Erie. Other well-known lakes include _____ Lake Okeechobee in Florida, Lake
           25
Pontchartrain in Louisiana, _____ Great Salt Lake in Utah, and Lakes Champlain
        26
and Placid in New York.

Many cities located on _____ lakes and other bodies of water also serve
         27
as _____ ports. Chicago, on Lake Michigan, is one such example. Tampa in
  28
Florida and New Orleans in Louisiana are both ports on _____ Gulf of Mexico.
                         29
San Francisco serves as a port on the Pacific Ocean while Boston does the same on

_____ Atlantic.
  30

Exercise 5 As you read the paragraph, fill in each blank with *the* or Ø.

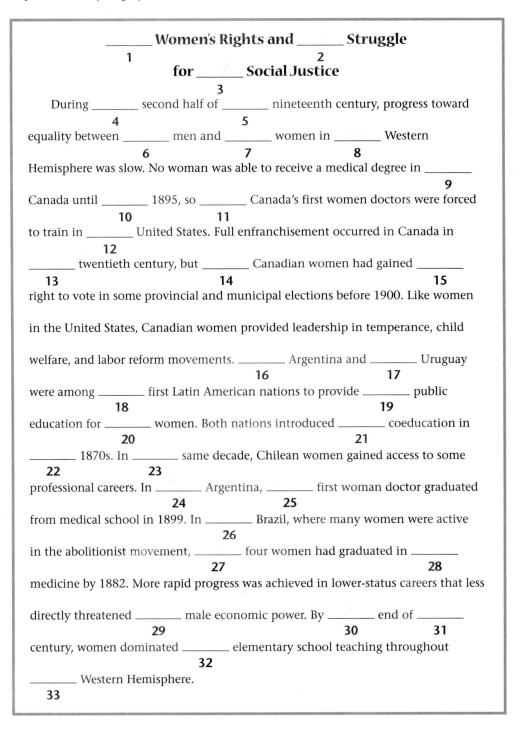

_____ Women's Rights and _____ Struggle
1   2
for _____ Social Justice
3

During _____ second half of _____ nineteenth century, progress toward
4   5

equality between _____ men and _____ women in _____ Western
6   7   8

Hemisphere was slow. No woman was able to receive a medical degree in _____
9

Canada until _____ 1895, so _____ Canada's first women doctors were forced
10   11

to train in _____ United States. Full enfranchisement occurred in Canada in
12

_____ twentieth century, but _____ Canadian women had gained _____
13   14   15

right to vote in some provincial and municipal elections before 1900. Like women

in the United States, Canadian women provided leadership in temperance, child

welfare, and labor reform movements. _____ Argentina and _____ Uruguay
16   17

were among _____ first Latin American nations to provide _____ public
18   19

education for _____ women. Both nations introduced _____ coeducation in
20   21

_____ 1870s. In _____ same decade, Chilean women gained access to some
22   23

professional careers. In _____ Argentina, _____ first woman doctor graduated
24   25

from medical school in 1899. In _____ Brazil, where many women were active
26

in the abolitionist movement, _____ four women had graduated in _____
27   28

medicine by 1882. More rapid progress was achieved in lower-status careers that less

directly threatened _____ male economic power. By _____ end of _____
29   30   31

century, women dominated _____ elementary school teaching throughout
32

_____ Western Hemisphere.
33

↑ Exercise 6   Read the following paragraph. There are twelve mistakes in article usage. The first one has been done for you. Find the additional eleven and correct them.

A Vacation to Remember

Ø
I'll never forget my first trip to ~~the~~ Florida. It was in the September of 1980.

I went to Naples for a week and rented one hotel room on beach. During my visit,

I had both positive and negative experiences. I got a sun poisoning. I walked on

the beach. I thought a manatee was the shark. I ate lots of good seafood. I collected

the shells. I went sailing in Gulf of Mexico. I watched sun set every evening. I saw

different kinds of palm trees. I experienced the real meaning of the humidity. I fell

in love with the climate. After my vacation, when I was back at the work, I made a

decision to move to Florida some day. It took more than fifteen years, but the one

day came when I packed my car and drove south. I never looked back.

Exercise 7   In each lettered item, one of the four underlined words or phrases is not correct. Circle the letter of the error and write the correction above the error.

1. If <u>you have</u> <u>the</u> good study skills, you will do well on <u>exams</u> and have
      A   **B**   **C**

    <u>confidence</u>.
    D

2. If <u>you are a little late in turning in</u> your <u>paper</u>, there's <u>a</u> good chance you will get
               A   **B**   **C**

    <u>the low grade</u>.
     D

3. <u>The</u> university library, <u>the only</u> building that can <u>offer quiet place</u> to study, serves
    A   **B**   **C**

    <u>as a meeting place</u> for many students.
         D

4. <u>When scheduling study time</u>, <u>good student</u> will allow <u>three hours of study time</u>
          A   **B**   **C**

    for each <u>hour of class</u> attended.
         D

Exercise 8   Circle the letter of the correct answer. Be prepared to explain your answers.

1. The professor believed that the student's paper was not her own original writing, so he wrote "plagiarized" across the top of the first page. However, according to the student, there was no proof of _____.

   A. plagiarism in research paper   C. the plagiarism in research paper

   B. the plagiarism in the research paper   D. plagiarism in the research paper

2. "I don't know which of these courses I should take. I need _____. Can you recommend one?"

   A. a good three-credit English course   C. good three-credit English course

   B. the good three-credit English course   D. a good three-credit English courses

3. _____ are awarded during a ceremony at the end of each semester.

   A. Degrees at an university   C. Degrees at a university

   B. A degree at universities   D. A degree at a university

4. Many universities have medical laboratories that carry out _____. These research studies conducted at universities often lead to _____ medical discoveries.

   A. the research ... exciting   C. the research ... the exciting

   B. research ... exciting   D. research ... the exciting

5. Be sure to take advantage of _____ that is offered to incoming freshman.

   A. the advising   C. an advising

   B. one advising   D. advisings

6. _____ thing that all students have to do at _____ of each semester is take their final exams.

   A. Last ... the end   C. The last ... the end

   B. Last ... end   D. The last ... end

7. _____ diploma is often a guarantee to _____ job.

   A. University ... a high-paying   C. University ... high-paying

   B. A university ... high-paying   D. A university ... a high-paying

8. In general, students' grade point averages, or GPAs, are higher than they were just _____ years ago. For this reason, _____ educators wonder how they can limit the grade inflation that they see in their schools.

   A. ten ... the many   C. the ten ... the many

   B. ten ... many   D. the ten ... many

Exercise 9 Write a paragraph about an important event in history. Identify the event, when it happened, why it happened, why it was important, who was involved, and so on. In your concluding sentence, write your opinion regarding this event or the importance of this event. Exchange paragraphs with a partner. Circle all the articles on your partner's paper and check for their correct use.

3 Pronouns and Possessive Adjectives

Pronouns are similar to nouns because they often take the place of subjects or objects. In this chapter, you will review several important types of pronouns. You will also learn about possessive adjectives, which are easily confused with pronouns.

✔ CHECK YOUR GRAMMAR

Two of the four underlined words contain an error related to pronouns and possessive adjectives. Can you explain why each of these underlined areas is (or is not) wrong? Discuss with a partner.

> ### The Impact of English Ideas
>
> The American Revolution and the events that followed <u>them</u> reflected the impact of English ideas on a pioneering society. The colonists worked well together at the local level in meeting <u>their</u> common needs. Beginning as <u>they</u> did—in a new environment—the colonists were critical of any limitation on <u>his</u> freedom.

Adapted from: Witt et al., *The Humanities*, p. 220.

3.1 Common Pronouns

These are the most common English pronouns:

Subject pronouns:	I	you	he / she / it	we	you	they	who
Object pronouns:	me	you	him / her / it	us	you	them	whom

In general, don't use a pronoun if you have yet to mention the noun. The word that the pronoun refers to is called the *antecedent* (coming before).

?
I don't like to eat **it.** (Object pronoun; we have no idea what *it* is; there is no antecedent. Remember: An antecedent is the noun that a pronoun refers to.)

My mother is making *lasagna*. I don't like to eat **it.** (In the first sentence, *lasagna* is the antecedent of the pronoun *it*.)

Note: If a noun and a pronoun connected with *and* are in the subject or object position in a sentence, the noun should be listed first.

Incorrect: ~~I and my classmates~~ will be studying for the final exam all weekend.

Correct: **My classmates and I** will be studying for the final exam all weekend.

Exercise 1 Read the following sentences. Change the underlined nouns to pronouns. Use the subject and object pronouns from the list on page 27. The first one has been done for you.

Our Busy Lives

My sister Sheila is in medical school. <u>Sheila</u> *(She)* is one of the busiest people I know.
<u> </u>
1

My brothers, on the other hand, want to become famous athletes, so <u>my brothers</u>
2

spend a lot of time practicing to become better at sprinting and running. I myself

am busy studying literature with Dr. Smith. He is a great professor, but his lectures are

repetitive. I am tired of listening to <u>Dr. Smith</u> and his lectures. When my sister comes
3

home on weekends, <u>my sister</u> often goes to the cineplex with <u>my brothers and me</u>.
4   **5**

Everyone in my family is usually too busy to do things together. However, my

family is planning a trip to Spain next year. <u>My family and I</u> have never been to
6

Spain, so we are very excited about seeing <u>Spain</u>. Madrid and Barcelona are two of
7

the most famous cities in Spain. <u>These cities</u> offer many things to do, and thousands
8

of tourists travel to <u>these cities</u> every year. If everything goes well, we will all take a
9

break from our busy lives and have a great vacation. I am certainly looking forward

to <u>this vacation</u>.
10

3.2 Object Pronouns Used After Prepositions

Use the object pronoun in prepositional phrases, even if the prepositional phrase comes at the beginning of the sentence.

> According to **them,** it's not easy to get into that field.
>
> Besides **me,** a lot of people are signing up for Dr. Winston's class.
>
> I will never forget our trip to France and the Eiffel Tower standing grandly in front of **us.**

Exercise 2 As you read the following sentences, put an object or a subject pronoun in the blanks. The first one has been done for you.

1. Rachel Williams, who is the Vice-President of Marketing for Ex-Co, was supposed to run today's important stockholders' meeting, but ___*she*___ was not able to attend the meeting.

2. Instead, Miguel Rodriguez, Ex-Co's well-known but not so popular CEO, stepped in to run the meeting. According to _____, the company's stock has lost 20 percent of its value this quarter, a negative trend that is expected to continue for at least another fiscal year.

3. This loss will most definitely affect the merchants. These merchants bargained for the sale of Ex-Co's goods, but _____ weren't successful at maintaining their target prices.

4. Most of Ex-Co's employees, however, blamed the company's losses on Paul Lee, the company's financial analyst. Because of _____, the proposed increases in salary didn't go through.

5. The bureaucracy in certain corporations is staggering. However, with a new restructuring plan, _____ should decrease as time goes by.

6. Ex-Co's employees don't have much confidence in this new plan. _____ want to organize a walkout if the changes are not implemented smoothly.

7. According to business analysts who follow the ups and downs of Ex-Co, all of these problems are not surprising. With the economy so sluggish, it is no surprise that employees are unhappy with the current situation. Knowing the company all too well, _____ do not see a happy ending for themselves or for Ex-Co.

3.3 Possessive Pronouns Versus Possessive Adjectives

It's easy to confuse possessive pronouns with possessive adjectives. Remember that possessive adjectives, like all adjectives, describe something. They are always used with a noun. Their function is to show ownership—to *whom* does the object belong?

Did you get **your** *car* repaired today?

Compare possessive adjectives with possessive pronouns, which take the place of nouns and are used alone. Nouns do not follow possessive pronouns.

I just got **my** *car* repaired. When will you get **yours** repaired?

This chart compares possessive adjectives with possessive pronouns:

Possessive Adjectives	Possessive Pronouns
my + NOUN	mine
your + NOUN	yours
his, her, its + NOUN	his, hers
our + NOUN	ours
your + NOUN	yours
their + NOUN	theirs

Exercise 3 Read the paragraph and fill in the blanks with the correct possessive adjective or possessive pronoun. The first one has been done for you.

Choosing Your University

(continued)

Choosing a university is not an easy task. First, you must decide what _your_ **1**

major is going to be. Why is this important? Many schools are famous for certain

fields of study, so a university that is famous for _____ business program might
2

not be a good choice for people who want English literature to be _____ field of
3

study. A friend of _____, James, decided to study at the University of Michigan
4

because it has an excellent language program. _____ parents wanted him to stay
5

in California and go to UCLA, but for the program he was interested in, going to

a school in Michigan made more sense. Another important factor is tuition. For

example, my brother, who worked part time throughout high school, was able to

get into a private university. The cost of _____ university is much higher than
6

_____, which, as a public university, costs me 70 percent less per year. _____
7   **8**

choice was purely economic. The bottom line is this: Whatever university you

decide on, make the best of _____ choice and take advantage of everything the
9

university has to offer. It can be one of the most important decisions of _____ life.
10

3.3.1   *Possessive Pronouns and Antecedent Agreement*

In writing, one of the most prevalent pronoun errors occurs with agreement. Make sure
that pronouns always agree with their antecedents in number (singular or plural), and in
gender. (See Section 3.1 for a definition of *antecedent*.)

The *boys* always ride to school on **their** bikes.

The possessive adjective *their* (plural) agrees with the noun *boys* (plural).

Britney usually calls **her** friends after school.

The possessive adjective *her* agrees with the noun *Britney* (singular, feminine).

Incorrect: Each *person* in this class should have ~~their~~ own textbook.

The possessive adjective *their* is plural, but its antecedent, *person*, is singular. You can correct this error in two ways:

1. Change the possessive pronoun to the singular *his or her.*

    Each **person** in this class should have **his or her** own textbook.

However, many writers do not like the use of "his or her" because it is wordy.

2. Make the subject plural: *people.*

    People in this class should have **their** own textbook.

An important additional benefit to using plural subjects is that verbs in the present tense do not need an *-s* ending. In other words, you are less likely to make mistakes with subject-verb agreement if the subject is plural. Remember this good strategy in your writing!

Editing

Exercise 4   The following paragraph contains seven errors concerning pronouns or possessive adjectives. Underline the errors and write a correction above each one.

Irrigation

Irrigation management is an interesting field, especially in places where water supplies are low. Irrigation experts have various tasks such as taking soil samples, checking existing water tables, and projecting the amount of rain for the future. These people usually get his degrees from irrigation institutes. Them study many years in order to become familiar with the various tasks involved in her profession. For some of they, a job with local water authorities is a good place to begin his career. Others prefer to find jobs as contractors, working independently to aid farmers with our irrigation needs. Whatever the job, irrigation experts are becoming increasingly important. Water is a precious commodity, and they cannot be taken for granted.

Reflexive Pronouns

When both the subject and the object refer to the same person or thing, you can use a reflexive pronoun as the object, or second noun. The reflexive pronoun refers to the subject. Here are the reflexive pronouns:

myself   yourself   himself   herself

ourselves   yourselves   themselves   itself

The *children* saw **themselves** on the television monitor.

The *skier* hurt **himself** when he veered off the main ski slope.

Do not use a reflexive pronoun after a preposition unless the pronoun is the same as the subject.

Incorrect: My *sisters* laughed at ~~myself~~ when I dyed my hair.

Correct: My *sisters* laughed at **me** when I dyed my hair.

Correct: I laughed at **myself** when I dyed my hair. (The subject pronoun *I* and the object of the preposition pronoun *myself* are the same person.)

Reflexive pronouns are never used as subjects.

The following are NOT grammatically correct English words:

hisself   ourselfs   theirselves

Editing

⚠ Exercise 5   Read each sentence. If it is correct, put a C in the blank. If there is an incorrect pronoun, put an X in the blank and make the correction above the error.

_____ 1. The defendant looked around and silently asked herself how the jury felt about her.

_____ 2. At the same time, the members of the jury were probably asking theirselves how they got chosen to participate in the trial.

_____ 3. The prosecuting attorney questioned the defendant about whether she had incriminated herselfs by not answering a previous question.

_____ 4. During closing remarks, the jury members wondered how many times the defense attorney had listened to himself practice that speech.

_____ 5. Since the trial took longer than expected, the judge asked that the jury members be sequestered in a hotel, without any access to outside information. This event put themselves in a difficult position.

_____ 6. With no access to newspapers, television, or any source of outside information, the members of the jury had to find other ways of entertaining themselves while they were sequestered.

_____ 7. The jury foreman promised hisself that he would remain calm during deliberations.

_____ 8. After the trial, one of the jury members said, "We certainly didn't enjoy ourselfs during this time, but serving on this jury was our civic duty."

Using Reflexive Pronouns for Emphasis

You may hear reflexive pronouns used to emphasize a point. In this case, the reflexive pronoun means the same thing as the noun or pronoun it refers to, or reflects.

I don't know what *you* want to do, but *I* **myself** want to go to the park.

It was *he* **himself** who built the tree house in the backyard.

We enjoyed the *play* **itself** but not the musical score.

When using reflexive pronouns, be careful with prepositions. Note the differences in meaning between these sentences:

Lisa painted **herself** green for the Halloween party. (Lisa painted her body.)

Lisa painted by **herself**. (Lisa painted alone; we don't know what she painted.)

Exercise 6 Fill in the blanks in the following paragraph with reflexive pronouns or with prepositions (for example, *for, at, of,* and *by*) and reflexive pronouns. The first one has been done for you.

Personal Ambition

Richard is an ambitious young man. He lives <u>by himself</u> and never asks for help
1
from anyone. He is an accomplished painter. In fact, he has recently painted a

self-portrait. He never officially studied art, but he _____ says that there is
2
nothing a person cannot learn by practicing. When Richard first started painting,

the results were not so good. Richard, always a good sport, just laughed _____ and
3
tried again. He doesn't feel sorry _____ when he makes a mistake. He learns from
4
his mistakes and goes on. At a special art auction held last week, one of his paintings

sold for more than $1,000! He was very proud _____ ! The buyers _____ were
5   **6**
surprised that Richard was a novice painter. Richard _____ was not; he knows
7
how much he can accomplish in his life.

3.5 *You, one,* and *they* Used as Indefinite Pronouns

You can use the indefinite pronouns *you, one,* and *they* in general terms.

One never knows what can happen during a long trip. (*One* refers to any person. This use is more formal than *you*.)

Credit card companies can harass **you** if **you** don't pay your bill on time. (*You* refers to any person. This use is considered informal. Some instructors may consider this word too informal for academic writing. Follow your course guidelines.)

They ski in the Alps, but I'd be afraid to. (*They* refers to people in general. Do not use in formal speech or writing. Instead, use a specific noun, such as "Many Swiss" instead of "They" in this example.)

Exercise 7 Read the following dialogue. Above the underlined indefinite pronouns, write the person or people these pronouns refer to. The first one has been done for you.

Joanne: Hi, Gina. What's new?

Gina: Don't ask! I'm mad!

Joanne: Why? Who are you mad at?

People who work in travel agencies
Gina: A travel agency. <u>They</u> never get anything right.
      1

Joanne: What happened?

Gina: I booked a flight and cruise to Mexico for

spring break.

Joanne: And?

Gina: You know the saying "<u>You</u> should always double-check everything"?
              2
Joanne: Sure. <u>You</u> never know the kinds of mistakes people will make.
        3
Gina: Well, I should've listened to that advice. I bought my tickets and thought

everything was fine until I noticed that the dates were all wrong! And my tickets are

nonrefundable. Now it's too late to change the tickets.

Joanne: Can you talk to someone at the agency? Complain maybe?

Gina: You know how <u>they</u> are … everything's about contracts and reading the fine print.
          4
I'm stuck with these tickets, and the travel dates, unfortunately, fall during final exams

this semester.

Joanne: Hmm. Maybe you could talk to your professors about changing the exam dates. <u>You</u>
                                                                    5
should never underestimate the flexibility of some instructors.

Gina: Maybe you're right. <u>You</u> never know! I'll give it a try.
              6

^ Exercise 8 In each item, one of the four underlined words or phrases is not correct. Circle the letter of the error and write the correction above the error.

1. Mike flew to Toronto to be with <u>her</u> sister. <u>It</u> had been over two years since <u>they</u>
             A   B   C

   had seen each <u>other</u>.
                    D

2. Everyone in the <u>airplane terminal</u> moved quickly out of <u>their airport lounges</u>
                        A   B

   except the people who <u>were</u> in the jetway at the <u>time</u>.
                             C   D

3. Mike took <u>so many</u> suitcases with <u>him</u> on vacation. He even brought <u>himself</u> laptop,
                A   B   C

   seven paperbacks, and his sister's CD player. <u>His sister and he</u> bought it a few years ago.
                                                     D

4. It was the airline union <u>that</u> worked to give <u>their</u> members a new deal including more
                              A   B

   sick leave, a higher salary, better benefits for <u>ramp workers</u> and their <u>families</u>, and a
                                                        C   D

   more solid pension plan.

Exercise 9   Circle the letter of the correct answer. Be prepared to explain your answers.

1. At the beginning of the semester, we asked our professor for his guidelines for writing our final research paper. Based on what _____ told us, we must cite at least ten articles and two books.

   A. he
   B. himself
   C. his
   D. Ø

2. Many of my classmates checked with fellow students who have taken this course with Dr. Thompson. It seems that a 20-page research paper is standard for most of _____ courses.

   A. Dr. Thompson
   B. himself
   C. his
   D. Ø

3. At our first class meeting, Dr. Thompson clearly stated, "It goes without saying that all students are supposed to do _____ own original research, which means that no one should use any material from any outside source without citing it appropriately in the paper."

   A. they
   B. them
   C. their
   D. theirs

4. Unfortunately, when reading the submissions, Professor Thompson found two students who had apparently copied substantial portions of _____ final papers from the Internet.

   A. they
   B. themselves
   C. their
   D. theirs

5. Not surprisingly, both students denied this serious charge. When Professor Thompson showed them the Internet site that closely resembled their papers, the students insisted that there was no proof of plagiarism in their research papers and that, in fact, _____ was the original and the Internet version was the plagiarized paper!

   A. they
   B. themselves
   C. their
   D. theirs

6. The students discussed this serious charge with the professor and then the department chair, but _____ were not satisfied with the result.

   A. they
   B. themselves
   C. their
   D. theirs

7. At this point, one of the two students wanted to drop the issue and accept the consequences, but the second student talked the first into continuing to fight their case. As a result, both students continued with _____ appeal.

A. they

B. themselves

C. their

D. theirs

8. Though it was apparent to most observers that the students had copied from the Internet source, the students continued, working up the chain of command. Eventually, even the college president _____ investigated the charges! Ultimately, the students' guilt was demonstrated, and they were expelled from the university for academic dishonesty. Plagiarism is serious.

A. she

B. by herself

C. herself

D. hers

Exercise 10   Write a paragraph about your best friend from childhood.

- Recall some specific characteristics about this person and his or her family.

- Think about some memories that you share.

- Identify the reasons that this person was or continues to be special to you.

Be sure to include as many pronouns as you can. Exchange paragraphs with a partner and underline the pronouns. Are they all correct?

_____

_____

_____

_____

_____

_____

_____

_____

_____

_____

_____

_____

_____

_____

_____

_____

_____

_____

_____

4 *Verb Tense Review*

This chapter reviews the <u>verb tenses</u> in English. In Chapter 5, you will work with specific problems that many writers have with verb tenses.

✔ CHECK YOUR GRAMMAR

Three of the five underlined words or phrases contain an error related to verb tenses. Can you explain why each of these underlined areas is (or is not) wrong? Discuss with a partner.

> ### Terrorist Attacks
>
> The September 11, 2001, attack on the World Trade Center by terrorists who <u>hijacked</u> two civilian airliners and <u>were using</u> them as missiles against the twin towers <u>had left</u> the nation stunned, angry, and determined to bring those who <u>orchestrated</u> the attack to justice. Unknown to American intelligence, in 1999 a group of terrorists in Germany led by Mohammed Atta <u>has already formulated</u> their plan to attack the United States.

From: C. Berkin, Miller, C., Cherny, R., and Gormly, J. (2006). *Making America: A History of the United States*, 4th ed. Boston: Houghton Mifflin, p. 1017.

4.1 Verb Tenses in English

The following chart gives you an overview of the twelve verb tenses in English. Then each tense is treated separately with examples of form and the most common uses, followed by practice exercises.

	REGULAR VERB	IRREGULAR VERB
Present:	I paint	I eat
Present progressive:	I am painting	I am eating
Present perfect:	I have painted	I have eaten
Present perfect progressive:	I have been painting	I have been eating

(continued)

	REGULAR VERB	IRREGULAR VERB
Past:	I painted	I ate
Past progressive:	I was painting	I was eating
Past perfect:	I had painted	I had eaten
Past perfect progressive:	I had been painting	I had been eating
Future:	I will paint	I will eat
Future progressive:	I will be painting	I will be eating
Future perfect:	I will have painted	I will have eaten
Future perfect progressive:	I will have been painting	I will have been eating

4.2   Present Tense

The present tense takes the form:

> VERB or VERB + *-s*   I **eat**.   He **eats**.

4.2.1   Uses

1. For general truths and facts that are not limited to a specific time

    Water **boils** at 100° Celsius.

2. For a repeated, habitual, or usual action

    They **play** tennis every Saturday morning.

3. For information from a book, a poem, research, or other work (this is often called the literary present)

    In the play, Romeo and Juliet **love** each other despite their family differences.

4. For a future event (but there should be a future expression, usually an adverb or adverbial phrase)

    The flight from Boston to New York **departs** in fifteen minutes.

5. For a future event in an adverb clause. (See Chapter 15 for adverb clauses.)

    It is unclear what the world population will be when the United Nations **celebrates** its 100th birthday in 2045.

Exercise 1   Write one sentence for each of the five uses of the present tense.[1]

Use 1. _____

_____

Use 2. _____

_____

Use 3. _____

_____

Use 4. _____

_____

Use 5. _____

_____

romeo and juliet

4.3   Present Progressive Tense

The present progressive tense takes the form:

am / is / are + VERB + *-ing*   **I am eating.**

4.3.1   *Uses*

1. For an action that is happening at this moment and that will have a definite end

   Doctors **are meeting** in Amsterdam to discuss treatments for AIDS.

2. For a longer action that is happening "now"

   "Now" can be a short time such as "at this second" or a longer time such as "today" or "this month / year / decade."

   Kevin **is working** on four projects this month.

3. For a repeated action that causes irritation or problems (often used with the word *always*)

   Politicians **are** always **discussing** ways of increasing government spending.

---

[1] For Exercises 1–13, you may find sentences from a source such as a magazine or the Internet.

4. For an event in the near future (used with an adverb indicating future)

Twenty students **are taking** TOEFL next Wednesday.

Remember that we usually put only action verbs in progressive tenses. Therefore, we can say *I am going, I am eating,* and *I am exercising,* but we do not usually say *I am knowing, I am having,* or *I am being.* However, it is possible to put nonaction (stative) verbs in the progressive whenever they have an "action" meaning.

I **am having** a problem.   He **is being** impolite.

Exercise 2   Write one sentence for each of the four uses of the present progressive tense.

Use 1. _____

_____

Use 2. _____

_____

Use 3. _____

_____

Use 4. _____

_____

4.4   Present Perfect Tense

The present perfect tense takes the form:

have / has + PAST PARTICIPLE   **I have eaten.**

4.4.1   Uses

1. For an action that started in the past and continues in the present

California **has been** a state since 1850.

2. For an action that has just been completed

We **have** just **finished** Unit 7.

3. For a past action that still has an effect on the present

The government **has raised** taxes, and many companies **have laid off** workers.

4. For an action that happened several times (no specific past time) and may happen again

> The government **has increased** the sales tax three times.

5. To indicate that you have (or don't have) the experience of doing something (no specific past time)

> **Have** you ever **read** *Hamlet*?

6. For a change or an accomplishment that has occurred (no specific past time)

> Because of the high demand for oil, the price of gasoline **has increased.**

> Scientists **have cloned** a sheep and a cat.

7. To indicate an unfinished action that may happen (no specific past time)

> The judge **has** not **decided** the fate of the criminal yet.

Exercise 3   Write one sentence for each of the seven uses of the present perfect tense.

Use 1. _____

_____

Use 2. _____

_____

Use 3. _____

_____

Use 4. _____

_____

Use 5. _____

_____

Use 6. _____

_____

Use 7. _____

_____

4.5 Present Perfect Progressive Tense

The present perfect progressive tense takes the form:

> have / has + been + VERB + -ing   **I have been eating.**

4.5.1 Uses

1. For an action that started in the past and is continuing in the present for a specific duration, with emphasis on the fact that it is still happening

   The president **has been discussing** this problem for more than two years.

2. For an action that started in the past and is continuing in the present for a nonspecific duration, meaning "recently" or "lately"

   Congress and the President **have been discussing** this problem.

Exercise 4   Write one sentence for each use of the present perfect progressive tense.

Use 1. _____

_____

Use 2. _____

_____

4.6 Simple Past Tense

The simple past tense takes the form:

> VERB + -ed   **I painted.**
>
> or   IRREGULAR form   **I ate.**

4.6.1 Uses

1. For an action or condition that was completed in the past

   Miners **discovered** gold in California in 1848.

2. For a series of finished actions

   Texas **became** a state in 1845, and California **joined** the U.S. in 1850.

Exercise 5   Write one sentence for each use of the past tense.

Use 1. _____

_____

Use 2. _____

_____

4.6.2	***Two Other Expressions for Past Time:*** used to *and* would

In English, *used to* and *would* also express past tense.

4.6.3	*Uses*

1. For a past habit or action that is no longer true: *used to* OR *would*

   When I was a young boy, I **used to play** tennis after school every day.

   When I was a young boy, I **would play** tennis after school every day.

2. For a past fact that is no longer true: *used to*

   When I was a young boy, my family **used to live** in Pennsylvania.

   Incorrect: When I was a young boy, my family **would live** in Pennsylvania.

Note that in the question form for *used to,* the final *-d* is dropped:

   "Did you **use to** live in Pennsylvania?"

and in the negative form for *used to,* the final *-d* is dropped as well:

   "I didn't **use to** like strawberry ice cream."

   Incorrect: "I didn't **used to** like strawberry ice cream."

Exercise 6   Write sentences for the uses of past time with *used to* and *would*. For Use 1, write one *used to* sentence and one *would* sentence. For Use 2, write one statement, one question, and one negative example using *used to*.

Use 1. used to _____

would _____

Use 2. statement _____

question _____

negative statement _____

4.7 Past Progressive Tense

The past progressive tense takes the form:

was / were + VERB + -*ing*   I **was eating.**

4.7.1 Uses

1. For an action in the past that was interrupted

   We **were eating** dinner when the phone rang.

2. For an action that was happening at a specific time

   At 7 p.m., we **were eating** dinner.

3. For background or atmosphere information

   When I boarded my flight, I immediately realized that it was not going to be a fun trip. Several people **were standing** in the aisles. A few children **were crying.** Another child **was standing** on the seat next to mine. A tired-looking flight attendant **was** already **staring** at her watch even before the door was closed.

Exercise 7   Write one sentence for each use of the past progressive tense. For Use 3, write one longer example using several verbs in the past progressive tense.

Use 1. _____

_____

Use 2. _____

_____

Use 3. _____

_____

_____

_____

_____

_____

_____

4.8   Past Perfect Tense

The past perfect tense takes the form:

> had + PAST PARTICIPLE   I **had eaten.**

4.8.1   *Uses*

1. For a past action or condition that ended before another past action or condition began

   The man told us that we could not play tennis because it **had rained** too hard.

2. For a past action or past condition that ended before a specific time in the past

   When Los Angeles became the capital of California in 1845, it **had been** a city for only ten years.

Often the past tense can be used instead of the past perfect tense. For example, when *before* or *after* is used in the sentence, you know which action happened first.

Kayleen **had taken** French before she took Spanish.

Kayleen **took** French before she **took** Spanish.

In contrast, expressions such as *by the time* often require the past perfect tense.

Incorrect: By the time he arrived, the meeting ~~began~~.

Correct: By the time he arrived, the meeting **had begun.**

Exercise 8   Write one sentence for each use of the past perfect tense.

Use 1. _____

_____

Use 2. _____

_____

4.9   Past Perfect Progressive Tense

The past perfect progressive tense takes the form:

> had + been + VERB + *-ing*   I **had been eating.**

4.9.1 Use

The past perfect progressive tense describes a continuing action that started in the past before another past action either began or interrupted the first action:

I **had been working** there for almost five weeks before I received my first check.

Exercise 9   Write a sentence using the past perfect progressive tense.

_____

_____

4.10 Future Tense

The future tense takes the forms:

am / is / are + going to + VERB	**I am going to** eat.
will + VERB	**I will eat.**

There are two ways to express the future in English: *be going to* or *will*. Many times you may use either verb without any difference in meaning. However, each form also has its special use, and there are times when only one is correct. In general, there are many more uses for *be going to* than for *will*. Unfortunately, many nonnative speakers have been taught that *will* is the better or "more correct" future form. For this reason, the most common error with future tense is for nonnative speakers to overuse *will*.

4.10.1 Uses

1. For a future plan: *be going to*

   As a result of his speech, I **am going to support** him in the next election.

   Most of my classmates **are going to go** to Hawaii for New Year's.

2. For a voluntary action: *will* (especially as a request or a response)

   Ben: **Will** you carry this bag for me, please?

   Sue: Sure, I **will.**

3. For a promise: *will*

   I **will send** you a postcard when I'm in Paris next week.

4. For a prediction: *will* or *be going to*

   In the next decade, consumers **will spend** more on electronic goods.

   In the next decade, consumers **are going to spend** more on electronic goods.

Exercise 10   Write a sentence for each use of *will* and *be going to.*

Use 1. _____

_____

Use 2. _____

_____

Use 3. _____

_____

Use 4. _____

_____

be going to _____

_____

4.11   Future Progressive Tense

The future progressive tense takes the form:

will + be + VERB + *-ing*   **I will be eating.**

4.11.1   *Uses*

1. For an "interrupted" action in the future

   I **will be watching** TV when you call at eleven tonight.

2. For picturing the future

   In 2050, families **will be living** in much larger houses. People **will** no **longer be communicating** by telephone. Students **will be learning** from home via the computer and new video machines.

Exercise 11   Write one sentence for each use of the future progressive tense. For Use 2, write one longer example using several verbs in the future progressive tense.

Use 1. _____

_____

Use 2. _____

_____

_____

_____

| 4.12 | **Future Perfect Tense** |

The future perfect tense takes the form:

> will + have + PAST PARTICIPLE   **I will have eaten.**

| 4.12.1 | *Uses* |

1. For a future action that is completed before another future action

   I will have worked here for more than five years when I get my promotion.

2. For a future action that is completed before a certain point of time in the future

   I will have worked here for more than five years by the year 2010.

Exercise 12   Write a sentence for each use of the future perfect tense.

Use 1. _____

_____

Use 2. _____

_____

| 4.13 | **Future Perfect Progressive Tense** |

The future perfect progressive tense takes the form:

> will + have + been + VERB + *-ing*   **I will have been eating.**

4.13.1   *Use*

The future perfect progressive tense describes a continuing action that will be finished at a specific time in the future:

> The pilots **will have been flying** for almost fifteen hours by the time we reach Zurich.

Exercise 13   Write a sentence using the future perfect progressive tense.

_____

_____

Exercise 14   Fill in the blanks with the correct forms for the verbs shown. A few answers have been provided for you.

	Work	**Talk**	**Eat**
Present:	he works	_____	_____
Present progressive:	_____	they are talking	_____
Present perfect:	_____	_____	_____
Present perfect progressive:	_____	_____	I've been eating
Past: used to	_____	_____	_____
would	_____	_____	_____
Past progressive:	_____	_____	_____
Past perfect:	_____	_____	_____
Past perfect progressive:	_____	_____	_____
Future:	_____	_____	_____
Future progressive:	_____	_____	_____
Future perfect:	_____	_____	_____
Future perfect progressive:	_____	_____	_____

Editing

⌃ Exercise 15 Read the following paragraph and look at the seven underlined verbs. Five of them contain an error. Circle the errors and write the corrections above. Explain to a partner why the other two are correct.

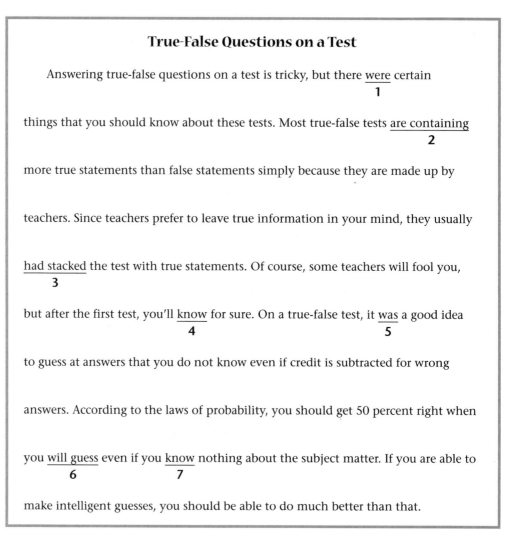

True-False Questions on a Test

Answering true-false questions on a test is tricky, but there <u>were</u> certain
                                                                    1

things that you should know about these tests. Most true-false tests <u>are containing</u>
                                                                          2

more true statements than false statements simply because they are made up by

teachers. Since teachers prefer to leave true information in your mind, they usually

<u>had stacked</u> the test with true statements. Of course, some teachers will fool you,
3

but after the first test, you'll <u>know</u> for sure. On a true-false test, it <u>was</u> a good idea
                                  4   **5**

to guess at answers that you do not know even if credit is subtracted for wrong

answers. According to the laws of probability, you should get 50 percent right when

you <u>will guess</u> even if you <u>know</u> nothing about the subject matter. If you are able to
     6   **7**

make intelligent guesses, you should be able to do much better than that.

Exercise 16 Read the whole paragraph. For each pair of blanks, fill in the first blank with the name of the correct verb tense and the second blank with the verb in that tense. The first one has been done for you.

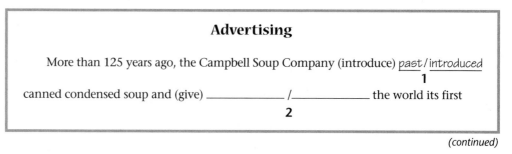

Advertising

More than 125 years ago, the Campbell Soup Company (introduce) <u>past</u>/<u>introduced</u>
                                                                                    1
canned condensed soup and (give) _____ /_____ the world its first
                                                         2

(continued)

convenience food. Since then, those well-known red-and-white labels and the sigh

"M'm! M'm! Good!" (become) _____ /_____ icons of American
3

culture. Although sales of the popular brand total $4.3 billion and Campbell's

brands currently (account) _____ /_____ for 80 percent of canned
4

soup sold in the United States, the company (face) _____ /_____
5

declines in domestic sales. Turning to global markets, Campbell executives (hope)

_____ /_____ that in the very near future, more than half of the
6

firm's profits (come) _____ /_____ from foreign sales.
7

Exercise 17 Read the following paragraph and underline the correct verb forms in parentheses. The first one has been done for you.

Tales from Literature

In the history of English, *tale* (<u>is</u>, had been) a close cousin of *tell*; stories
1

(have, will have) a much longer association with voices than with pages. Some of
2

the greatest and most familiar tales (are being, were) told for centuries before they
3

(had been, were) written down by folklorists such as the Brothers Grimm. When
4

we read them, we notice how much there (has been, is) to hear. The peasants
5

and townspeople who (recite, recited) their tales for the Brothers Grimm
6

(had, will have) memorized them word for word as a magician might memorize
7

a spell (and indeed, in medieval German and English, the word *spell* might mean

either a story or an incantation). A story (changes, would change) gradually
8

over decades of telling, but a traditional tale was not to be loosely paraphrased.

The telling, that is, the spell, required certain syllables in a certain order. In this

respect, the traditional tale is more like a poem or song than it (is, was) like most
9

modern novels, which (will not be, are not) intended to be read aloud, let alone
10

memorized.

Exercise 18   Circle the letter of the correct answer. Be prepared to explain your answers.

1. New Belgium Brewing (NBB), America's first wind-powered brewery, _____ to make both a better beer and a better society.
   A. aims
   B. had aimed
   C. was aiming
   D. used to aim

2. Founded by husband-and-wife entrepreneurs Jeff Lebesch and Kim Jordan, the company _____ European-style beers with intriguing brands such as Fat Tire and Sunshine Wheat.
   A. offered
   B. had offered
   C. is offering
   D. offers

3. Lebesch _____ up with this idea for brewing beers with unique names while touring Belgium on a bicycle.
   A. comes
   B. came
   C. is coming
   D. used to come

4. Returning home with a special yeast strain, Lebesch experimented in his basement and _____ a beer that he named Fat Tire Amber Ale in honor of his bicycle trip.
   A. was creating
   B. had created
   C. created
   D. will create

5. By 1991, he and his wife _____ in bottling and delivering five Belgian-style beers to stores in and around their hometown of Ft. Collins, Colorado.
   A. are succeeding
   B. succeed
   C. will have succeeded
   D. had succeeded

6. Caring for the environment, NBB employees _____ paper and as many other supplies as possible.
   A. have recycled and reused
   B. had recycled and reused
   C. recycled and reused
   D. recycle and reuse

7. Lebesch and Jordan _____ the entrepreneurial spirit of the workforce through employee ownership. In fact, employees share in decisions, serve as taste testers, and receive detailed information about NBB's financial performance.
   A. unleash
   B. have unleashed
   C. had unleashed
   D. would unleash

8. If the success of NBB continues, no one doubts that NBB _____ to be one of

America's best business success stories.

    A. will continue   C. have continued

    B. had been continued   D. used to continue

Exercise 19   Choose a copy of a paragraph in English from a magazine, newspaper, or the Internet. Underline the verbs and identify their tenses. Then bring your work to class to check with a partner.

■ ORIGINAL WRITING

Exercise 20   Write two paragraphs about two people who have been important in your life. Try to use both affirmative and negative verb forms. Underline all of the verbs and be prepared to identify the verb tense for each.

- In the first paragraph, write about someone who is no longer living. Tell who the person was, when he or she was born, where he or she lived, his or her relationship to you, and why this person was important to you.

- In the second paragraph, do the same thing, but write about someone who is still living.

_____

_____

_____

_____

_____

_____

_____

_____

_____

_____

_____

_____

5 Problems With Verb Tenses

This chapter focuses on three of the most common problems that writers have with verb tenses: (1) <u>incorrect forms</u>, (2) <u>shifts in verb tense</u>, and (3) <u>confusing verb tenses</u>. As you study this chapter, you can refer to Chapter 4 for examples of the forms of the verb tenses.

✓ CHECK YOUR GRAMMAR

Five of the eight underlined words or phrases contain an error related to verb tenses. Can you explain why each of these underlined areas is (or is not) wrong? Discuss with a partner.

Thematic Apperception Test

Harvard psychologist Henry Murray <u>has developed</u> the Thematic Apperception Test (TAT) in the 1930s (Murray, 1938). The test <u>consists</u> of a set of pictures depicting ambiguous scenes that <u>may be interpreted</u> in different ways. In this test, a subject <u>had been asked</u> to tell a story about the scene, what <u>led</u> up to these events, and what the eventual outcome <u>had been</u>. Murray <u>believed</u> that the stories that people <u>tell revealed</u> aspects of their own personalities.

From: J. Nevid (2007). *Essentials of Psychology: Concepts and Application.* Boston: Houghton Mifflin, p. 496.

5.1 Problems With Verb Forms

English has twelve verb tenses (see Chapter 4 for more information), but five verb tense forms often give writers the most trouble:

5.1.1. Progressive tenses

5.1.2. Passive voice and past participle

5.1.3. Perfect tenses, past participle, and *have*

5.1.4. *Do* and the form of the verb

5.1.5. Modals and the verb

Study the following rules, errors, and correct examples. Do you sometimes make these errors in your writing? Do you know when and why?

5.1.1   *Progressive Tenses and -ing*

With a progressive tense, it is easy to forget the *-ing*. The rule is:

Use *be* + PRESENT PARTICIPLE (base verb plus *-ing*) for a progressive tense.

Don't forget the *-ing*.

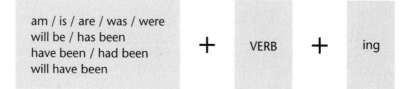

| am / is / are / was / were
will be / has been
have been / had been
will have been | **+** | VERB | **+** | ing |

While passengers on long international overnight flights **are sleeping,** the pilots **are working** hard to make the flight as smooth as possible.

5.1.2   *Passive Voice and Past Participle*

In passive voice, some writers forget to use the past participle form of the verb. The rule is:

Use *be* + PAST PARTICIPLE (base verb plus *-ed*) for the passive voice.

| am / is / are / was / were
will be / has been
have been / had been
will have been | **+** | PAST PARTICIPLE |

After the exams **have been graded,** they **will be returned** to the students.

5.1.3   *Perfect Tenses, Past Participle, and* have

For perfect tenses, you need to use the past participle with the correct form of *have* (*have, has, had, will have*). The rule is:

Use *have* + PAST PARTICIPLE for perfect tenses.

have / has / had	**+**	PAST PARTICIPLE

We **had visited** Los Angeles before the last earthquake struck, but we **have not gone** back since then. (The past participle of *go* is irregular: *gone.*)

5.1.4   Do *and the Form of the Verb*

With *do / does / did*, don't put an *-s* or *-ed* on the verb. The rule is:

Use the base form of the verb with *do / does / did.*

Do not add any endings to a verb following *do / does / did.*

do / does / did	**+**	SUBJECT	**+**	VERB

How many people **do** you **expect** to attend the gathering this Saturday evening?

5.1.5   *Modals and the Verb*

With modals, such as *would, may, can,* some writers make the mistake of adding the word *to* before the verb or adding an ending (*-s, -ed, -ing*) to the verb. The rule is: Use only the base form of the verb after modals. Do not use *to* after modals. Do not add any endings to the verb.

will / would / can / could should / must / may / might had better	**+**	SIMPLE VERB (base form)

Some scientists **will participate** in the experiment, but others **may refuse** to do so.

Exercise 1 As you read the paragraph, underline the correct verb forms. The first one has been done for you.

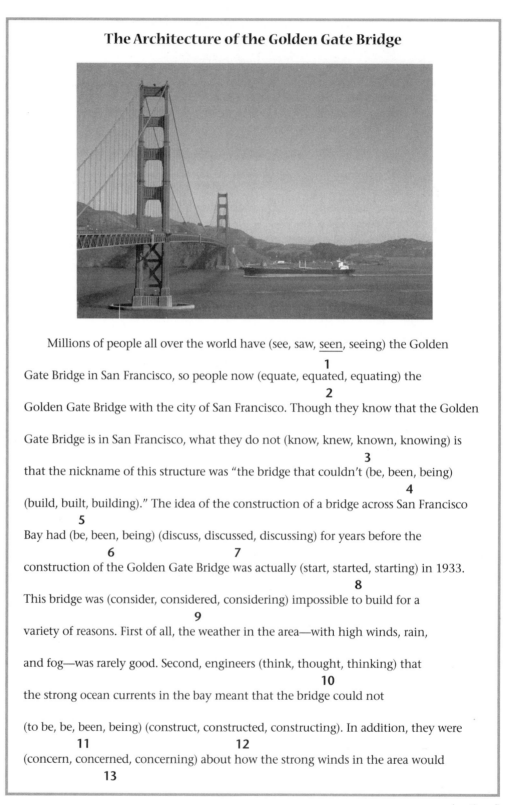

The Architecture of the Golden Gate Bridge

Millions of people all over the world have (see, saw, <u>seen</u>, seeing) the Golden
                                                                                    1
Gate Bridge in San Francisco, so people now (equate, equated, equating) the
                                                                              2
Golden Gate Bridge with the city of San Francisco. Though they know that the Golden

Gate Bridge is in San Francisco, what they do not (know, knew, known, knowing) is
                                                                              3
that the nickname of this structure was "the bridge that couldn't (be, been, being)
                                                                                  4
(build, built, building)." The idea of the construction of a bridge across San Francisco
   5
Bay had (be, been, being) (discuss, discussed, discussing) for years before the
              6   **7**
construction of the Golden Gate Bridge was actually (start, started, starting) in 1933.
                                                                               8
This bridge was (consider, considered, considering) impossible to build for a
                                9
variety of reasons. First of all, the weather in the area—with high winds, rain,

and fog—was rarely good. Second, engineers (think, thought, thinking) that
                                                                          10
the strong ocean currents in the bay meant that the bridge could not

(to be, be, been, being) (construct, constructed, constructing). In addition, they were
              11   **12**
(concern, concerned, concerning) about how the strong winds in the area would
              13

(continued)

(to affect, affect, affected, affecting) any large structure. Finally, it was the Depression.
14

The poor economy was (cause, caused, causing) people to experience incredible
15

difficulties, so many people thought that it would (to be, be, been, being) foolish
16

to spend such a large amount of money on such an impossible project. Getting the

funds to build a bridge of this magnitude was a monumental task. In fact, it took

four times as long to collect enough money to build the bridge as it actually took to

build the bridge. Despite all these hindrances, the bridge was (erect, erected, erecting)
17

in four and a half years at a cost of 36 million dollars. The cost was high not only in

monetary terms but also in human life: fourteen lives were (lose, lost, losing) during
18

the construction of the Golden Gate Bridge.

Exercise 2   As you read the paragraph, fill in each blank with the correct form of the verb in parentheses. The first one has been done for you.

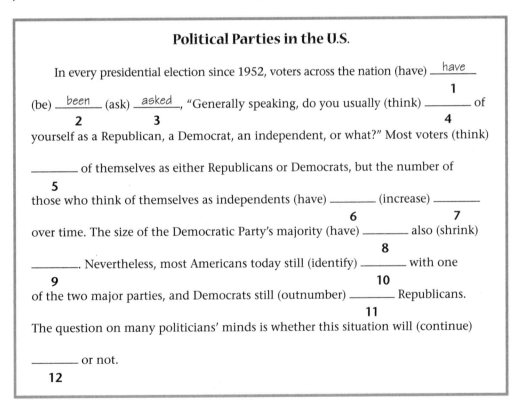

Political Parties in the U.S.

In every presidential election since 1952, voters across the nation (have) __have__
1

(be) __been__ (ask) __asked__, "Generally speaking, do you usually (think) _____ of
2   **3**   **4**

yourself as a Republican, a Democrat, an independent, or what?" Most voters (think)

_____ of themselves as either Republicans or Democrats, but the number of
5

those who think of themselves as independents (have) _____ (increase) _____
6   **7**

over time. The size of the Democratic Party's majority (have) _____ also (shrink)
8

_____. Nevertheless, most Americans today still (identify) _____ with one
9   **10**

of the two major parties, and Democrats still (outnumber) _____ Republicans.
11

The question on many politicians' minds is whether this situation will (continue)

_____ or not.
12

5.2   Maintaining the Same Verb Tense

In a nutshell, this is the rule for being consistent with verb tenses: Do not change verb tense in a paragraph unless you have a specific reason for doing so.

A common error made by writers is an incorrect shift in verb tense. For example, if your paragraph is about the history of a country, most of the verbs will be in the past tense. If your paragraph tells how a machine works, most of the verbs should be in the present tense. Pay careful attention to the topic that you are writing about because a topic usually has a certain range of verb tenses normally associated with that topic.

5.2.1   *When a Tense Shift Is Correct*

Sometimes a shift in verb tense is necessary, but it is important to consider the time of the action of the verb and its relationship to other actions or events in the paragraph. You may want to state a present fact, such as

> Nuclear reactors **are** a huge threat to our well-being.

then explain why you believe this by supporting it with a past historical fact:

> The horrible nuclear accident at Chernobyl in 1986 **killed** almost three thousand people in the immediate and surrounding areas as well as in faraway lands.

This shift from present tense to past tense is logical because the historical event occurred in the past, but nuclear reactors still exist.

5.2.2   *Switching Between Present Tense and Past Tense*

Shifting between the present and past tense of a verb is the most common shift error.

> *Error 1:*   You begin a narrative paragraph in the past tense, shift to present tense, and then shift back to past tense.

> *Error 2:*   You start explaining something in the present tense and unexpectedly shift to past tense.

The solution to this problem is to *think* about the time of each action that you are writing about and to *proofread* your work carefully with this time in mind.

⚠ Exercise 3   As you read the paragraph, find and correct ten errors in shifting verb tenses. Be sure to take into account the time of the action.

Buying a Used Car

One of the worst experiences that I have ever gone through was buying a used car. I had heard many things—both good and bad—about buying a used car, but I never think anything bad would happen to me. I respond to an advertisement in the local newspaper. After I was calling the person and I made arrangements to see the car with him, I went to the owner's house and take the car for a test drive. The car seemed fine, but of course I took it to a car repair shop to have a professional mechanic look it over. Once he tells me that the car seems okay to him, I paid $2,900 cash for the car. The owner assured me that everything in the car was working fine. Unfortunately, less than a month after I buy the car, the engine started making noises. Soon after, the car stopped running completely. I called the owner, but legally, he did not have any obligation to me. I quickly learn the meaning of the phrase "as is." In the end, I have to pay an additional $2,000 to have a new engine installed. Therefore, my used car ends up costing me almost $5,000. In hindsight, I could have used that sum as a large down-payment on a brand-new car.

Exercise 4   As you read the paragraph, find and correct seven errors in shifting verb tenses. Be sure to take into account the time of the action.

Censoring Music

One of the basic rights that we enjoy is freedom of speech, and this includes our right to listen to any kind of music that appealed to us. However, some of the music that is currently being played on the radio is obscene and should be banned. I don't have any children, but I do have* a seven-year-old niece. While I was driving her to school the other day, we were talking and listening to the radio. One of the songs on the radio is about sex and had some foul language in it. My niece asks me what one of the words meant. Clearly, what children heard has an influence on them. While I agree with the concept of free speech, I also thought that everyone had an obligation to set limits and not cross those lines. When songs deal with sex and use foul language, I think that the limit will be breached. This is not censoring; it is common sense.

Exercise 5   As you read the paragraph, find and correct thirteen errors in shifting verb tenses. Be sure to take into account the time of the action.

Working as a Server

Everyone has eaten in a restaurant, but I wonder how many people really know how hard a server's job is. I have been a server for almost five years. At first, it was a part-time job, but now it is my main job. I worked at a small upscale restaurant called the White Wolf Café. The restaurant served dinner from 5 p.m. to 10 p.m., but my shift runs from 4 p.m. to midnight. I get to work a few minutes before 4:00. After I have clocked in, I start folding napkins. Sometimes I had to help set silverware on the tables, but sometimes someone else takes care of that task. Though

(continued)

---

* Do/does/did + VERB is the emphatic form: I **do have** a car. I **did study** the material.

---

we open at 5:00, hardly any customers showed up till around 5:30 or 6:00. For the rest of the evening, my job entailed greeting customers who are sitting in my section, which consisted of six tables. I explain things on the menu, take people's drink orders, take their food orders, and made sure that customers have what they need. I think that I am a good server because I am good at anticipating what people needed before they ask for it, and customers appreciated my service. The work is hard, but I enjoy working with people. The only negative aspect of this job is dealing with rude or difficult customers, but this was part of every job that deals with the public. We stopped serving food from the kitchen at 10:00, but some customers did not leave until 11:00. I have to stay until midnight to clean up and then organize some things for the next day. My job as a server is not an easy one, but I love this job and cannot imagine doing anything else.

Exercise 6   Analyze Real Language for Verb Tenses

Select a paragraph from an article or website that you find interesting. Underline all of the verbs in the excerpt. Work with a partner to identify and give a reason for the tense of each verb. Remember that some verb tense shifts, for example, are correct in moving from a present fact to the past history of how that fact came about. In your excerpt, can you find examples of verb tense shifts? Explain why the writer made these shifts.

5.3   Confusing Verb Tenses

In English, there are twelve verb tenses. (See Chapter 4.) Some tenses are easy to use; others are more difficult. A few verb tenses are easily confused with others. Most of the confusion centers around four verb tenses, all of which have a connection to past time.

5.3.1   *Past Tense*

Use the past tense when you are referring to an action that is finished:

Lincoln **governed** the United States during a difficult period.

Common errors that happen when you mean to use past tense:

Past progressive:	Lincoln **was governing** ... (indicates a longer action that was interrupted)
Past perfect:	Lincoln **had governed** ... (indicates that one past action happened before another past action)

5.3.2   *Present Perfect Tense*

- Use the present perfect tense when you are referring to an action that began in the past and continues now:

  The U.N. **has solved** world problems for five decades.

- Use the present perfect tense when you are referring to an action that is important now:

  The government **has reformed** the tax system.

- Use the present perfect tense when you are referring to a past action with an indefinite time, especially an accomplishment:

  Scientists **have discovered** how aspirin works.

Common errors that happen when you mean to use present perfect tense:

Present progressive:	The U.N. **is solving** ... (indicates an action that is continuing right now)
Past tense:	Scientists **discovered** ... (indicates an action that is finished, with no relationship to the present; often used with a specific past time)

Present perfect is often used for a past action when that action is relevant or important to the new information being presented. Consider this example from a conversation:

Ann:	It's hot in here!
Pedro:	I know, but **I've turned on** the air conditioner, so we have to wait a few minutes.

The action of turning on the air conditioner is clearly a past action, but we use present perfect tense to show that it has a relationship to Ann's first statement "It's hot in here!"

5.3.3   *Past Progressive Tense*

- Use the past progressive tense when you want to set the scene or atmosphere in prose:

  What a scene! A mother **was trying** to quiet her children.

- Use the past progressive tense when you are referring to a longer action that was interrupted:

  The cashier **was studying** a receipt when the phone rang.

  The flight **was going** smoothly when the pilot received a radio message about possible bad weather.

Common errors that happen when you mean to use past progressive tense:

Incorrect: The cashier **is studying** a receipt when the phone rang. (Use of the present tense makes the verb tenses inconsistent.)

Incorrect: The flight **went smoothly** when the pilot received … (Use of the past tense implies a sequence of events instead of one event that was interrupted by another event.)

5.3.4   *Past Perfect Tense*

Use the past perfect tense when you are referring to a past action that happened before another action:

I **had** never **lived** abroad before, so living in Malaysia was difficult.

A common error that happens when you mean to use past perfect tense:

Past tense: I never **lived** abroad … (Indicates that you are talking about one event that was not necessarily completed before the second event.)

Exercise 7   Read the paragraph and underline the correct verb tenses. Distinguish between using the past tense, the present perfect tense, and the past perfect tense. Be sure to take into account the time of the action. The first one has been done for you.

My Life as an ESL Teacher

My name is Carl Davids, and I am an ESL teacher. I (was, <u>have been</u>, had been) an
1

ESL teacher since 1985. I (taught, was teaching, have taught) English in the United
2

States and several foreign countries. In fact, I (had, have had, was having) more
3

teaching jobs overseas than here in the United States. In 1985, I (started, have started)
4

teaching in a large English program at a big university. Most of my students

then (were, have been, had been) Spanish speakers or Arabic speakers. After that,
5

I (moved, was moving, had moved) to a smaller city in a different state and
6

(got, was getting, had gotten) a teaching position at a small college.
7

I (worked, have worked, had worked) there for five years. In 1992,
8

I (was deciding, decided, have decided) to accept a job in Saudi Arabia.
9

I (have never worked, had never worked, never worked) in a foreign country before, so
10

this (had been, was, has been) a big shock in many ways. I (stayed, have stayed) there
11   12

(continued)

for one year. I (taught, have taught) English to officers in a military program. The
13

following year I (moved, have moved) to Malaysia to work at a brand-new English
14

program just outside Kuala Lumpur. For many reasons, it (was, has been) the
15

best teaching experience that I (had, have had) in my life. I (stayed, have stayed) in
16

Malaysia for three years. After Malaysia, I (took, have taken) a job in Japan. In late
17

1997, I finally (came, have come) back to the United States. In early 1998,
18

I (was finding, found, have found) a great teaching job at a university in
19

California where I (was, have been, had been) since then. I have great memories
20

of my years overseas. In fact, I (went, was going, have gone) back to Malaysia and
21

Japan twice and hope to be able to go back again next summer. When I first chose

this career years ago, I was not so sure that it was the right career for me, but

I (was enjoying, had enjoyed, enjoyed, have enjoyed) my years of ESL tremendously
22

and am certain that I made the right choice.

Exercise 8 Each of the following statements contains a puzzle. Read each one and then answer the questions. Be sure to identify the verb tenses in your answer and explain what they mean. The first one has been done for you.

1. Karen was writing a book in 1995. Lynn wrote a book in 1997. One of these books was

   published in 1998. Whose book was it? ___Lynn's___ How do you know?

   The past tense verb "wrote" shows that the book was completed, while the past

   progressive tense verb "was writing" shows that the writing continued and may still

   continue.

2. Tom has been ill since last week. Jerry was sick last week. Which person might not be

   ill now? _____ How do you know?

   _____

   _____

   _____

3. Mohammed lived in Pakistan for twelve years. Twi has lived in Turkey since 1999. Hussein used to live in Syria. Which of these people might live in the U.S. now? _____ How do you know?

_____

_____

4. When the lights went out last night, Kevin was studying. Jack had studied. Who is probably better prepared to take the test today? _____ How do you know?

_____

_____

5. Luke, Kyle, and Rick share an apartment. At 9:15 last night, the phone rang. Luke had taken a shower, Kyle was going to take a shower, and Rick was taking a shower. Which one could not answer the phone? _____ How do you know?

_____

_____

6. Explain what the time of the action means in each sentence:

   a. When the phone rang, I was eating. _____

   _____

   b. When the phone rang, I ate. _____

   _____

   c. When the phone rang, I had eaten. _____

   _____

   d. When the phone rang, I was going to eat. (More common: When the phone rang, I was about to eat.) _____

   _____

   e. When the phone rang, I had been eating. _____

   _____

Exercise 9   Circle the letter of the correct answer. Be prepared to explain your answers.

1. Along with creativity in the visual arts, the late fifth century B.C. _____ an increase
   in drama.

   A. was seen   C. had been seeing

   B. is seeing   D. saw

2. Drama, as we know it in the West, _____ in fact a creation of the Greeks.

   A. is   C. had been

   B. has been   D. had been being

3. Theatergoing was more than a festive activity for Athenians; it _____ as an
   important part of a citizen's education and was supported by the state.

   A. is regarding   C. is regarded

   B. was regarding   D. was regarded

4. Tragedies and comedies, as well as other theatrical events, _____ performed annually
   at the festival of Dionysus.

   A. are   C. have been

   B. were   D. had been

5. The ruins of the better preserved theater at Epidaurus and the theater of Dionysus on the Akropolis _____ us a clear idea of the circular orchestra—where the chorus sang and danced—and the *theatron*, the horseshoe-shaped area for the audience.

   A. give   C. gave

   B. were giving   D. had given

6. A *skene*, or backdrop against which the actors _____, was set up in the back of the orchestra, facing the audience.

   A. perform   C. are performing

   B. performed   D. were performed

7. Acoustics in this theater _____ still remarkable.

   A. are   C. have been

   B. were   D. had been

8. In fact, a clear voice from the orchestra is deflected by the stone sides and _____ without any form of artificial amplification.

   A. can hear   C. can be heard

   B. can to hear   D. can to be heard

From: Witt et al., *The Humanities,* p. 100.

Exercise 10 Write a paragraph about either (1) an important current event or (2) an important recent problem.

- Tell what the current situation is, why or how this event or problem happened (including when it began), and what is going to happen next.

- Use both affirmative and negative forms.

Try not to shift tenses unnecessarily or confuse any tenses. Underline all of the verbs. Exchange paragraphs with a partner and check each other's work for correct verb tenses.

_____

_____

_____

_____

_____

_____

_____

_____

_____

_____

_____

_____

_____

_____

_____

_____

_____

_____

_____

Subject-Verb Agreement

6

This chapter covers <u>subject-verb agreement</u>, including these problematic categories:

- basic subject-verb agreement
- subjects separated from verbs
- indefinite pronouns as subjects
- quantity words as subjects
- plural nouns that take singular verbs

✔ CHECK YOUR GRAMMAR

Two of the three underlined words contain an error related to subject-verb agreement. Can you explain why each of these underlined areas is (or is not) wrong? Discuss with a partner.

Hieroglyphic Systems

Both Mesopotamian cuneiform and Egyptian hieroglyphics <u>was</u> cumbersome systems of writing. In fact, only scribes with many years of training <u>could</u> write them. A form of writing corresponding to our alphabet (from *alpha* and *beta*, the first letters of the Greek alphabet) <u>seem</u> to have developed in response to the need of soldiers, traders, and merchants for a more efficient and easier writing system.

From: Witt et al., *The Humanities*, p. 31.

6.1   Basic Subject-Verb Agreement

This is the main rule to remember about subject-verb agreement: <u>A subject must agree with its verb in number (singular or plural)</u>. The rules on the next page show how to form singular and plural verb tenses. In the examples notice how the verb changes to plural when the subject is plural.

1. For a singular third-person subject in present tense, the verb must have an *-s* ending. For all other subjects, the verb does not end in *-s*. (Modals never add any ending.)

singular	**plural**
I live	we live
you live	you live
he / she / it lives	they live

Singular: The **President** of the U.S. **lives** in the White House.

Plural: The President's immediate family **members live** there, too.

2. For the irregular verb *be*, the singular uses *am, are,* and *is* for present tense and *was* and *were* for past tense.

singular		**plural**	
I am	I was	we are	we were
you are	you were	you are	you were
he / she / it is	he / she / it was	they are	they were

Singular: **President John Kennedy was** assassinated on November 22, 1963.

Plural: On that day, **President and Mrs. Kennedy were** visiting the city of Dallas.

3. In the following examples, the auxiliary verbs *has* and *have* (present perfect) must agree with each subject.

singular	**plural**
I have	we have
you have	you have
he / she / it has	they have

Singular: **The White House has** had the name "White House" since 1801.

Plural: U.S. **presidents have** lived in the White House since 1800.

4. In "there + verb" constructions, the word *there* is never the subject. The subject comes after the verb.

Singular: There **seems** to be some **question** about the origin of this container.

Plural: There **were** several **international officials** visiting the city yesterday.

Exercise 1   Read the following paragraph. Underline the subjects once and the verbs twice.

Communication

A good story is essential to a good speech. A good story certainly helps a speaker to grab and maintain people's attention. Sources for good stories for speeches are everywhere. You can find stories in children's books and in holy books. You can highlight the exploits of heroes from mythology or movies in order to make

---

(continued)

a point. Sports celebrities and historical figures often have life stories that you can use to inspire and teach. Personal incidents from your childhood and life-changing events are excellent sources for stories for speeches. In fact, all of us are surrounded by stories. Good speakers keep their eyes and ears open for presentation topics. When they read a compelling story in a newspaper or magazine, they clip it. When they hear someone tell a great story, they write it down.

Adapted from: I. Engleberg and Daly, J. (2005). *Presentations in Everyday Life: Strategies for Effective Speaking,* 2nd ed. Boston: Houghton Mifflin, p. 300.

6.2 Subjects That Are Separated From the Verb

You may find it more difficult to see the connection between the subject and the verb if there is extra information between them. The extra information can be a prepositional phrase (Chapter 7), an adjective clause (Chapter 14), or a reduced clause (Chapters 14–16). In general, this intervening information does not affect the verb.

> The little *girl in the light blue jumper and matching tennis shoes* **is crying.** (prepositional phrase)
>
> The new board *members who decided to vote down the proposed stock split* **are renegotiating** their positions. (adjective clause)
>
> The *thundershowers pounding the coastline* **have caused** some damage to the sand dunes. (reduced adjective clause)

Exercise 2   Read the following paragraph. Underline the subjects once and the verbs twice.

Business Management—The Subway Story

In 1965, when Fred DeLuca, age seventeen, borrowed $1,000 from Dr. Peter Buck to open a sandwich shop, he did not realize that the two of them were launching an immensely successful global business. At the time, DeLuca and thousands of other college students were thinking about earning money to pay for college. The surprising result was a franchised organization with its name on 16,000 restaurants in seventy-four countries. Today Subway has more U.S. restaurants than McDonald's, and it is second only to McDonald's in the number of outlets worldwide. Nearly four decades after Subway's founding, its growth and enthusiastic customer acceptance around the globe have made DeLuca a billionaire.

Adapted from: W. Pride, Hughes, R., and Kapoor, J. (2005). *Business,* 8th ed. Boston: Houghton Mifflin, p. 97.

6.3   Indefinite Pronouns as Subjects

The list below shows common indefinite pronouns. Though these pronouns often refer to more than one person or thing, they take a singular verb when they act as the subject.

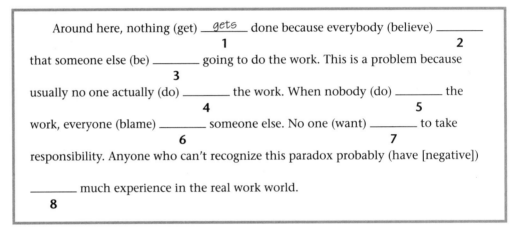

	every-	some-	any-	no-
-one	everyone	someone	anyone	no one
-body	everybody	somebody	anybody	nobody
-thing	everything	something	anything	nothing

Is *anyone* coming to the party tomorrow night?

Something **has** to be done about the increasing crime rate!

If you believe in yourself, *nothing* **is** impossible.

Exercise 3   As you read the following paragraph, fill in each blank with the correct form of the verb in parentheses. Be sure the verbs agree with their subjects. The first one has been done for you.

> Around here, nothing (get) __gets__ done because everybody (believe) _____
>   1   2
> that someone else (be) _____ going to do the work. This is a problem because
>   3
> usually no one actually (do) _____ the work. When nobody (do) _____ the
>   4   5
> work, everyone (blame) _____ someone else. No one (want) _____ to take
>   6   7
> responsibility. Anyone who can't recognize this paradox probably (have [negative])
> _____ much experience in the real work world.
>   8

6.4   Expressions of Quantity

Quantity expressions can be troublesome when it comes to subject-verb agreement. The rules below govern quantity expressions with both singular and plural verbs.

- When a quantity word is followed by a prepositional phrase, the verb usually agrees with the quantity word.

  One of the presidential candidates **is** in town today.

  Three of my classes **were** canceled yesterday!

- Some expressions of quantity can take either a singular or a plural verb depending on whether the noun in the prepositional phrase is singular or plural.

	Singular	Plural
All of the …	**All** of the *restaurant* **was** full.	**All** of the *restaurants* **were** full.
A lot of …	**A lot** of the *money* **was** torn.	**A lot** of the *bills* **were** torn.
Some of the …	**Some** of the *pizza* **has** been eaten.	**Some** of the *pizzas* **have** been eaten.
One-half (third, quarter) of the …	**One-third** of the *population* **is** going to vote.	**One-third** of the *people* **are** going to vote.

- The quantity word *none* takes a singular verb. Remember that *none* means "not one" (and "one" is singular).

> I looked at all the paintings. ***None* is** interesting to me.

> ***None*** of the ***paintings* is** interesting to me. (formal)

In spoken English, most people use a plural verb when a plural noun follows *none*. Never use a plural verb with *none* in formal academic writing.

> *Informal use only:* ***None*** of the ***paintings* are** interesting to me.

Exercise 4 Look around your classroom as you complete these sentences. Be sure to consider quantity when choosing a verb. The first one has been done for you.

1. One of my classmates _is sleeping in class._____.

2. None of my friends _____.

3. Some of the people in class _____.

4. Everyone _____.

5. Some of the desks _____.

6. No one in the class _____.

7. One-half of the class _____.

8. One-half of the students _____.

When you use the following quantity words alone as subjects, without objects of prepositions after them, they take the verbs indicated below.

Singular	Plural
One **is** / **makes**	Both **are** / **need**
A little **is** / **falls**	A few **are** / **fall**
Each **is** / **needs**	
Every **is** / **has**	

Exercise 5   As you read the paragraph, underline the correct form of the verb twice in parentheses.

Careers in Information Technology

The number of people choosing a career in information technology

(is increasing, are increasing) year by year. This decision is a smart one, for most
      1

companies now (need, needs) someone with advanced computer knowledge. Web
      2

design, computer graphics, and software development (is, are) just some of the areas
      3

that (is, are) in demand. Anyone with the skill to manipulate a keyboard and be
      4

creative (has, have) the opportunity to find an excellent employer. For those who
      5

(is not, are not) happy working for someone, other opportunities (exist, exists).
      6   **7**

Consulting (is, are) an excellent way to make a good living but not be tied down
      8

to one job. People who like to make their own hours, choose their contracts, and

decide how much they are willing to work (thrive, thrives) on consulting work.
      9

Overall, a career in information technology, one of the most booming sectors that

(has developed, have developed) over the last ten years, (is, are) a smart choice.
      10   **11**

6.5   Connecting Words and Phrases and Subject-Verb Agreement

The next two sections show some common connecting words and phrases. The agreement of the verb depends on the particular connecting word or phrase.

- With the connecting words *neither+nor* and *either+or*, the verb must agree with the subject that is closer to the verb.

  Neither the *professor* nor her ***students* are** in the library.

  Neither the *students* nor the ***professor* is** in the library.

  Either my *mother* or my ***uncles* are** taking a vacation next week.

  Either my *uncles* or my ***mother* is** taking a vacation next week.

- With the connecting phrases *along with* and *together with*, the verb must agree with the first noun mentioned.

  The ***professor***, along with her students, **is** in the library.

  The ***students***, along with their professor, **are** in the library.

  The anatomy ***books***, together with the corresponding instructor's guide, **look** brand new.

  The instructor's ***guide***, together with the corresponding anatomy books, **looks** brand new.

Exercise 6 The phrases in the first column are subjects, and the phrases in the second column are verbs plus objects or prepositional phrases. Match the second column of verb phrases with their corresponding subjects. One answer will not be used. The first one has been done for you.

_____c_____ 1. The committee members, along with the company president,

_____ 2. Some of the more recent history books

_____ 3. None of the storm victims

_____ 4. Either the romantic comedies or the action film

_____ 5. Everyone in the modern dance class

_____ 6. Two-thirds of the band members

_____ 7. Anyone born in the United States

_____ 8. Half of the class

a. want to change musical style.

b. is eligible to become president.

c. are evaluating the annual report.

d. is excited about the performance.

e. discuss oppression of Native Americans.

f. are going to win the movie award.

g. is going to get government aid.

h. is scheduled to be shown on TV tonight.

i. isn't ready for the exam.

6.6 *A number of* Versus *the number of*

The phrases *a number of* and *the number of* have different subject-verb agreement rules:

- The quantity phrase *a number of* always takes the plural form of the verb.

  A number of consulting firm addresses **were** left to me by my old boss.

- *The number of* takes the singular verb ending.

  The number of consulting firm addresses in the directory **is** extremely short.

- *A number of* literally means "quite a few" or "many," while *the number of* refers to the actual number or quantity of items, so *a number of* is plural and *the number of* is singular.

6.7 Some Nouns That Look Plural But Take a Singular Verb

Some nouns seem to be plural because they end in *-s* (mathematics) or because they have a number in them (fifty dollars). However, nouns like these take a singular verb.

1. Names of areas of study usually take a singular verb even when the noun has an *-s* ending.

   Mathematics is not an easy subject for many people, including myself.

2. Country names with the plural *-s* ending take the singular verb form.

   The Netherlands is also known as Holland.

3. Expressions of money, time, and distance take the singular verb form.

   Fifty dollars for a dinner for one person **seems** like a lot of money to me.

Editing
Exercise 7   The following paragraph contains six errors in subject-verb agreement. Read the paragraph and correct the errors. The first one has been done for you.

Setting Budgets

Kim, along with three of her friends, ~~are~~ *is* going to move to New York City next

summer. They are all very excited about the move, but they are having some money

problems. One of the biggest problems are the amount of money that they have to

spend on rent. There are four of them, and a two-room apartment in Manhattan

cost almost $3,000. Three thousand dollars are a lot of money to spend every

month. Because of this, the friends has been saving money for the past three years.

Kim's money, together with the others' funds, is probably going to be enough to

---

(continued)

pay for half a year. In this way, they don't have to worry too much about finding jobs right away. Kim and her friends wants to be stage performers on Broadway, but they will have to work hard to make it. They have to make a reasonable budget for themselves and stick to it.

Editing

⚠ Exercise 8

In each sentence, one of the four underlined words or phrases is not correct. Circle the letter of the error and write the correction above the error.

1. The members <u>of the</u> swim team <u>was disqualified</u> for <u>having had</u> too <u>many false</u> starts

          A   **B**   **C**   **D**

   during the last state competition.

2. My landlord, <u>together with</u> the other <u>owners</u> of our apartment building, <u>is getting</u>

               A   **B**   **C**

   ready to set up a renovation contract, so the apartments <u>is going to</u> look much better.

                                               D

3. Many of the TV <u>shows</u> that <u>are aired</u> these days are reality-type shows; the <u>general</u>

               A   **B**   **C**

   public, however, <u>are not so</u> happy with the content.

                      D

4. Everyone who <u>was present</u> in class yesterday <u>was</u> surprised by the <u>instructor's</u> pop quiz.

               A   **B**   **C**

   A lot of <u>the student</u> were unprepared for the quiz.

         D

Exercise 9   Circle the letter of the correct answer. Be prepared to explain your answers.

1. There _____ dozens of public and presentation speaking books on the shelves of most retail bookstores.

   A. is   B.   are

2. Some of their titles _____ practical—*Speaking Your Way to the Top, Writing Great Speeches*, and *High-Impact Presentations*.

   A. is   B.   are

3. Perhaps one-half of the titles _____ somewhat bizarre—*I Can See You Naked, I'd Rather Die Than Give a Speech*, and *What to Say When You're Dying on the Platform*.

   A. is   B.   are

4. Clearly, any one of these titles _____ some insight into the subject of speech making.

   A. provides   B.   provide

5. The practical titles _____ a compelling need for presentation speaking skills in business and career settings.

   A. presumes   B.   presume

6. The weird titles appeal to those speakers who are anxious about speaking in front of an audience. That is, someone with a fear of getting too much attention _____ likely to buy this type of book.

   A. is   B.   are

7. Both sets of titles _____ merit.

   A. has   B.   have

8. However, taking a closer look at any of these books quickly reveals that there _____ not a clear way to measure their effectiveness.

   A. is   B.   are.

Exercise 10   Write a paragraph about a career in which you are interested. Discuss the background necessary for getting into this line of work and the job opportunities. Use at least five quantity words or connecting phrases such as:

no one	everyone	together with	a number of
most of	some	either … or …	neither … nor …

Underline the quantity words in your writing. If they are used as the subject, put two lines under their corresponding verbs. Exchange paragraphs with a partner and check each other's work for correct subject-verb agreement.

7 *Prepositions*

In this chapter, you will review and practice the most commonly used <u>prepositions</u> in English. Prepositions come in two basic types: single-word prepositions, such as *in* and *by*, and multiword prepositions, such as *in front of*. Their use can be literal, such as *on the table*, or idiomatic, such as *on the contrary*.

 ## CHECK YOUR GRAMMAR

Four of the eight underlined words contain an error related to prepositions. Can you explain why each of these underlined areas is (or is not) wrong? Discuss with a partner.

Space Bubble

Every person is surrounded <u>for a psychological bubble</u> of space. The size of the bubble depends <u>in the person's cultural background</u>, emotional state, and the activities <u>in which he or she is participating</u>. <u>Throughout Northern Europe</u>, people tend to prefer a larger zone <u>of personal space</u> and often avoid <u>of touching</u> and close contact. They require <u>of more room</u> around them and structure their lifestyles to meet the need <u>for this space</u>, both in public and in private.

Adapted from: R. Berko, Wolvin, A., and Wolvin, D. (2007). *Communicating: A Social and Career Focus*, 10th ed. Boston: Houghton Mifflin, p. 74.

7.1 Common Prepositions

We can group many prepositions into categories such as time, location, or direction. Some prepositions, such as *at*, are in all three of these categories. Other prepositions need to be memorized and are used with specific nouns, verbs, or adjectives. The exercises in this chapter will offer you practice with different kinds of prepositions. In the chart on the next page, you can see the most common English prepositions. How many do you recognize?

about	beside	inside	past
above	besides	in spite of	since
across	between	into	through
after	beyond	instead of	throughout
against	but	like	till
ahead of	by	near	to
along	close to	next to	toward(s)
among	despite	of	under
around	down	off	underneath
as	during	on	unlike
at	except	onto	until
back to / from	far from	on top of	up
before	for	opposite	upon
behind	from	out	with
below	in	outside	within
beneath	in back / front of	over	without

7.2   A Few Basic Rules

These few basic rules about prepositions will help you as you work through this chapter.

1. A preposition is a word that shows the relationship between a noun or a noun equivalent—a noun phrase, a clause (see Chapter 18), or a gerund phrase (see Chapter 10)—and another word in a sentence.

    The girls' soccer team played **on** the new field. (*On* shows the relationship of the noun *field* to the verb *played*.)

2. A preposition always has an object. The object can be a noun, a pronoun, or a noun-equivalent (a noun phrase, a clause, or a gerund phrase). Together they form what is called a *prepositional phrase*. In the following examples, the preposition is bold and the object is circled. The prepositional phrase is in a box.

    They received a notice **from** Mr. Taft. (object = noun)

    They received a notice **from** him. (object = pronoun)

    They received a notice **from** a young lawyer. (object = noun phrase)

    They received a notice **from** a young lawyer who works downtown. (object = noun phrase + adjective clause)

    They received a notice **about** cleaning their yard. (object = gerund phrase)

3. Some prepositions may be used as adverbs or as particles. Their meanings can be either literal or idiomatic.

> He walked **up** the stairs. (preposition; literal meaning)

> Stand **up**. (adverb)

> Look **up** the rule. (particle; used with the verb *look* to form one unit of meaning— *look up*—which is idiomatic)

7.3   Prepositions of Time

Prepositions of time can be about a specific time, a general time, or a length of time.

7.3.1   *Specific Time*

Here is a list of prepositions of specific time:

after	during	past
at	for	since
before	from	till
between	in	to
by	on	until

Use these prepositions when you know the specific time, such as *at 6:00* or *before noon*. Here are more examples:

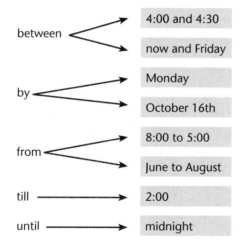

between	4:00 and 4:30
	now and Friday
by	Monday
	October 16th
from	8:00 to 5:00
	June to August
till	2:00
until	midnight

Expressions of Specific Time

It's 10 to / till 3.	It's ten minutes **to** 3:00.
It's 20 after / past 7.	It's twenty minutes **after** 7 o'clock.
in time	They arrived **in time** to see the opening act. (not too late)

on time	They arrived **on time** for the meeting. (at the required time)
out of time	That's it. We're **out of time**. (The allotted time is over [for us.])
at the end of	The report is due **at the end of** the day. (when the time ends)

Exercise 1   On a separate sheet of paper, write a short paragraph about how you spend a typical day. Use at least six prepositions and expressions of specific time. Underline the prepositions.

7.3.2   *General Time*

Use prepositions of general time—*at, by, in, on*—when you refer to the time of day, a day of the week, a month, a season, or a year.

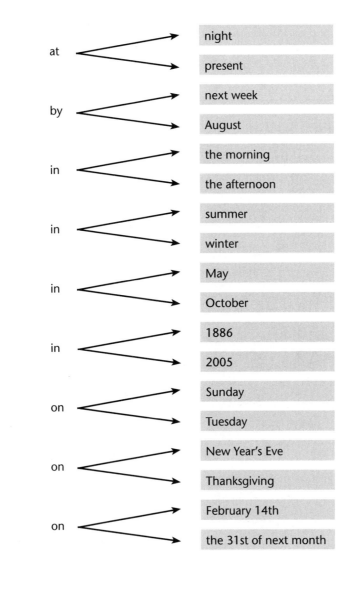

at → night / present

by → next week / August

in → the morning / the afternoon

in → summer / winter

in → May / October

in → 1886 / 2005

on → Sunday / Tuesday

on → New Year's Eve / Thanksgiving

on → February 14th / the 31st of next month

Exercise 2 Write six sentences about two or more special holiday events and how you have celebrated them. Use each of these prepositions of general time at least once: *at, by, in*, and *on*. Circle the prepositions.

1. _____

_____

2. _____

_____

3. _____

_____

4. _____

_____

5. _____

_____

6. _____

_____

7.3.3 *Length of Time*

The prepositions *at, during, since, through*, and *for* indicate a span of time rather than one specific time or a general time.

In English "a half" comes *after* the number as in "two and a half weeks," not "two weeks and a half."

Exercise 3 Fill in the blanks with the correct preposition of specific time, general time, or length of time. The first one has been done for you.

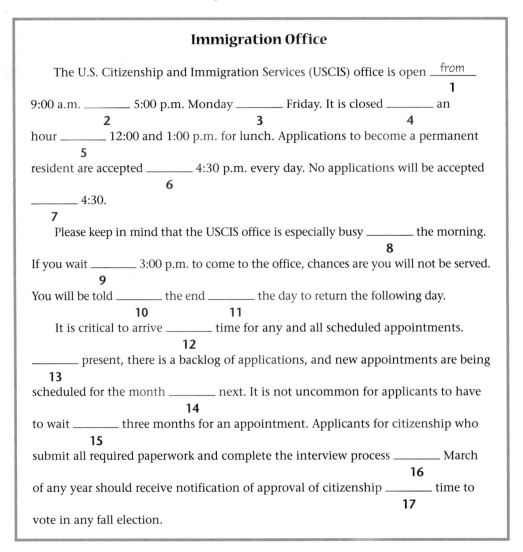

Immigration Office

The U.S. Citizenship and Immigration Services (USCIS) office is open __from__

                                                                      1

9:00 a.m. _____ 5:00 p.m. Monday _____ Friday. It is closed _____ an

              2   **3**   **4**

hour _____ 12:00 and 1:00 p.m. for lunch. Applications to become a permanent

        5

resident are accepted _____ 4:30 p.m. every day. No applications will be accepted

                                6

_____ 4:30.

    7

Please keep in mind that the USCIS office is especially busy _____ the morning.

                                                                        8

If you wait _____ 3:00 p.m. to come to the office, chances are you will not be served.

              9

You will be told _____ the end _____ the day to return the following day.

                      10   **11**

It is critical to arrive _____ time for any and all scheduled appointments.

                                12

_____ present, there is a backlog of applications, and new appointments are being

    13

scheduled for the month _____ next. It is not uncommon for applicants to have

                              14

to wait _____ three months for an appointment. Applicants for citizenship who

          15

submit all required paperwork and complete the interview process _____ March

                                                                        16

of any year should receive notification of approval of citizenship _____ time to

                                                                        17

vote in any fall election.

7.4 Prepositions of Location

Prepositions of location tell where something is. Here are the most common ones:

above	behind	close to	near	throughout
across	below	far from	next to	under
across from	beneath	in	on	underneath
ahead of	beside	in back of*	opposite	
among	between	in front of*	outside	
at	by	inside	over	

_____

* Pay careful attention to the word *the* in expressions with these prepositions of location.

in back of

in the back of

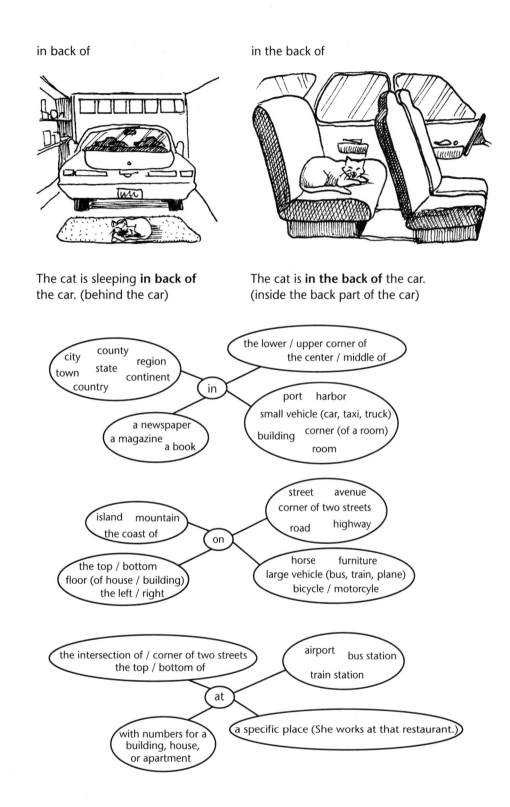

The cat is sleeping **in back of** the car. (behind the car)

The cat is **in the back of** the car. (inside the back part of the car)

in
- city   county
- town   state   region
- country   continent
- a newspaper   a magazine   a book
- the lower / upper corner of
- the center / middle of
- port   harbor
- small vehicle (car, taxi, truck)
- building   corner (of a room)
- room

on
- island   mountain
- the coast of
- the top / bottom
- floor (of house / building)
- the left / right
- street   avenue
- corner of two streets
- road   highway
- horse   furniture
- large vehicle (bus, train, plane)
- bicycle / motorcyle

at
- the intersection of / corner of two streets
- the top / bottom of
- airport   bus station
- train station
- with numbers for a building, house, or apartment
- a specific place (She works at that restaurant.)

Use the preposition *between* with two people or things:

Between you and me, I'm really getting tired of this place.

Use *among* for three or more people or things:

Among all my friends, Joan is the hardest-working one.

7.4.1 *Idiomatic Expressions With Prepositions of Location*

Here is a list of idiomatic prepositions of location:

in bed (sleeping)	on the bed (sitting)
at home	at work
at / in school	at / in church at / in the office
at the hospital (visiting, working)	in the hospital (a patient)

Editing

⚠ Exercise 4 As you read the paragraph, choose the correct preposition in parentheses and underline it. The first one has been done for you.

Susana's Trip

    Susana was (in, <u>at</u>) home on Tuesday, standing (<u>in front of</u>, in the front of) the
          1   **2**
window (in, on) her living room (at, on) the eighteenth floor of Ocean Towers,
       3   **4**
her apartment building. As she gazed out the window, she saw the marina

(behind, below) her.
   5

    Scattered (outside, throughout) the marina were small boats, some tied to the
            6
docks and others sitting (between, among) the many buoys (at, in) the harbor.
               7   **8**
(On, In) her left, Susana saw a cruise ship sailing into port. She watched as the
 9
tugboat (beneath, behind) the ship guided it to its berth. Passengers (in, on)
       10   **11**
the ship were (over, outside) standing (at, on) the decks and waving to people
           12   **13**
(at the bottom of, below) them.
       14
    Susana wished she could take a cruise. It had always been her dream. She

imagined herself (at, on) an island, surrounded (by, close to) deep blue water and
          15   **16**
(across from, far from) everyone and everything.
   17
    Suddenly, Susana heard the sound of the intercom (in front of, near) the front
                             18
door. It was the doorman, buzzing to let her know that the taxi she had called for

had arrived. In a couple of hours, she would be (on, at) the airport, sitting (on, at)
           19   **20**

(continued)

a plane headed for the Arctic Circle, (in the top of, at the top of) the world. The
21
Arctic Circle was as (far to, far from) a tropical island as a person could get. Susana
22
shivered as she closed the door to her apartment and waited (near to, next to) the
23
elevator. She'd rather be headed for a vacation (on, beside) that island!
24

7.5 Prepositions of Direction or Movement

These prepositions indicate a specific direction or a movement in a direction:

across	back to / from	in / into	past
along	by	off	through
around	down	onto	to
at	for	out of	toward
away from	from	over	up

Here are some examples:

If you go **across** the road, you'll see the entrance to the trail. (*across* applies to a flat area, such as a road, a parking lot, or a bridge)

You'll have to go **over** a hill before you see the pond. (*over* refers to an up/down movement, such as over a hill, a fence, or a bridge)

When you go **through** the Millers' garden, you'll know it's the end of the trail. (*through* indicates something having two sides or entrance/exit, such as a window, a garden, or a city)

7.5.1 *Expressions With Prepositions of Direction or Movement*

Here are some expressions using prepositions of direction or movement:

1. arrive **in** a city, state, country

   I arrived **in** Dallas yesterday.

2. arrive **at** other places (restaurant, school, or work)

   I arrived **at** the bank late.

3. go **to** or leave **for** a place

   I left **for** the airport at noon.

4. go **from** a place **to** another place

   I went **from** Miami **to** New York.

Exercise 5 Read the following directions for the treasure map. Underline the thirteen prepositions that show *direction* or *movement*. Correct the five that are wrong. The first one has been underlined for you.

Treasure Map

First, climb <u>out of</u> the boat. Walk along the pier out of the shore. When you get

to the shore, turn east and go past the palm trees. Near the palm trees are some huge

boulders. Climb by the boulders and head for the tower. Walk around the tower and

through the bushes that run into the stream. Go across the stream, away from the

tower. Soon you will see a flag on a pole. Dig until you find the box buried beneath

the pole. Head back from your boat at the dock.

Exercise 6 In the space provided, write a paragraph describing a trip that you have taken or would like to take. Use at least eight direction / movement prepositions in your paragraph. Be sure to underline them.

_____

_____

_____

_____

_____

_____

_____

_____

_____

_____

_____

_____

_____

_____

_____

_____

_____

_____

_____

7.6 Prepositions in Idioms

Some prepositions occur with nouns to form idiomatic expressions. Review the phrases on the next page. You must learn these combinations as a unit. There is no rule to explain when to use a certain preposition with a specific noun.

PREPOSITION + NOUN			
at	on	out of	in
odds	hold	control	a hurry
risk	sale	order	control
war	vacation	time	danger
work	loan	shape	debt
	one hand		luck
	the other hand		love
			shape
			trouble
			pain
			person
			public
			private

For more information on preposition combinations, see Chapter 13.

Editing

Exercise 7   Read the following paragraph. Using the list of nouns below, choose a noun and write it in the appropriate space. Add the correct preposition. Refer to the previous list of preposition + noun combinations if you need help. The first one has been done for you.

control	~~odds~~	debt	hurry	love	vacation

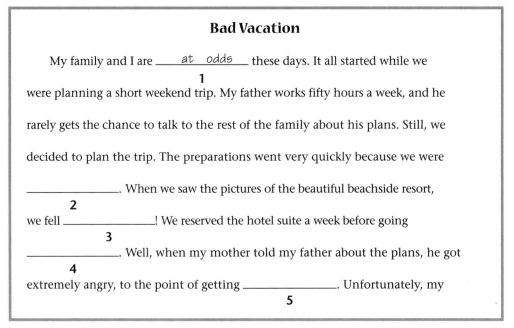

Bad Vacation

My family and I are ___*at odds*___ these days. It all started while we

1

were planning a short weekend trip. My father works fifty hours a week, and he

rarely gets the chance to talk to the rest of the family about his plans. Still, we

decided to plan the trip. The preparations went very quickly because we were

_____. When we saw the pictures of the beautiful beachside resort,

2

we fell _____! We reserved the hotel suite a week before going

3

_____. Well, when my mother told my father about the plans, he got

4

extremely angry, to the point of getting _____. Unfortunately, my

5

(continued)

family had forgotten that that particular weekend was his mother and father's 50th wedding anniversary. Needless to say, we didn't go to the beach that weekend. In addition, we're _____ because the weekend trip was non-refundable.
                              6
Next time we'll remember to ask if everyone in the family is available to go on a spontaneous trip.

Editing

▲ **Exercise 8**   In each item, one of the four underlined words or phrases is not correct. Circle the letter of the error and write the correction above the error.

1. Our dog Ginger loves to roam <u>around</u> the house. Currently, she's sleeping
                                    A

    <u>in the back of</u> the van, so be careful not to hit her <u>as you leave</u> the driveway. You
         B   **C**

    <u>don't want to</u> run her over.
         D

2. We got Ginger <u>in</u> 2003 when she was six weeks old. She was so scared to be <u>in a new</u>
                   A   **B**

    environment that she <u>spends</u> most of her time <u>in the bedroom</u> closet.
                              C   **D**

3. Now Ginger owns the house and acts like the queen <u>of the</u> castle. You can find her
                                                          A

    <u>under the bed</u>, <u>on the couch</u>, and even <u>below the pool</u>.
         B   **C**   **D**

4. Even though we've tried to train her to stay <u>off the furniture</u>, she rarely listens. Right
                                                     A

    now she's sleeping <u>on bed</u>. Yesterday she escaped <u>from</u> the back yard. We found her
                          B   **C**

    two hours later <u>on the corner</u> of Main Street and Himes Avenue.
                         D

Exercise 9   Circle the letter of the correct answer. Be prepared to explain your answers.

1. Charles moved _____ Nevada in 2003.

   A. at   C. since

   B. in   D. to

2. _____ his first year, he lived in a small apartment about a mile from his aunt's

   house.

   A. At   C. Since

   B. During   D. When

3. _____, he decided to buy a condominium so he could be on his own.

   A. After   C. Out of

   B. After that   D. On the contrary

4. Charles got a job _____ a local community college, and he works there _____

   weekends.

   A. at … on   C. in … at

   B. on … at   D. at … in

5. Charles loves the weather _____ Nevada, but he's planning on moving to California

   _____ a year.

   A. at … at   C. in … in

   B. at … in   D. in … at

6. He's been accepted at San Diego State University, where classes will begin _____

   August.

   A. on   C. at

   B. in   D. since

7. He has already found a really great apartment. Luckily for Charles, his new apartment

   is _____ from the campus.

   A. near   C. between

   B. across   D. beside

8. Charles is not sure if he will like California better _____ Nevada, but he is looking

   forward to his new situation.

   A. in   C. from

   B. for   D. than

Exercise 10   Write a paragraph describing a specific event you attended or an experience you had. Be sure to identify when and where the event or experience occurred. Include how you reacted, how you felt, what you thought, and what you did. Before you begin, make a list of the prepositions from this chapter that you will try to use. In your paragraph, circle the prepositions from the list that you were able to use. Exchange paragraphs with a partner and check each other's work for correct use of prepositions.

_____

_____

_____

_____

_____

_____

_____

_____

_____

_____

_____

_____

_____

_____

_____

_____

_____

_____

_____

_____

_____

8 *Word Forms*

In this chapter, you will find charts with different <u>word forms</u> for the major parts of speech: <u>nouns</u>, <u>adjectives</u>, <u>adverbs</u>, and <u>verbs</u>. Study the charts before you do the exercises that follow them.

✔ CHECK YOUR GRAMMAR

Four of the eight underlined words contain an error related to word forms. Can you explain why each of these underlined areas is (or is not) wrong? Discuss with a partner.

Modernist Movements

Closely allied with the various <u>modernist</u> <u>movements</u> in the <u>visualize</u> arts,

<u>musicians</u>, and dance, <u>write</u> and theater <u>artists</u> in the opening decades of the

twentieth <u>century</u> showed many of the same formal and thematic <u>concernings</u>.

From: Witt et al., *The Humanities*, p. 390.

8.1   Adjective Endings

The following is a list of commonly used endings for adjectives. Refer to them as you complete Exercise 1.

Ending	Meaning	Examples
-able	able to	enjoy**able**, wash**able**
-al	having the quality of	crimin**al**, gener**al**, music**al**
-an / -ian	belonging or relating to	Americ**an**, reptil**ian**
-ant	having the quality of	reluct**ant**, defi**ant**
-ar / -ary	relating to	spectacul**ar**, ordin**ary**
-ate	characterized by	consider**ate**, passion**ate**
-ative / -itive	having the quality of	talk**ative**, prim**itive**

(continued)

Ending	Meaning	Examples
-ed	past participle	bored, interested
-en	past participle	written, stolen
-en	made of	golden, wooden
-ent	having the quality of	consistent, dependent
-ese	of a place or country	Chinese, Portuguese
-esque	in the style of	picturesque, grotesque
-ful	full of	beautiful, joyful
-ible	able to	edible, visible
-ic / -ical	related to, nature of	heroic, conical
-ine	having the nature of	feminine
-ing	present participle	boring, interesting
-ish	having the character of	childish, sheepish
-ive	tending to, causing	active, explosive
-lent	full of	succulent, virulent
-less	without	harmless, childless
-like	like, similar to	childlike, ladylike
-ly	having the qualities of	matronly, worldly
-ory	relating to	mandatory, obligatory
-ous / -ious	full of	contemptuous, gracious
-proof	protected from	foolproof, childproof
-y	tending to	creamy, unhealthy

Exercise 1 Read the paragraph, which contains twenty-five adjectives. Many of them have endings from the list on the previous page. The first two adjectives have been underlined for you. Find and underline the other twenty-three.

Central Asia

Central Asia offers possibilities for <u>imaginative</u> travelers to experience new horizons. The many cities available to travelers include the pristine mountains of Kyrgyzstan, the historic cities found in Uzbekistan, and the picturesque countrysides of Kazakhstan. The relatively unknown areas offer alternative venues to the more popular areas of Europe, South America, and Asia. As the local economies are growing slowly, Central Asian prices are relatively cheap. Visitors can witness not only natural beauty but also towns and cities rich in history. Opulent mosques and palaces can be seen in the regional capitals of Central Asia. For a truly unforgettable experience, Central Asia has numerous venues of interest for the brave traveler.

8.2 Noun Endings

This list gives commonly used noun endings. Refer to them as you complete Exercise 2.

Ending	Meaning	Examples
-acy	condition	demo**cracy**, fall**acy**
-age	action, state	marri**age**, us**age**

(continued)

Ending	Meaning	Examples
-an / -ian	person related or belonging to	Moroccan, librarian
-ance / -ence	condition, state	attendance, excellence
-ant / -ent	person who	participant, student
-ar	person who	liar, scholar
-ation	action, state	inauguration, exploration
-dom	being or having position of	freedom, kingdom
-ee	person who receives something	grantee, refugee
-er / -or	person who does	dancer, employer, professor
-ery	relating to, quality	bribery, slavery, robbery
-ese	belonging to or native of	Vietnamese, Chinese
-hood	state of	brotherhood, childhood
-ics	science, art, or practice	mathematics, academics
-ing	gerund (action)	swimming, bowling
-ion / -sion / -tion	action, state, result	opinion, occasion, reception
-ism	belief, practice	socialism, skepticism, symbolism
-ist	person who believes or does	capitalist, terrorist
-ment	result of action	argument, achievement
-mony	action or result	ceremony, hegemony
-ness	quality, state	darkness, politeness
-or	activity, quality, or state	behavior, demeanor
-ship	condition, quality	partnership, scholarship
-ty / -ity	quality, condition	eligibility, community

Exercise 2   In each sentence, write the correct noun ending. The first one has been done for you.

1. The inaugur_ation_ of the new university president was quite an event.

2. Memb_____ of the media were present to film the occa_____ .

3. Current stud_____ were also on hand to witness the cere_____ .

4. The university president spoke of the import_____ of academic excell_____ .

5. She also mentioned strengthening the partner_____ between the university and the commun_____ .

6. After the ceremony, a recep_____ was held in the University Center.

8.3 Verb Endings

Here are some commonly used endings for verbs. Refer to them as you complete Exercise 3.

Ending	Meaning	Examples
-ate	cause, make	grad**uate**, compli**cate**
-en	made of, make	black**en**, rip**en**, wid**en**
-ify	make	beaut**ify**, simpl**ify**
-ize	make	critic**ize**, symbol**ize**

Exercise 3   As you read the paragraph, fill in the missing verbs using the clues in parentheses.

The IRS

Many Americans have trouble understanding the difficult tax forms they need to fill out every year. The Internal Revenue Service should (make simple) _____ these forms. Taxpayers often (give criticism) _____ the IRS for continuing
1   2
to use these forms. The highly advanced legal language on these tax forms (gives complications) _____ the process of
3
answering the questions correctly. If taxpayer resentment (becomes wider) _____,
4
perhaps the IRS will really think about paperwork reduction and reform.

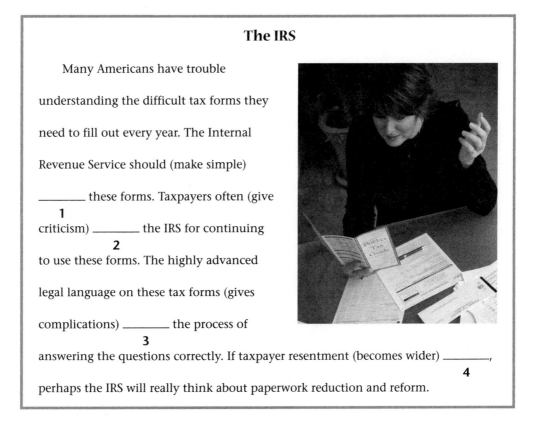

8.4 Adverb Endings

Most words ending in -*ly* are adverbs. They answer the question "how?"

Ending	Meaning	Examples
-ly	manner of	happ**ily**, strange**ly**

Some adverbs have irregular forms that you have to memorize:

　　　well　　hard　　worse　　late　　fast

⚠ Exercise 4 Read the dialogue and look for ten word form errors in the underlined phrases. Write a correction above each error. The first two have been done for you. (Number 1 is correct as it is.)

Mario: Hi, Ian. I haven't seen you in <u>a while</u>!
1

                             really
Ian: I know. I've <u>been ~~real~~ busy with</u> school and other things.
                                2

Mario: What other things? Did <u>you get a job</u>?
                                      3

Ian: Of course not! You know <u>my opinionate</u>: always concentrate <u>on academize subjects</u>.
                                               4   5

Mario: That's right. So … what's been keeping you <u>so actively</u>?
                                                                      6

Ian: Well, it's related to <u>my professorship</u>, Dr. Cleaver.
                                      7

Mario: What about her? Are you helping her out <u>with research</u>?
                                                                 8

Ian: Actually, it's about <u>my scholar</u>. I must put in at least twenty hours per week in the
                                      9

research lab to maintain <u>my eligible</u>. It's <u>mandatory</u>.
                                      10   11

Mario: I see <u>what you mean</u>. It must be tough to keep up with <u>all that work</u>. Are you
                                12   13

getting paid, at least?

Ian: A little. That's the <u>good news</u>, I guess. With my own pocket money, I don't have to be
                                      14

so <u>dependence on my parents</u>.
              15

Mario: Well, <u>you've only got</u> one more year till you <u>graduation</u>. I think you should look on
                       16   17

the bright side.

Ian: I guess you're right. Boy, things really have changed since <u>our childlike</u>, huh?
                                                                             18

Mario: You can say *that* again.

8.5	**Word Forms Across Parts of Speech**

The chart on the next page gives you the forms a word takes in different parts of speech. Refer to this information as you complete Exercise 5.

Noun	Verb	Adjective	Adverb
description	describe	descriptive	descriptively
—	—	appropriate	appropriately
desire	desire	desirable	—
finance	finance	financial	financially
development	develop	developed / developing	—
time	time	timely	—
information	inform	informative	—
preference	prefer	preferential / preferred	—
fear	fear	fearful	fearfully
qualification	qualify	—	—
benefit	benefit	beneficial	beneficially
lead/leader	lead	leading	—
strength	strengthen	strong	strongly

Exercise 5   Write eight sentences using at least two words in each sentence from the chart above. Circle those words. The first sentence has been done for you.

1. The (leader) of the trade union offered a (beneficial) package to the members.

2. _____

   _____

3. _____

   _____

4. _____

   _____

5. _____

   _____

6. _____

   _____

7. _____

   _____

8. _____

   _____

Exercise 6   Read the following paragraph. From the list below, choose the correct word form to insert in each blank. The first one has been done for you.

produce	production	class	classy	classic
poor	poorly	involved	involvement	involve
excellence	excellent	popularity	popularly	popular
China	Chinese	newness	new	newly

> ### Unlucky Avenger
>
> A new action film was released last Friday by Tri-Moon Pictures. Titled *Unlucky Avenger*, this movie opened in Los Angeles to ~~excellent~~ _____ reviews. It stars the _____
>   **1**   **2**
>
> action hero Xin-Yeo in his first U.S. _____. The plot of the film is not _____. It
>   **3**   **4**
>
> is the _____ good versus evil idea that has been so _____ in the past decade,
>   **5**   **6**
>
> especially with U.S. audiences. Mr. Xin-Yeo plays a _____ young man who gets
>   **7**
>
> involved in a series of seemingly unrelated incidents. His _____, however, ruins
>   **8**
>
> the plans of the enemy. *Unlucky Avenger* will open nationwide next month.

Exercise 7   Rewrite each sentence, changing the underlined word or words to the word form indicated in parentheses. You may have to make other changes to the sentence. The first one has been done for you.

1. Some symbols are related to <u>literature</u> (change to adjective), some to <u>politics</u> (change to adjective), and others to <u>religion</u> (change to adjective).

   Some symbols are literary, some political, and others religious.
   _____

2. For example, an object made of <u>gold</u> might represent the sun or power and wealth. (change to adjective)

   _____

   _____

3. Animals are often <u>symbols</u> of traits or represent beliefs. (change to verb)

   _____

4. A parrot suggests the image of a person who likes to <u>talk a lot</u>. (change to adjective)

   _____

   _____

5. In the United States, the donkey symbolizes the party that supports a <u>democratic</u>

   system. (change to noun)

   _____

   _____

6. Some symbols may be easy to understand, such as the owl, which represents being <u>wise</u>,

   (change to noun) or the pineapple, which depicts being <u>hospitable</u>. (change to noun)

   _____

   _____

7. Sometimes symbols are warnings. For example, the Jolly Roger, the flag flown from

   pirate ships, evokes the threat of a possible <u>violent</u> condition. (change to noun)

   _____

   _____

8. The same symbol, the skull and crossbones, is used on substances full of <u>poison</u>

   (change to adjective), warning people that the contents are not able to be <u>eaten</u>

   (change to adjective) and are, in fact, quite full of <u>harm</u> (change to adjective) if eaten.

   _____

   _____

9. A symbol does not necessarily have the same meaning for all people. In fact, some

   writers make their symbols very <u>complicated</u> (change to verb), causing readers to <u>argue</u>

   (change to noun) among themselves.

   _____

   _____

10. For more information on the practice of using <u>symbols</u> (change to another noun form),

    talk to the reference person who works in the <u>library</u> (change to another noun form).

    Perhaps there's a title "Symbolism Made <u>Simple</u>" (change to verb) on the shelves.

    _____

    _____

Exercise 8   Use a dictionary to find as many word forms as you can for each word below taken from a recent news story. Be sure to include a notation for the part of speech of the variations you list (n = noun; v = verb; adj = adjective; adv = adverb).

1. (v) marry: _____

2. (adj) popular: _____

3. (n) problem: _____

4. (n) immediacy: _____

5. (adj) current: _____

6. (v) labor: _____

7. (v) sympathize: _____

8. (n) president: _____

Editing
▲ **Exercise 9**   In each item, one of the four underlined words or phrases is not correct. Circle the letter of the error and write the correction above the error.

1. The <u>argumentative</u> presented by the <u>prosecuting</u> attorney was not <u>accepted</u> by the
      A   **B**   **C**

   judge in last week's murder <u>case</u>.
                                D

2. The <u>defense</u> attorney attempted to present her <u>client</u> as an <u>ordinarily</u> and <u>simple</u>
       A   **B**   **C**   **D**

   person.

3. If the <u>prosecutor</u> had shown that the <u>defendant</u> was, in fact, a very <u>complicate</u>
       A   **B**   **C**

   individual, the <u>judgment</u> might have been different.
                      D

4. The judge later <u>criticism</u> the <u>prosecuting</u> attorney for lack of <u>preparation</u> in this
                      A   **B**   **C**

   important <u>criminal</u> case.
              D

Exercise 10   Circle the letter of the correct answer. Be prepared to explain your answers.

1. As the company's receptionist, Louise needs to be _____ to visitors.

   A. gracious   C. graceful

   B. graciously   D. gracing

2. Unfortunately, Louise's _____ behavior often gets her into trouble at work.

   A. childless   C. child

   B. children   D. childish

3. Many of her coworkers think that she is _____ when dealing with customers.

   A. inconsiderate   C. inconsiderately

   B. inconsiderably   D. inconsideration

4. The first impression that she makes is especially _____ for the company's _____
   customers.

   A. important ... prospective   C. importance ... prospective

   B. important ... prospectively   D. importance ... prospectively

5. Louise's job requires her to tell customers why they do not _____ for the company's
   special services or discounts.

   A. qualification   C. qualify

   B. qualificate   D. qualified

6. Her current methods of handling customers are _____ for her _____, who is
   unhappy with Louise's rudeness.

   A. problematic ... supervisor   C. problematic ... supervision

   B. problem ... supervision   D. problem ... supervisor

7. The company is _____ on her to offer friendly and efficient service to all _____
   clients.

   A. dependence ... potentially   C. dependence ... potential

   B. dependent ... potential   D. dependent ... potentially

8. Unlike some of her coworkers, Louise dresses _____ for her job. The problem is her
   behavior, which clearly needs to be more _____.

   A. appropriately ... professional   C. appropriate ... professional

   B. appropriately ... professionally   D. appropriate ... professionally

Exercise 11   Write a paragraph or short essay about a current event. You may use a topic featured on television news, in the newspaper, or at your school. Give a short background of the issue. Describe the problem, when it happened, why it exists, and who is involved. Pay close attention to word forms as you write. Exchange paragraphs with a partner and check each other's work for correct word forms.

_____

_____

_____

_____

_____

_____

_____

_____

_____

_____

_____

_____

_____

_____

_____

_____

_____

_____

_____

_____

9 Modals: Present, Future, Past

Modals are used with verbs to express many different meanings, such as the speaker's attitude or point of view about an action. You use modals in your everyday English speaking and writing now, but this review helps ensure that you are using modals correctly. In this chapter, a brief review of modals for the present and future is given before the longer explanations about past modals. Especially in writing, it is important to use the correct modal at the appropriate time while avoiding common mistakes.

✔ CHECK YOUR GRAMMAR

Three of the four underlined modal phrases contain an error related to modals. Can you explain why each of these underlined areas is (or is not) wrong? Discuss with a partner.

Internet Business

For a new Internet business, a good e-business plan should to offer detailed answers to basic questions. To begin, the planners need to determine if an Internet business will meet the needs of a group of customers. Furthermore, the planning process should provides planners with information than can helping them to identify and select groups of potential buyers, direct development of the online product or service, as well as the promotion, pricing, and distribution effort.

From: Pride et al., *Business,* p. 120.

9.1 Modals

Modals can be a single word or a multiword unit. Some single-word modals have a multiword counterpart.

Single	Multiword
will	be going to
must*	have to*
should	ought to
can OR could	be able to
should**	had better**
may	
might	
would	
shall	

* The modals *must* and *have to* are used for necessity, but *must* is much more formal.
** The modals *should* and *had better* are similar in meaning but cannot always be used interchangeably. *Had better* is much stronger and implies a warning of some kind.

9.2 Meanings of Modals

One of the most difficult aspects of modals is their meanings. Each modal has a unique meaning, but one modal may also have multiple meanings and usages.

Meaning	Modal Example Sentences
Permission	**May** I *leave* as soon as I finish the exam? (formal)
	Can I *leave* as soon as I finish the exam? (informal)
	Would you *mind* if I asked you your age?
Request	**Could** you please *sign* the purchase order for me?
	Will you *hold*, please?
	Would you *get* the door for me, please?
Certainty, Probability, and Possibility	He **will** *leave* at noon. (100% certain)
	He **can** *leave* at noon if he wants. (100% possible)
	He **must** *be* from France. (probable or logical conclusion)
	He **should** *arrive* at 6 p.m. (strong expectation)
	He **may/might/could** *arrive* at 6 p.m. (possible)

Meaning	Modal Example Sentences
Ability	He **can** *run* one mile in five minutes.
	(OR: He **is able to** *run* one mile in five minutes.)
Necessity	You **must** *get* a visa to enter that country.
	(OR: You **have to** *get* a visa to enter that country.)
Advice and Suggestions	Ella **should** *work* harder than she does.
	(OR: Ella **ought to** *work* harder than she does.)
	I don't think that you **should** *watch* so much TV.
	(OR: I don't think that you **ought to** *watch* so much TV.)
	He **had better** *finish* that report by 9:00 tomorrow morning or his boss will be upset. (very strong suggestion that implies that something bad will happen if the advice is not taken)
	If you're unhappy, just quit. You **could** *start* your own business. (offer advice or suggestion; speaker is unsure if listener may take advice; used in affirmative sentences)
	People **might** *want* to file their taxes early. (indirect suggestion)
Prediction, Intention, and Expectation	This new plan **will** *succeed.* (prediction or expectation) (OR: This new plan **is going to** *succeed.*)
	The president **will** *allocate* more money to schools. (intention)
	(OR: The president **is going to** *allocate* more money to schools.)
	The movie **is supposed to** *be* on Channel 8 at 10:00 p.m. (a planned event; conveys expectation)
	The final exam **should** *be* easy. (expectation)
	(OR: The final exam **ought to** *be* easy.)

9.3   A Few Basic Rules

These few basic rules about modals will help you as you work through this chapter.

1. The verb following the modal is always the base or simple form.

> The professor **must** *plan* the final exam soon.

Do not use *to* between the modal and the verb, as in this error:

> *Incorrect:*   The professor **must** ~~to~~ *plan* the final exam soon.

Do not add endings to the verb, such as -*s, -ing, -ed,* as in these errors:

> *Incorrect:*   The professor **must** *plans* the final exam soon.

> *Incorrect:*   The professor **must** *planning* the final exam soon.

> *Incorrect:*   The professor **must** *planned* the final exam soon.

2. Use only one single-word modal with a verb.

> The committee **might** *approve* the plan today.

Do not use two single-word modals together, as in this error:

> *Incorrect:*   The committee **might** ~~could~~ *approve* the plan.

It is sometimes possible to use a phrasal modal for the second meaning above:

> The committee **might be able to** *approve* the plan.

3. Negative modals are formed in this order: MODAL + *not* + VERB.

> She **should not** *be* here.

Do not use the auxiliary *do/does/did* to make a negative modal:

> *Incorrect:*   She ~~doesn't should~~ *be* here.

4. Questions with modals are formed in this order: MODAL + SUBJECT + VERB.

> **Could** you please *answer* the phone?

Do not use the auxiliary *do/does/did* to make a question with a modal:

> *Incorrect:*   ~~Do you could~~ please *answer* the phone?
>
> *Correct:*   **Could** you please *answer* the phone?

5. Modals can be used with the progressive forms (verb ending in *-ing*).

> We **must** *be going.*
>
> I **should** *be studying* for tomorrow's exam.
>
> The plane **will** *be leaving* in a few minutes.

6. Some modals have contracted forms, but contractions should be avoided in formal writing.

can not OR cannot	can't
will not	won't
Subject + will	*Subject*'ll (They**'ll** *be* late.)
Subject + had better	*Subject*'d better (I**'d better** *leave* now.)

9.4   Forms of Past Modals

Past modals consist of three parts: (1) the *modal*, (2) the word *have*, and (3) the *past participle* of the verb. It is the past participle that makes the whole verb past tense. (Reminder: The past participle for regular verbs is the base form of the verb + *ed*. The past participle of irregular verbs is often formed with *-en* [*spoken*] or *-ne* [*done*].)

The following sentences give an example of each past modal in this chapter.

> We **should have** *hired* more workers last year. Now our production has decreased.
>
> Sam **must have** *gone* to the beach yesterday. He has a sunburn today.

Hurricane Katrina **could have** *hit* New Orleans directly, but it affected areas to the east of the city more.

She **might have** *left* her keys on the table, but she is not sure.

It **may have** *rained* last night. Look, the grass looks wet.

You **would have** *gotten* the job for sure if you had applied for it.

With past modal constructions, you must always use the past participle of the verb after MODAL + *have*.

Incorrect:	She **must have** ~~*take*~~ the 7 p.m. flight to New York.
Correct:	She **must have** *taken* the 7 p.m. flight to New York.

With past modal constructions, never use *had*; always use *have*:

Incorrect:	She **must** ~~**had**~~ *taken* the 7 p.m. flight to New York.
Correct:	She **must have** *taken* the 7 p.m. flight to New York.

9.5 The Modal *should* in the Past

Use *should* + *have* + PAST PARTICIPLE to form the past modal.

1. We use *should have* + PAST PARTICIPLE when the action (of the verb) did not happen and someone is sorry (regrets) that the action did not happen.

   I failed the test. **I should have** *studied* last night. (The speaker did not study. The speaker regrets not studying last night.)

2. We use the negative form, *should not have* + PAST PARTICIPLE, when the action (of the verb) happened and someone is sorry (regrets) that the action happened.

   My stomach hurts! I **shouldn't have** *eaten* those four doughnuts. (The speaker ate four doughnuts. The speaker regrets eating them.)

Exercise 1 Underline the *should have* + PAST PARTICIPLE construction in each sentence. Then put a check mark (✔) beside all of the sentences underneath that are true. The first one has been done for you.

1. She <u>should have cooked</u> the beans and the rice in separate pots.

   ___✔___ a. She cooked the beans and rice in the same pot.

   _____ b. She cooked the beans and rice in two pots.

2. Tom is sure that he shouldn't have traveled to Taiwan in the summer.

   _____ a. Tom traveled to Taiwan.

   _____ b. Tom regrets traveling to Taiwan.

3. You should have told me this news sooner.

_____ a. The speaker now knows the news.

_____ b. The speaker still doesn't know the news.

4. I'm sorry for not inviting you to my party. I should have sent you an invitation.

_____ a. The speaker invited the person to the party.

_____ b. The speaker did not invite the person to the party.

5. Many people think that the U.S. shouldn't have dropped atomic bombs on Japan.

_____ a. Many people agree with the use of atomic bombs in World War II.

_____ b. Many people disagree with the use of atomic bombs in World War II.

6. That shirt shouldn't have faded after just one washing.

_____ a. The shirt lost some color when it was washed.

_____ b. The shirt looked better after it was washed.

Exercise 2   Write a sentence that uses *should have* or *should not have* + PAST PARTICIPLE to express the same idea. The first one has been done for you.

1. Joe bought a used car. He regrets buying it.

   Joe should not have bought a used car. _____

2. You did not get a new umbrella. You are sorry about this.

   _____

   _____

3. Instead of taking a taxi, we took a bus from the airport. Taking a bus took much longer and was not as good as taking a taxi.

   _____

   _____

4. Toshio regrets quitting his job today.

   _____

   _____

5. Last night I went to bed after midnight. I regret doing this.

_____

_____

9.6 The Modal *must* in the Past

Use *must + have +* PAST PARTICIPLE to form the past modal.

1. Use *must have +* PAST PARTICIPLE when you are almost certain that the action happened. Based on the facts or current situation, you conclude that the action happened.

> Joe looks really tired today. He **must have** *gone* to bed late last night. (The speaker thinks that Joe went to bed late last night.)

2. Use the negative form, *must not have +* PAST PARTICIPLE, when you are almost certain that the action did not happen.

> Irene failed her spelling test. She **must not have** *studied* very much. (The speaker thinks that Irene did not study very much.)

Exercise 3   To complete these sentences, write the correct construction using *must (not) have +* PAST PARTICIPLE with the verb in parentheses. The first one has been done for you.

1. No one ordered any dessert after dinner. Everyone (be) _____ *must have been* _____

   full.

2. When I saw Ben this morning, he didn't know who had won the football match last

   night. He (watch) _____ it on TV.

3. Paula's French is outstanding. I know she's a good language learner, but she (have)

   _____ a great French teacher, too.

4. Ellen returned four of the five dresses that she bought yesterday. They (fit)

   _____ her very well.

5. Rick didn't follow the teacher's directions for this assignment. He (understand)

   _____ the directions clearly.

6. Look at the decorations on these cakes! They're so elaborate! It (take)

   _____ a long time to make them!

9.7 The Modal *could* in the Past

Use *could have* + PAST PARTICIPLE to form the past modal.

1. Use *could have* + PAST PARTICIPLE when the speaker had the opportunity to do something, but you are not sure he did it. You can also use it when the action was possible, but you are not sure if it really happened.

    After dinner, I felt really sick. It **could have** *been* the fish. It tasted a little strange. (The speaker thinks that one possible reason for being sick was the fish.)

2. Use the negative form *could not have* + PAST PARTICIPLE, when you are almost positive that the action did not happen. This form implies that it was impossible for the action to have occurred.

    The evidence proves that the woman **couldn't have** *killed* her husband because she was traveling in a different country when he was killed. (According to the evidence, it was impossible for the woman to have killed the man.)

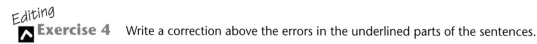

Editing

Exercise 4   Write a correction above the errors in the underlined parts of the sentences.

1. If you missed eight of the ten questions on the test, you <u>could have passed</u> it.

2. No one believes that the man <u>could have kill</u> his boss.

3. My late grandfather was extremely rich. He didn't own a BMW, but he <u>couldn't have easily bought</u> one or more of them.

4. I <u>could visit</u> many more places in Paris if I had had more time.

5. I <u>could have lent</u> you my car yesterday because I needed it all day.

6. I could have lent you my car because I <u>needed</u> it all day yesterday.

7. When we went to France last year, we <u>could have fly</u> on the Concorde.

8. It <u>couldn't rain</u> this morning. I would have noticed if the ground had been wet!

9.8 The Modal *might* in the Past

Use *might have* + PAST PARTICIPLE to form the past modal.

1. Use *might have* + PAST PARTICIPLE when the action was possible, but you are not sure if it happened. (This is the same meaning as *may have* or *could have* + PAST PARTICIPLE.)

    After dinner, I felt really sick. It **might have** *been* the fish. It tasted a little strange. (The speaker thinks that one possible reason for being sick was the fish.)

2. *Might have* + PAST PARTICIPLE has a second meaning. It can be a suggestion about a past event, like *could have*. Sometimes it is a form of complaint.

> Mother: The train trip took us several hours. I don't know why we came by train.

> Ana: We **might have** *flown.* It would have been so much faster.

3. The negative form, *might not have* + PAST PARTICIPLE is used when the negative situation was possible, but you are not sure if it happened. (This is the same meaning as *may not have* + PAST PARTICIPLE.)

> The teacher believes that Joe **might not have written** his paper by himself. (The teacher believes it is possible that someone helped Joe write his paper.)

Exercise 5 Read each sentence. Then write a sentence that means the same as the first sentence. Use *might have* or *might not have* + PAST PARTICIPLE. The first one has been done for you.

1. It is possible that it rained last night. I'm not sure.

   It might have rained last night. _____

2. When you called last night, maybe David wasn't home then.

   _____

3. Why did Hector leave the party? Maybe he didn't feel well.

   _____

4. The student's answers are all wrong. Maybe he didn't understand the directions.

   _____

   _____

5. Perhaps the doctor prescribed the wrong medicine.

   _____

6. Why did the accident happen? Maybe the pilot turned onto the wrong runway.

   _____

   _____

9.9 The Modal *may* in the Past

Use *may have* + PAST PARTICIPLE to form the past modal.

1. Use *may have* + PAST PARTICIPLE when the action was possible, but you are not sure if it happened.

   After dinner, I felt really sick. It **may have** *been* the fish. It tasted a little strange.
   (The speaker thinks that one possible reason for being sick was the fish.)

2. The negative form *may not have* + PAST PARTICIPLE is used when the negative situation was possible, but you are not sure if it happened.

   The teacher believes that Joe **may not have** *written* his paper by himself.
   (The teacher believes it is possible that someone helped Joe write his paper.)

Exercise 6   Read each sentence. Then write a sentence that means the same as the first sentence. Use *may have* or *may not have* + PAST PARTICIPLE. The first one has been done for you.

1. Perhaps Jennifer went to her cousin's house.

   Jennifer may have gone to her cousin's house.

2. It's possible that Ned didn't like the gift that Linda gave him.

   _____

   _____

3. Maybe some passengers survived the plane crash.

   _____

   _____

4. Maybe he didn't hear the announcement.

   _____

   _____

5. It's possible that the secretary has already received the documents.

   _____

   _____

6. Perhaps it was too late for Alan to buy a cheap ticket for the flight.

   _____

   _____

The Modal *would* in the Past

Use *would have* + PAST PARTICIPLE to form the past modal.

1. Use *would have* + PAST PARTICIPLE when the action did not happen. This meaning is for the main clause in conditional sentences: another condition was missing, and that's why the second action did not happen.

   The young couple **would have** *purchased* the house if it had had two bathrooms. (The house did not have two bathrooms, so the young couple didn't purchase it.)

2. The negative form *would not have* + PAST PARTICIPLE is used when the action actually happened, but it would not have happened if something else had occurred first.

   The pie **wouldn't have** *tasted* so sweet if I had added the correct amount of sugar. (The pie tasted too sweet because the speaker added the wrong amount of sugar.)

NOTE: Sometimes the *if*-clause is not stated; it is understood. You can find more information about *if*-clauses in Chapter 12.

Exercise 7   Fill in the blanks with *would have* + PAST PARTICIPLE of the verbs in parentheses. The first one has been done for you.

1. (start, [negative]) Perhaps if Lincoln had not become the 16th president, the Civil War

   <u>would not have started</u> in 1861.

2. (like) People _____ the party better if you had had good

   music.

3. (be, [negative]) The spaghetti _____ crunchy if you had

   cooked it a little longer.

4. (win) If Kostov had done better in the second set, perhaps he _____

   _____ the match.

5. (be) The outcome of the election _____ the same if people

   had voted on computers instead of using the old methods.

6. (have, [negative]) If you had taken the medicine correctly, you _____

   _____ any problems with your stomach.

Exercise 8   Underline the six past modal forms in this paragraph and explain their meanings to a partner.

My Oldest Memory

My oldest memory is of a time when I was a very young child. I couldn't have been more than five years old. In fact, I might have been as young as three. I remember that I was with a woman who was our neighbor. It must have been around 6 or 7 o'clock because it was getting a little dark. The woman told me that we were going to walk to the store on the corner to get an ice cream cone. Just as we left the front steps of our house, the light above the store went out. It had just closed. We should have left earlier. If we had left the house a few minutes earlier, then we might have gotten to the store in time. If we had done that, then I could have had some ice cream. To this day, I cannot remember exactly who the woman was, but I certainly remember the day that I didn't get any ice cream.

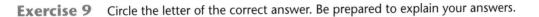

Exercise 9   Circle the letter of the correct answer. Be prepared to explain your answers.

1. As I sat waiting for my flight to take off, I read this statement on the information card: "In an emergency, all passengers _____ the directions of the crew."

   A. must follow   C. might follow

   B. must have followed   D. might have followed

2. I overheard a mother tell her son, "If you need to use your cell phone, you _____ do it now because you _____ make a call during the flight."

   A. had better … cannot   C. must … do not able to

   B. had better to … cannot   D. must to … do not able to

3. A passenger seated next to me told me about a problem on her previous flight. As the passengers were boarding the plane, an alarm went off. She thought that one of the passengers may _____ an emergency door by mistake.

   A. open   C. have opened

   B. have open   D. to open

4. About an hour after takeoff, the flight attendant gave each of us a small sandwich, but I could not eat mine because the cooks had put spicy mustard on all of them. They really _____ such spicy mustard.

   A. should have added   C. shouldn't have added

   B. should add   D. shouldn't add

5. One passenger said that his worst flight was aboard a 747 with Southwest Airlines, but a flight attendant who was standing nearby corrected him. She said, "Are you sure it was a 747 with Southwest? Actually, if it was a Southwest jet, it _____ been a 747 because that airline does not have any jumbo jets."

   A. might not have   C. might not had

   B. could not have   D. could not had

6. The pilot announced, "Ladies and gentlemen, we are very near the Salt Lake City Airport. We _____ shortly, so please follow the flight attendants' instructions at this point."

   A. land   C. could land

   B. must land   D. will land

7. A man next to me remarked, "I hate having to wait for my luggage. I wish they could just take my luggage directly to my car. That _____ great!"

   A. would be

   B. should be

   C. would have been

   D. should have been

8. As we were exiting the airplane, an agent told us that we _____.

   A. should pick up our baggage at carousel 7

   B. might have waited ten minutes for our baggage

   C. must to have our baggage claim tickets in our hands

   D. were able ask for assistance at the baggage claim area

Exercise 10   Write a paragraph about an important event in history or in your life. Tell what happened and why it happened. Tell how it could have been different. Consider what should have been done to make it different (if it was something negative). Use at least five of the past modals from this chapter. Use both affirmative and negative forms. Exchange paragraphs with a partner. Circle all the past modals on your partner's paper and check for their correct use.

_____

_____

_____

_____

_____

_____

_____

_____

_____

_____

_____

_____

_____

_____

_____

_____

_____

_____

_____

_____

_____

_____

10 Gerunds *verb ⊕ ing . (noun)* and Infinitives

Two verb forms in English are used as nouns: <u>gerunds</u> and <u>infinitives</u>. Gerunds are verbs ending in *-ing*. Infinitives are *to* + VERB. How do you know when to use an infinitive and when to use a gerund? This chapter will answer that question.

✔ CHECK YOUR GRAMMAR

Four of the eight underlined words contain an error related to gerunds and infinitives. Can you explain why each of these underlined areas is (or is not) wrong? Discuss with a partner.

Reading Skills

<u>To read</u> is much more than <u>run</u> your eyes across the page and <u>recognizing</u> words. It involves <u>grasping</u> the meaning of what is written, <u>understanding</u> the relationship of each sentence and paragraph to all the others. <u>Getting</u> more from your reading, you will need <u>skim</u>, reflect, <u>read</u>, and review each chapter.

From: V. Ruggiero. (2002). *Becoming a Critical Thinker*, 4th ed. Boston: Houghton Mifflin, p. xvi.

10.1 Forming Gerunds and Gerund Phrases and Infinitives and Infinitive Phrases

Here are the basic forms of gerunds and infinitives:

Gerund	Infinitive
VERB + -ing	*to + VERB*
swimming	to swim
laughing	to laugh

A gerund phrase includes the gerund and its related information.

Taking *good class notes* makes it easier to review for exams.

An infinitive phrase includes the infinitive and its related information.

To take *good class notes,* you should read about the subject in advance.

Exercise 1 Read the following paragraph on stress. Underline all the gerunds and infinitives. The first one has been done for you. There are ten more.

Handling Stress

To relieve stress, you must first understand which brain hemisphere is stressed. Feeling depressed or emotionally overwrought means your stress is in the right hemisphere. This is the creative, emotional, holistic side of your brain. To cut stress, switch to your matter-of-fact left hemisphere. How? Doing math or writing factual prose calms down the emotional right brain. Another option is to organize something; it has the same calming effect. Feeling time-stressed and overburdened means the left hemisphere of your brain is stressed. Singing or playing a sport will allow you to switch to your right brain and to reduce your stress.

From: Berko et al., *Communicating,* p. 188.

10.2   Gerunds and Gerund Phrases

Although gerunds, like infinitives, are formed with verb stems, they function like nouns. A gerund phrase is a gerund followed by a noun or pronoun.

1. Gerunds and gerund phrases as **subjects**

   Eating *vegetables* is a good way to stay healthy.

A gerund as the subject of a sentence takes a singular verb. When multiple gerunds are used as the subject, they take a plural verb.

   Eating *vegetables* and **exercising** are excellent ways to stay healthy.

When a gerund has multiple objects, the subject is singular.

   Eating *broccoli, carrots, and tomatoes* is an excellent way to stay healthy.

2. Gerunds and gerund phrases as **direct objects** (see Section 10.2.1)

   However, many people dislike **preparing** *vegetables.*

3. Gerunds and gerund phrases as **subject complements** (after the verb *be*)

   One easy preparation method is **eating** *them raw with a simple sauce.*

In this case, the gerund is often inverted to the subject position without changing the meaning of the sentence.

   Eating *vegetables raw with a simple sauce* is one easy preparation method.

4. Gerunds and gerund phrases as **objects of prepositions** (see Chapter 7)

Another method of **preparing** *vegetables* is stir-frying.

5. To form the negative of a gerund, simply place *not* immediately before the gerund.

***Not* cooking** *vegetables* allows you to prepare a meal faster.

Exercise 2 Complete the following sentences with a gerund or gerund phrase using some of the words below or your own words. In the parentheses, write the function of the gerund in the sentence. The gerund can serve as the subject, direct object, subject complement (after the verb *be*), or object of a preposition. The first one has been done for you.

	Verbs			Nouns	
clean	fry	slice	counter	new recipes	salt
cook	mop	taste	dishes	olive oil	seafood
cut	peel	try	fruit	praise	tomatoes
eat	receive	use	meat	salad	vegetables

1. I'm tired of ____cooking____ meals every day of the week. (*object of preposition*)

2. Lisa's favorite hobby is __eating__. (_sbj complement_)

3. __tasting__ is one of the benefits all cooks enjoy! (_sbj_)

4. It's almost impossible to make a meal without __cutting__. (obj. prep)

5. While some people enjoy __cleaning__, I think it's a boring activity. (direct obj.)

6. My mother is great at __cooking__, but I'm not so good at it. (obj. prep)

7. I don't mind __moping__, but I am tired of __cleaning__ every week! (direct obj) (obj. preposition

10.2.1 *Verbs Commonly Followed by Gerunds*

1. These verbs frequently have a gerund or a gerund phrase following them:

appreciate	delay	dislike	involve	practice	risk
avoid	detest	enjoy	miss	quit	stop
consider	discuss	finish	postpone	recommend	suggest

My mother *appreciated* **getting a puppy** for her birthday.

2. Whenever a verb follows a preposition, the verb takes the gerund form. The common expressions in the following chart have a gerund or gerund phrase following them. (For a longer list of prepositions after certain verbs and adjectives, see Sections 13.3.2 and 13.3.3 in Chapter 13.)

be afraid of	be interested in	be worried about	dream about	thank (someone) for
be good at	be responsible for	argue about	excel at	think about
be used to	be accustomed to	believe in	talk about	think of

Common error:	We **are interested in** ~~take~~ summer classes.
Correct:	We *are interested in* **taking** summer classes.
Common error:	Did she **thank you for** ~~drive~~ her to work this morning?
Correct:	Did she *thank you for* **driving** her to work this morning?

3. Other common expressions include:

- *by* + *gerund* to explain how something is done

  You can pass this class **by reading** the text and **keeping up** with assignments.

- *go* + *gerund* to describe activities

  Would you rather **go bowling** or **go swimming** this afternoon?

Exercise 3 Complete each sentence with the verb or expression in parentheses and add an appropriate gerund or gerund phrase. The first one has been done for you.

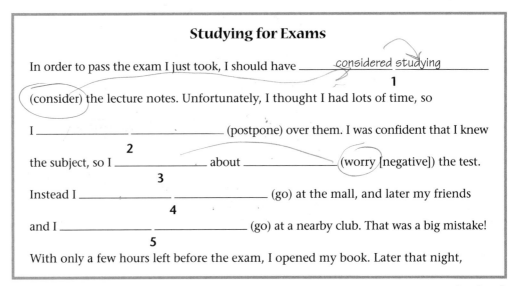

Studying for Exams

In order to pass the exam I just took, I should have _____considered studying_____
                                                                        1
(consider) the lecture notes. Unfortunately, I thought I had lots of time, so

I _____ _____ (postpone) over them. I was confident that I knew
        2

the subject, so I _____ about _____ (worry [negative]) the test.
                        3

Instead I _____ _____ (go) at the mall, and later my friends
                4

and I _____ _____ (go) at a nearby club. That was a big mistake!
            5

With only a few hours left before the exam, I opened my book. Later that night,

(continued)

while sleeping, I _____ about _____ (dream) the

6

test. I woke up from that nightmare and _____ _____ (finish)

7

the rest of the chapter. Then I went to school and took the exam. I learned my

lesson the hard way. What do I recommend? I _____ not _____

8

(recommend) what I did. Instead, I _____ _____ (suggest)

9

your notes regularly. By reviewing them every day, you won't _____

about _____ (worry) any exam!

10

10.3   Infinitives and Infinitive Phrases

Infinitives consist of two words: *to* + VERB. An infinitive phrase is the infinitive followed by any noun or pronoun and modifying words.

1. Infinitives and infinitive phrases as a reduction of the phrase *in order to* (showing purpose)

    To build its international business, the company spent millions on advertising in sixteen different languages. = [In order] **to build** its international business, the company spent …

2. Infinitives and infinitive phrases as subjects

    To live *in a large city* requires a lot of patience and nerve. (less common)

Compare with the gerund as the subject paired with the same verb. (Infinitives can be subjects, but gerunds are much more common as subjects.)

    Living *in a large city* requires a lot of patience and nerve. (more common)

Remember: When an infinitive phrase begins a sentence, it is probably a "purpose" phrase, not the subject:

    To live *in a large city*, you need a lot of patience. ([in order] to + verb = purpose)

3. Infinitives and infinitive phrases as direct objects

    Mario wanted **to stay** *at the beach*, but it began **to rain**.

4. Infinitives and infinitive phrases after phrases beginning with *it* (*it* + *be* + ADJECTIVE or NOUN + INFINITIVE)

    It is impossible **to get** *a cheap apartment* in a large city.
        ADJECTIVE   INFINITIVE

    Many people say that **it is a good idea** **to save** *money for the future*.
                   NOUN   INFINITIVE

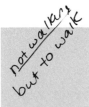
not walking
but to walk

Here are some common adjectives and nouns that are preceded by *it* + *be* and followed by an infinitive:

bad	dangerous	difficult	easy
fun	hard	important	impossible
interesting	necessary	relaxing	a good idea
a bad idea	a pity	a shame	a waste

5. Infinitives and infinitive phrases with the verb *take* (*it* + *take* + NOUN + INFINITIVE)

    It takes a lot of **energy to find** *the perfect job.*

6. Infinitives and infinitive phrases after certain adjectives

    Habiba was **happy to learn** *that she'd been accepted to graduate school.*

Here are some common adjectives followed by infinitives.

afraid	glad	relieved	sorry
ashamed	happy	reluctant	surprised
bound	lucky	sad	sure
careful	proud	shocked	willing

Note that *accustomed to* always takes a gerund.

    I am **accustomed to waking up** at 5 a.m. every day.

7. To form the negative of an infinitive, simply place *not* immediately before the infinitive.

    You should be **careful not to strain** *your eyes* in front of the computer.

Exercise 4   Complete the sentences with an infinitive phrase. In the parentheses, write the function of the infinitive in the sentence. Choose from one of the four following options: *direct object, after a phrase with* it + ADJECTIVE, *to show purpose,* or *after certain adjectives.* The first one has been done for you.

1. Margaret and her sister Jenna went to college <u>to become their family's first college</u>

    <u>graduates. (to show purpose)</u>

2. They were afraid _____

    _____, but their family encouraged them. (_____

    _____)

3. Margaret and Jenna wanted _____

    _____ at a prestigious university in

    California, but it was too expensive. (_____

    _____)

4. Then they found a university that was willing _____

_____ them a scholarship.

(_____)

5. It was impossible _____

_____ such a wonderful opportunity. (_____

_____)

6. During their first semester, they went to the library _____

_____. (_____

_____)

7. In the beginning, it wasn't easy for Margaret and Jenna _____

_____. However, they

were proud _____

_____. (_____

_____) (_____)

10.3.1   *Verbs Commonly Followed by Infinitives*

These verbs frequently have an infinitive or an infinitive phrase following them:

afford	agree	ask	decide	demand	deserve
expect	hesitate	hope	learn	need	offer
plan	pretend	promise	refuse	wait	want

When no one else volunteered, Manny **offered** to go.

The students **demanded** to see *the program director* when the course was canceled.

⌃ Exercise 5 The following paragraph contains seven errors in gerund and infinitive use. Find and correct the errors. The first one has been done for you.

Searching for a Cure

As doctors continue to searching for a cure for

the common cold, they have found some things that

make people more vulnerable to catching a cold.

One negative influence is to argue. People who argue

are more likely to get colds than those who do not.

Another characteristic is be a "loner." People who

have strong social networks tend to be happier and

therefore more resistant to colds. Finally, to stress

over a job can lead to colds. There are many workers

who do not feel confident enough to get their job done right. Some researchers

believe that this lack of self-confidence can lead to lowered immune systems. To

resisting colds, people should look at the quality of their lives. While patients wait

for a cure for the common cold, they can begin bolster their bodies by to deal with

the treatable issues mentioned above.

10.3.2 *Verbs That Need Nouns or Pronouns Before the Infinitive*

These verbs often need either a noun or a pronoun before the infinitive.

advise	allow	cause	convince	forbid	force
invite	permit	remind	teach	tell	warn

We all *warned Jason* **to stop** eating so much junk food.

    (noun before infinitive)

My father *taught me* **to play** tennis when I was young.

    (pronoun before infinitive)

Somebody

you, me, Kim

Exercise 6 Complete each sentence with the correct forms of the words in parentheses. The first one has been done for you.

Piano Lessons

When I was a child, my mother (advise / me / study) <u>advised me to study</u> hard every

day. She (not want / me / lose out) _____ on a quality

education. For this reason, she (forbid / me / watch) _____ _____

_____ too much television. Instead, she would (tell / me / practice) _____

_____ the piano. I absolutely hated my mother's forcing (me / play)

_____, but I always did what I was told. She would

(invite / her friends / listen) _____ to my home

concerts, and it always made me so nervous! Well, today I must thank her. As a

well-known pianist who travels around the world, I am happy that she (convince /

me / appreciate) _____ hard work. I would never have

gotten where I am today without her focus on education and practice.

10.4 Verbs Commonly Followed by Either Gerunds or Infinitives

The following verbs often have either a gerund or an infinitive following them. The meaning is similar for both.

begin	attempt	continue	hate
love	prefer	start	like

Jeanne prefers **carrying** her own luggage. (gerund)

Jeanne prefers **to carry** her own luggage. (infinitive)

The verbs *forget, regret, remember, stop,* and *try* are also followed by either a gerund or infinitive. However, the meaning is different for each usage.

forget	I forgot **taking** this picture of the Eiffel Tower. In fact, I took several. (*forget* + GERUND refers to an earlier action that occurred)
	I forgot **to take** a picture of the Eiffel Tower. Maybe I'll do it on my next trip. (*forget* + INFINITIVE refers to an action that did not occur)
regret	I regret **telling** you last week that you would be laid off. I was wrong. (*regret* + GERUND refers to an earlier action)
	I regret **to tell** you today that you will be laid off next week. (*regret* + INFINITIVE refers to an action in the present)

remember	Now I remember **taking** this picture. It was on May 8th. (*remember* + GERUND refers to an earlier action)
	I remembered **to take** this picture. I did not forget to do this. (*remember* + INFINITIVE refers to an action at the same or later time)
stop	I was driving my car. I stopped **to make** a phone call. (*stop* + INFINITIVE means to interrupt an action to do something else)
	My phone bill got too high, so I stopped **making** so many calls. (*stop* + GERUND means to finish an action in progress)
try	You have hiccups? You should try **holding** your breath. (*try* + GERUND means to experiment with a solution to a problem)
	The doctors tried **to save** her life, but she died. (*try* + INFINITIVE means to make an effort to do something that is usually difficult)

Exercise 7   Fill in the blank with the appropriate gerund or infinitive form of the verb in parentheses.

1. Paula forgot _____ (tell) her husband she hadn't fed their cat. Her husband didn't feed the cat either, so the poor thing meowed all day long!

2. Paula forgot _____ (tell) her husband she hadn't fed their cat, so she worried all day long. However, her husband had fed the cat before he left for work.

3. Do you remember _____ (stop) the newspaper delivery for this week that we're on vacation?

4. I remembered _____ (stop) the mail, but I don't remember _____ (stop) the paper.

5. After getting my last credit card bill, I stopped _____ (spend) so much time at the mall. I need to follow my budget more closely.

6. I stopped _____ (spend) some time at the mall today. I've been pretty good about watching my money and decided to splurge and buy some new shoes.

7. Each week we try _____ (save) a little money to put toward a vacation. We hope to go to Japan next summer.

8. Each week we try _____ (save) the planet by volunteering to pick up trash along the highway.

9. The committee regrets _____ (inform) you that your request for a hearing has been denied. You may appeal this decision if you wish.

10. The committee regrets _____ (inform) you that your request for a hearing was denied. It has, in fact, been granted.

Exercise 8   Circle the letter of the correct answer. Be prepared to explain your answers.

1. Even small changes can result in weight loss. For example, my personal trainer cautioned me _____ real cream in my coffee.

   A.   to avoid using   C.   avoid to use

   B.   avoid using   D.   to avoid use

2. He told me that _____ certain foods such as cream and cookies would really help me lose weight quickly.

   A.   not to eat   C.   not eating

   B.   I do not eat   D.   doesn't eat

3. In fact, I stopped _____ dessert because the scales told _____!

   A.   eating ... me to stop   C.   to eat ... me stop

   B.   to eat ... to stop   D.   eating ... me stopping

4. _____ vegetables is a good way to stay healthy, but I dislike _____ many of them.

   A.   To eat ... to prepare   C.   To eat ... preparing

   B.   Eating ... to prepare   D.   Eating ... preparing

5. Do you _____ to go to the gym alone or with a workout buddy?

   A.   prefer   C.   enjoy

   B.   suggest   D.   appreciate

6. For many people, _____ out with someone else increases their motivation and ultimately yields better physical results.

   A.   work   C.   working

   B.   they work   D.   if they work

7. If you have a friend to work out with, you are not likely _____ working out from one day to the next.

   A.   for postpone   C.   to postpone

   B.   for postponing   D.   to postponing

8. When I first started working out, running on the treadmill was difficult because my body was not accustomed _____ for so long.

   A.   for run   C.   for running

   B.   to run   D.   to running

Exercise 9   Write a paragraph about something special that you have achieved in your life. Give some background that includes how old you were during this time and why it was important for you to achieve this goal. Explain the events that led to this success. How did you feel after this achievement?

Review the uses of gerunds and infinitives in this chapter. Try to include at least four infinitives or infinitive phrases and four gerunds or gerund phrases in your paragraph. Exchange paragraphs with a partner. Review your partner's paper, circling all the gerunds and infinitives and checking for their correct use.

11 Passive Voice and Participial Adjectives

<u>Passive voice</u> can be difficult to understand. Before you study this chapter, you may find it a good idea to review the verb tenses in Chapter 4 and Chapter 5. This will help you understand passive voice better.

✔ CHECK YOUR GRAMMAR

Four of the seven underlined words or phrases contain an error related to passive voice and participial adjectives. Can you explain why each of these underlined areas is (or is not) wrong? Discuss with a partner.

Audience Feedback

Your ability to listen to yourself <u>can be enhanced</u> by two skills: translating audience feedback and listening. Good speakers silently ask and <u>are answered</u> questions as they speak. If an audience seems <u>confused</u>, the speaker may slow down and re-explain a concept. If the audience looks <u>boring</u>, the speaker <u>may be added</u> an <u>interesting</u> or <u>amused</u> story to rekindle their interest.

Adapted from: Engleberg and Daly, *Presentations in Everyday Life*, p. 39.

11.1 Passive Versus Active Voice

When a verb is in the active voice, the subject is the actor. In other words, the subject is doing the action.

The ***dog* bit** the man. (Who did the action? The dog.)

In contrast, when a verb is in the passive voice, the subject is the receiver of the action of the verb. The actor may (or may not) be expressed by a *by* + ACTOR expression.

> The man **was bitten** *by the dog.* (Who did the action? The dog.)

In the first example (active voice), the speaker emphasizes the dog. In the second example (passive voice), the speaker emphasizes the man. The noun in the subject position is the one that the speaker emphasizes. When should you use the passive voice? Use it when the receiver of the action is more important than the one who did the action.

11.2   Form of Passive Voice

Passive voice always consists of a form of the verb *be* followed by the past participle of the action verb: *be* + PAST PARTICIPLE.

> Penicillin **was discovered** in 1928.

The following chart gives you an overview of the passive voice of verb tenses in English.

Tense	Active Voice	Passive Voice
Present:	I write it	It is written
Present progressive:	I am writing it	It is being written
Present perfect:	I have written it	It has been written
Past:	I wrote it	It was written
Past progressive:	I was writing it	It was being written
Past perfect:	I had written it	It had been written
Future:	I will write it	It will be written
Future perfect:	I will have written it	It will have been written
Present modal:	I can write it	It can be written
	I should write it	It should be written
Past modal:	I could have written it	It could have been written
	I may have written it	It may have been written

The progressive forms are almost never used in the passive voice.

An easy thing to remember about forming the passive voice is that the verb usually has one more word (**+1**) than the active voice verb.

Active	Passive + 1
They **answer** their mail immediately.	Their mail **is answered** immediately.
They **have not called** Jack.	Jack **has not been called.**
They **could have sent** the package.	The package **could have been sent.**

Infinitives and gerunds can also be used in passive voice.

Infinitives	Gerunds
Simple: *to* + *be* + PAST PARTICIPLE	Simple: *being* + PAST PARTICIPLE
We waited **to be served.**	**Being selected** was an honor.
Perfect: *to* + *have been* + PAST PARTICIPLE	Perfect: *having been* + PAST PARTICIPLE
I was happy **to have been** selected.	I denied **having been arrested.**

Exercise 1 Put a check mark (✔) by the passive verb forms. The first one has been done for you.

✔ 1. have been eaten   _____ 8. will be taking   _____ 15. haven't been slicing

_____ 2. have been eating   _____ 9. will be taken   _____ 16. needed to be told

_____ 3. cannot fly   _____ 10. can be taking   _____ 17. needed to tell

_____ 4. cannot be flying   _____ 11. should be needed   _____ 18. enjoyed being taken

_____ 5. cannot be flown   _____ 12. should be needing   _____ 19. enjoyed taking

_____ 6. were taken   _____ 13. hadn't been sliced   _____ 20. dislike being asked

_____ 7. were taking   _____ 14. weren't sliced   _____ 21. dislike asking

Exercise 2 Underline the passive verb forms in this news report. The first one has been done for you. There are six more.

Commencement Address

In today's news, Prime Minister Clark gave a speech at the graduation ceremony at Dover University. As the guests were being seated, an orchestra played quietly. The prime minister was introduced by the president of the university, who was visibly moved by the prime minister's attendance at today's event. Prime Minister Clark received his degree from Dover University in 1979. Today's trip to the university was his first trip back to the area since then. When Clark's name was announced to the audience, a loud cheer could be heard for the lost son who had finally returned to Dover University. In his speech at this event, the prime minister noted the important role that today's graduates will play in shaping the future of our country. "A country is only as strong as its educated. You are our educated; thus, you are our strength. We are counting on you for leadership as we enter a new era." Some

---

(continued)

thought that the possibility of war with neighboring countries might come up, but serious topics such as this were not mentioned at all. Having been addressed, the students then came forward to receive their diplomas.

11.3 How to Change Active Voice to Passive Voice

To change the active voice to passive voice in a sentence with SUBJECT / VERB / OBJECT word order, follow these four easy steps. (See Chapter 13 for word order.)

1. Begin with a sentence that has an active verb.

   Mark Twain **wrote** *The Adventures of Tom Sawyer* in 1876.

Identify the receiver of the action—*The Adventures of Tom Sawyer*. Move this receiver to the subject position in a new sentence.

   The Adventures of Tom Sawyer ...

2. Identify the verb—*wrote*—and its tense (simple past). After the subject, put the verb *be* in the same verb tense.

   The Adventures of Tom Sawyer **was** ...

3. Next, add the past participle of the verb you identified in Step 2.

   The Adventures of Tom Sawyer **was written** ...

4. Finally, include the original person or thing that did the action (the agent) in a *by* phrase.

   The Adventures of Tom Sawyer **was written** by Mark Twain ...

Then add the rest of the information (if there is any) from the original sentence.

   The Adventures of Tom Sawyer **was written** by Mark Twain in 1876.

In some cases, you may want to omit the agent if the main emphasis is on the receiver (the new subject) or if the agent or actor is obvious or unknown.

   The Adventures of Tom Sawyer, not *A Tramp Abroad*, **was written** in 1876.

Exercise 3 Underline the complete verb in each sentence and identify it as *active* or *passive*. Then rewrite the sentence by changing the voice of the verb from either active to passive or from passive to active. Remember that when you change active to passive, you may not necessarily include the agent in a *by* phrase. The first one has been done for you.

1. ___active___ In Unit 12, students <u>must use</u> a range of written sources to understand the causes of World War I.

   In Unit 12, a range of written sources must be used to understand the causes of World War I.

2. ___active___ Video and other media <u>facilitate</u> the presentation and understanding of the events leading up to and following World War I.

3. _____ In the accompanying course textbook, the constantly changing nature of world governments over several decades has been emphasized in great detail by the authors.

4. _____ Both the illustrations and the written material in the text are protected by Title 17 of the United States Copyright Law.

5. _____ The introduction to the first chapter was written in 1999 by Charles Kingly, a well-known university history professor.

11.4 Three Common Errors With the Passive Voice

Writers tend to make three mistakes with the passive voice: in form, in use, and with intransitive verbs (verbs that do not take an object and therefore cannot be in passive voice).

1. Error with past participle form. Remember that the verb *be* must be followed by the past participle of the action verb.

   Incorrect verb form: The book **was writing** in 1998.

   Incorrect verb form: The book **was wrote** in 1998.

   Correct past participle: The book **was written** in 1998.

2. Error with use. Remember that passive voice is used when the receiver of the action is more important than the agent (doer of the action). You should mention the agent only if it is important to the meaning or if it is not obvious.

   Incorrect: Arabic **is written** by Arabic speakers from right to left. (*by Arabic speakers* is not necessary information)

Some writers use passive voice too often, especially just after they have learned it. Active voice is generally much more effective than passive voice. Use passive voice when

- you want the receiver of the action to be the main topic of your words:

   Smoking **is prohibited** in this area.

- you don't know who did the action:

   The First United Bank **was robbed** early this morning.

- the subject of the active sentence would be *people* or *one:*

   Abraham Lincoln **was considered** an honest man.

- reporting unwelcome news or avoiding blame:

   Taxes **will be increased.**

   All of my important e-mails **were deleted!**

- the topic has already been mentioned:

   Ethanol production is the latest hot topic for discussion. *It is seen* as a possible solution to the country's dependence on oil.

The following two examples describe the same event, but the writer's emphasis is different in each.

Active voice: **The dog** bit the thief.   (The writer's focus is *the dog.*)

    The thief quietly opened the window of the house. He climbed into the residence as carefully as possible so that he would not make any noise. He did not know, however, that there was a vicious dog watching over the house. The dog heard the noise of the intruder and reacted quickly. Like a bolt of lightning, the dog jumped up and barked ferociously. Then the dog lunged at the man. In a split second, **the dog bit the thief**, which ended the robbery.

Passive voice: **The thief** was bitten by the dog.   (The writer's focus is *the thief.*)

    The thief quietly opened the window of the house. He climbed into the residence as carefully as possible so that he would not make any noise. He did not know, however, that there was a vicious dog watching over the house. The thief heard the loud clicking of claws on the floor. The thief could not escape. **He was bitten by the dog,** which ended the robbery.

3. <u>Error with intransitive verbs.</u> English has two kinds of verbs: transitive and intransitive. Transitive verbs are followed by an object. For example, the verb *announce* must always have an object. You cannot say "Yesterday they announced." This sentence must have an object, as in "Yesterday they announced their engagement" or "Yesterday they announced the winners' names." Here are some transitive verbs:

announce (an engagement)	buy (a gift)	like (a person or thing)
discover (a cure)	find (a good deal)	take (a nap)

Intransitive verbs are not followed by an object. Here are a few intransitive verbs:

come	die	go	happen	seem	occur	*appear* ~

Intransitive verbs do not have grammatical voice, so they cannot be changed from active to passive voice. Study the following examples.

Transitive Verb, Active Voice	⇨	Transitive Verb, Passive Voice
They discovered a cure …	⇨	A cure **was discovered** …
The machine accepts coins …	⇨	Coins **are accepted** …

Intransitive Verb, Active Voice	⇨	No Passive Possible
The accident happened …	⇨	~~was happened~~
The man died …	⇨	~~was died~~

Exercise 4   Read the sentences. Find the error in each sentence and identify why it is an error (refer to Section 11.4). Then correct the error. The first one has been done for you.

1. World War II was won.

    Error: _____ no agent _____   Why: _____ agent is important _____

    Correction: World War II was won by the Allies.

2. World War II was occurred more than fifty years ago.

    Error: _____   Why: _____

    Correction: _____

3. World War II was fighting in Africa, North America, Europe, and Asia.

    Error: _____   Why: _____

    Correction: _____

4. Thousands of soldiers were died in World War II.

    Error: _____   Why: _____

    Correction: _____

5. For years after the War, countries were completely rebuilt by the people.

    Error: _____   Why: _____

    Correction: _____

6. Even today, some of the signs of the war can still be seen by people.

    Error: _____   Why: _____

    Correction: _____

⚠ Exercise 5

Read the following paragraph from a business textbook. If the underlined verb phrase is incorrect, write your corrected edit on the line. If it is correct, write *correct* on the line.

1. _____   5. _____   9. _____

2. _____   6. _____   10. _____

3. _____   7. _____

4. _____   8. _____

CPA Credentials

Most accounting firms <u>are included</u> on their staffs at least one certified public
                         1
accountant, or CPA, an individual who <u>has met</u> state requirements for accounting
                                       2
education and experience and <u>has been passed</u> a rigorous two-day accounting
                              3
examination. The examination <u>is prepared</u> by the American Institute of Certified
                              4
Public Accountants and covers accounting practice, accounting theory, auditing,

taxation, and business law. State requirements usually <u>are included</u> a college
                                                         5
degree in accounting and from one to three years of on-the-job experience.

Once an individual becomes a CPA, he or she <u>must be attended</u> continuing-
                                             6
education programs to maintain state certification. These specialized programs

<u>design</u> to provide the current training that <u>is needed</u> in today's changing business
 7   **8**
environment. In addition, CPAs <u>must be taken</u> an ethics course to satisfy the
                                9
continuing-education requirement. Details regarding specific state requirements for

practice as a CPA <u>can obtain</u> by contacting the state's board of accountancy.
                   10

⚠ Exercise 6

Read these two paragraphs from an education textbook. If the underlined verb phrase is incorrect, write your corrected edit on the line. If it is correct, write *correct* on the line.

1. _____   5. _____   9. _____

2. _____   6. _____   10. _____

3. _____   7. _____

4. _____   8. _____

Education in the 1600s

Education <u>has changed</u> drastically since colonial days. In the 1600s, some girls

1

received elementary instruction, but formal colonial education was mainly

for boys, particularly those of the middle and upper classes. Both girls and boys

<u>might have had</u> some preliminary training in the four Rs—reading, 'riting [writing],

2

'rithmetic [arithmetic], and religion—at home. Sometimes, for a small fee, a

housewife <u>was offered</u> some training to children in her own home. In these cases,

3

she <u>would be taught</u> a little reading and writing, basic prayers, and religious beliefs.

4

In these dame schools, girls also <u>learned</u> some basic household skills, such as

5

cooking and sewing. The dame schools often <u>are provided</u> all the formal education

6

that some children, especially girls, ever received.

Throughout the colonies, poor children <u>were often apprenticed</u> or indentured

7

to local tradesmen or housewives. Apprenticeships <u>lasted</u> for three to ten years,

8

generally ending around age twenty-one for boys and eighteen for girls. During that

time, an apprentice <u>would learn</u> the basic skills of a trade and <u>might also teach</u> basic

9   **10**

reading and writing, and perhaps arithmetic, as part of the contractual agreement.

11.5 Stative Passive and Passive With *Get*

The stative passive is formed with the verb *to be* + PAST PARTICIPLE. In the stative passive, the past participle functions as an adjective and describes a state or situation. Stative passive constructions are not used with the *by* phrase.

> The door to the office **is closed.**
>
> Jay and Jenny **are married.**
>
> The class **was gone** when I arrived.
>
> Their new house **was made** of brick.

The passive with *get* is formed with a form of the verb *get* + ADJECTIVE or *get* + PAST PARTICIPLE. The past participle functions as an adjective and describes the subject. The use of passive voice with *get* is informal and often describes a process. Although you will hear the *get* construction frequently in informal conversation, you should remember that this construction is not preferred in formal academic writing. Follow your instructor's guidelines.

> Jay and Jenny **are getting married.**
>
> I **got hired** as an advertising copy writer.
>
> A number of people **got hurt** in the accident.
>
> She woke up late and **got dressed** in ten minutes.

Exercise 7 Complete the sentences with a stative passive or passive with *get*. Use words from the following list. The first one has been done for you.

confuse	crowd	~~lose~~	schedule	~~turn~~
better	depress	hungry	~~sick~~	worry

be + PAST PARTICIPLE

1. I don't have any idea where I am. I think I ___am lost.___

2. The tourists didn't understand the directions you gave them. They _____.

3. We should have taken a taxi. The subway _____ and I feel like I'm in a

   sardine can.

4. Hurry up. The tour bus _____ to leave in 3 minutes!

5. This hotel is so cheap that the heat _____ off on March 1st, no matter what

   the temperature is.

get + ADJECTIVE or PAST PARTICIPLE

6. We've been looking at paintings of fruit all day! I _____.

7. Our flight leaves in two hours and you haven't packed yet. I _____.

8. What's wrong with you? You're sneezing and coughing. Are you _____?

9. Our vacation is almost over. I'm _____.

10. How is that blister on your foot? Is it _____?

11.6 Participial Adjectives

The verb forms known as participles can also be used as adjectives.

The present participle, which is used to form progressive tenses, can also act as an adjective with an active meaning.

> The engine noises were **frightening** the passengers. (present participle in progressive tense)
>
> The passengers were nervous because of the **frightening** noises. (present participle as adjective)
>
> The engine noises were **frightening.** (present participle as adjective)

The past participle, which is a necessary part of forming the passive voice, can also act as an adjective with a passive meaning.

> The car was **stolen** by two young men. (past participle in passive voice)
>
> The police found the **stolen** car a week later. (past participle as adjective)

11.6.1 Present Participles Used as Adjectives

As you have seen, present participles are verb forms that end in -ing:

> interesting   confusing   surprising   annoying   losing

Present participles used as adjectives:

- are active
- refer to the cause of the experience
- describe what the effect is
- often describe inanimate (nonliving) nouns

> The audience heard the results. The audience did not expect the results. = The results were **surprising.** No one could believe the **surprising** results.
>
> The teacher explained the lesson. The students did not understand anything. = The explanation was **confusing.** The **confusing** explanation did not help.

11.6.2 Past Participles Used as Adjectives

Past participles are verb forms that end in -ed or an irregular form:

> interested   confused   surprised   annoyed   lost   known

Past participles used as adjectives:

- are passive
- refer to the person who feels or has the experience
- describe how the person is affected
- usually describe animate (living) nouns

> The audience heard the results. The audience did not expect the results.
>
> (The audience was **surprised**. The **surprised** audience was silent.)
>
> The teacher explained the lesson. The students did not understand anything.
>
> (The students were **confused**. The **confused** students need more help now.)

Exercise 8 Fill in each blank with the correct adjective or participial adjective form of the verb in parentheses. The first one has been done for you.

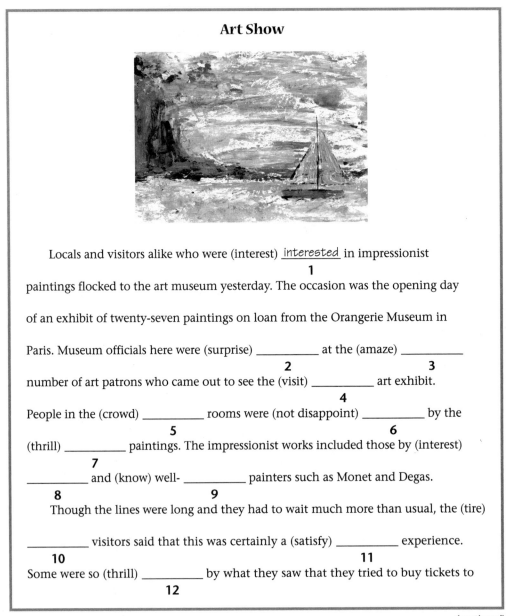

Art Show

Locals and visitors alike who were (interest) <u>interested</u> in impressionist
                                                        1

paintings flocked to the art museum yesterday. The occasion was the opening day

of an exhibit of twenty-seven paintings on loan from the Orangerie Museum in

Paris. Museum officials here were (surprise) _____ at the (amaze) _____
                                               2   **3**

number of art patrons who came out to see the (visit) _____ art exhibit.
                                                         4

People in the (crowd) _____ rooms were (not disappoint) _____ by the
                        5   **6**

(thrill) _____ paintings. The impressionist works included those by (interest)
           7

_____ and (know) well- _____ painters such as Monet and Degas.
    8   **9**

Though the lines were long and they had to wait much more than usual, the (tire)

_____ visitors said that this was certainly a (satisfy) _____ experience.
    10   **11**

Some were so (thrill) _____ by what they saw that they tried to buy tickets to
                         12

(continued)

come again. Unfortunately, tickets for subsequent days are already (sell) _____

13

out, so those without tickets in hand will be (disappoint) _____ by the news.

14

At the end of this long day, museum officials were (exhaust) _____ but

15

happy because of the successful opening day.

Exercise 9   Read the situations below. Then describe each situation and how people might feel or react. Use passive voice and participial adjectives in your descriptions. Use a participial form of the verbs below in your answer. The first one has been done for you.

~~bore~~   dishearten   excite   frustrate   terrify

convince   embarrass   frighten   interest   thrill

1. Moviegoers standing in line to get tickets

   Standing in line for tickets was boring. The boring ticket line barely moved.

   or The moviegoers were bored. The bored moviegoers started to get impatient.

2. Spectators watching a World Cup soccer match

   _____

   _____

3. Being in an earthquake

   _____

   _____

4. A student failing a test

   _____

   _____

5. Spilling your drink in a restaurant

   _____

   _____

6. Theme-park visitors riding a roller coaster

   _____

   _____

7. A victim falling for a con-artist's story

_____

_____

8. Students not understanding a grammar structure

_____

_____

9. Tourists traveling to new countries

_____

_____

10. A runner winning a marathon

_____

_____

⋀ Exercise 10 Read the paragraph below. There are seven errors in participial adjectives. Find the errors and correct them. The first one has been done for you.

Culture Shock

Culture shock is a feeling often experienced by people who move to another

country to live or study. There are distinct phases or stages of culture shock. During

excited
the first stage, the "honeymoon" stage, the ~~exciting~~ newcomer is eager to explore
                                              1

and learn about the new culture. The person may even feel as though he or she is

an <u>invited guest</u> in the country. Soon, however, that <u>comforting feeling</u> disappears.
    2   **3**

Earlier <u>amused cultural differences</u> suddenly become stressful. <u>Repeating remarks</u>
        4   **5**

by others about differences between the two cultures may be interpreted as

(continued)

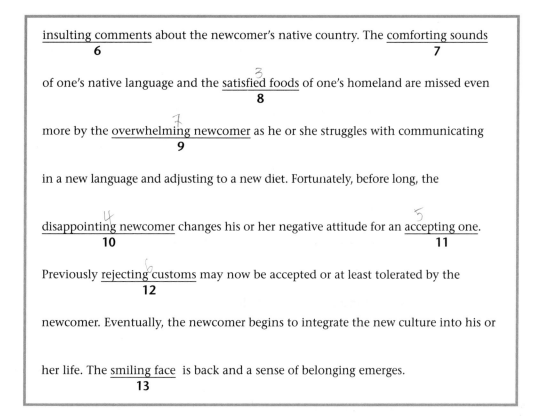

insulting comments about the newcomer's native country. The comforting sounds
6   7

of one's native language and the satisfied foods of one's homeland are missed even
                                    8

more by the overwhelming newcomer as he or she struggles with communicating
            9

in a new language and adjusting to a new diet. Fortunately, before long, the

disappointing newcomer changes his or her negative attitude for an accepting one.
10   11

Previously rejecting customs may now be accepted or at least tolerated by the
          12

newcomer. Eventually, the newcomer begins to integrate the new culture into his or

her life. The smiling face is back and a sense of belonging emerges.
          13

Editing
Exercise 11   One of the four underlined words or phrases is not correct. Circle the letter of the error and write a correction above the error.

1. The students' raw scores are calculating by dividing the number of
                              A   B

   correct answers by the total number of questions.
          C   D

2. For many reasons, it is important to ensure that tests are being properly
                      A   B

   administering by school officials.
          C   D

3. Simpler than either the median or the mean, the mode is the value that
            A   B

   is appeared the most frequently in a set of test score data.
          C   D

4. It was discovered that the State Comprehensive Testing Office providing
      A   B

   incorrect test scores for more than three million students in the state.
          C   D

Exercise 12   Circle the letter of the correct answer. Be prepared to explain your answers.

1. The development of a good test _____ several steps, each of which _____ a great deal of time.

   A.   is included ... is required   C.   is included ... requires

   B.   includes ... is required   D.   includes ... requires

2. For example, a test must _____ before it can _____ to schools.

   A.   validate ... distribute   C.   be validated ... distribute

   B.   be validated ... be distributed   D.   validate ... be distributed

3. Before educational testing employees begin working on test validation, they _____ three months of training, which costs the company more than $8,000 per employee.

   A.   are receiving   C.   receive

   B.   are received   D.   were received

4. This training is necessary because only _____ test writers can understand the complexity of high-stakes _____ tests.

   A.   experiencing ... state-mandating   C.   experienced ... state-mandated

   B.   experiencing ... state-mandated   D.   experienced ... state-mandating

5. To keep up with changes and trends in testing, educational testing administrators must routinely _____ publications that discuss new methods and processes.

   A.   review   C.   reviewed

   B.   be reviewed   D.   have been reviewing

6. Some tests for university-bound students have multiple sections that can _____ several hours to complete.

   A.   take   C.   be taken

   B.   be taking   D.   have taken

7. On the English proficiency test that our university gives, the first parts of the test _____ to see if students _____ gerunds and articles.

   A.   are designing ... understand   C.   are designing ... are understood

   B.   are designed ... are understood   D.   are designed ... understand

8. Just two years ago, the test _____. An improvement in the second version of the test is the inclusion of relevant and _____ material.

A. revised ... interested

B. revised ... interesting

C. was revised ... interested

D. was revised ... interesting

Exercise 13 Write one to three paragraphs that report the news about an event. The event can be real or imagined. Tell what happened, when it happened, and why it happened. Try to give numbers and examples of details of the event. When possible, describe people's reactions to the event. Were they surprised? Terrified? Annoyed?

Try to use passive voice when possible. Underline your passive voice examples. Remember that passive voice is not as common as active voice or intransitive verbs in real English, so make sure that you do not have a disproportionate percentage of passive voice examples in your writing. Exchange paragraphs with a partner. Review your partner's paragraph, checking for correct use of passive voice.

_____

_____

_____

_____

_____

_____

_____

_____

_____

_____

_____

_____

_____

_____

_____

_____

_____

_____

12 *Conditionals*

In this chapter, you will learn about a simple but powerful word that we use to express conditions, or whether results are real or possible depending on other circumstances. That word is *if*.

✓ CHECK YOUR GRAMMAR

Three of the five underlined words or phrases contain an error related to conditionals. Can you explain why each of these underlined areas is (or is not) wrong? Discuss with a partner.

> ### Forming a Union
>
> Forming a union for workers can be complicated. There are set rules for forming a union. <u>If at least 30 percent of the eligible employees sign authorization cards</u>, the organizers generally <u>requested</u> that the firm recognize the union as the employees' bargaining representative. Usually the firm rejects this request, and a formal election is held to decide whether to have a union. <u>If the union obtains a majority</u> in the election, it <u>became</u> the official bargaining agent for its members, and the final step, certification, <u>took place</u>.

From: Pride et al., *Business*, p. 349.

12.1 Conditionals With *if*

We use adverb clauses with the conjunction (joining word) *if* to convey conditional ideas, that is, when the occurrence of one event depends on the occurrence of another event. (See Chapter 15 for more information about adverb clauses.)

The English language features four types of conditional sentences:

Conditional 1: A situation that is always true

    A. **If** the price of gas goes up, the cost of a bus ticket goes up, too.

    B. **If** the President does not like a bill, he vetoes it before it becomes a law.

Conditional 2: A real or possible condition for the future

    C. **If** I study tonight, I will get a good score on the final exam tomorrow.

    D. **If** Karkovia invades Bratlova, the army of Bratlova might fight back with nuclear weapons.

Conditional 3: An unreal or imaginary condition

    E. **If** Bolivia possessed a seacoast, the country's economy would be very different.

    F. **If** cars were able to run on water, the world would have a better environment.

Conditional 4: A past condition with hypothetical results

    G. **If** the paparazzi had not chased Princess Diana, she would not have died in 1997.

    H. **If** AIDS had been cured early, millions of people would have survived.

12.1.1   *Punctuation With* if *Conditionals*

As with other adverb clauses, the if-clause can either begin or end the sentence. We use a comma when the adverb clause comes first in the sentence. Thus, when an if-clause begins a sentence, a comma is required.

    *C. **If** I study tonight, I will get a good score on the final exam tomorrow.

    OR: I will get a good score on the final exam tomorrow **if** I study tonight.

    H. **If** AIDS had been cured early, millions of people would have survived.

    OR: Millions of people would not have died **if** AIDS had been cured early.

Exercise 1   In each sentence, underline the if-clause. Circle the verb inside the if-clause and the verb inside the main clause. Add a comma where necessary. The first one has been done for you.

1. If the air temperature (drops) below freezing, the forecast (will be) snow.

2. If the temperature is above freezing then rain is much more likely.

3. You should seek shelter immediately if you are outside during a thunderstorm.

4. If a tornado appears to stay in the same place and is growing larger this may mean that it is coming toward you.

---

* Throughout Chapter 12, example sentences are recycled for better comprehension. For example, C and H are also at the top of this page and on subsequent pages.

5. If you have seen a tree move or waves on the water you have seen the effect of wind.

6. If air that has been heated by the sun during the day cools enough at night the moisture in the air condenses and forms fog.

7. If the wind in a tropical storm reaches 74 miles per hour that storm becomes a hurricane.

8. In Medieval Europe, people used to ring church bells if they saw lightning or heard thunder.

12.2 Conditional 1: A Situation That Is (or Was) Always True

In the first type of conditional sentence, both the if-clause and the main clause describe situations that are or were always true. These situations are either in the present tense or in the past tense.

Note about verbs: To express situations that are always true, verbs in both the main clause and the if-clause are in the present tense. To describe a similar situation in the past, verbs in both clauses are in the past tense.

Conditional 1 in the Present Tense

   A. If the price of gas *goes* up, the cost of a bus ticket *goes* up, too.

   B. If the President *does not like* a bill, he *vetoes* it before it becomes a law.

Conditional 1 in the Past Tense

   K. If I *was* late for work, my boss *got* really angry at me.

   L. If people *wanted* to sail from Miami to Los Angeles before the Panama Canal was opened in 1914, they *sailed* all the way around the southern tip of South America.

Note that in this type of conditional sentence, the meaning of *if* is similar to *when* or *whenever*.

   M. **When** the price of gas *goes* up, the cost of a bus ticket *goes* up, too.

   N. **Whenever** I *was* late for work, my boss *got* really angry at me.

Exercise 2   Read each condition below. Fill in the blank with a logical result of the information in the if-clause. Add commas where necessary. The first one has been done for you.

   1. If you drop an egg, it breaks. _____

   2. If you can't drive a car, you _____.

   3. If water drops below 32 degrees, it _____.

4. As a child, if I didn't like what my mother cooked for dinner, my mother _____ .

_____

5. If I received a bad grade in high school, I _____ .

6. If I need to mail a letter, I _____ .

7. In the past, if children misbehaved in public, their parents _____ .

_____

8. Hundreds of years ago, if there was a solar eclipse, people _____ .

_____

12.3 Conditional 2: A Real or Possible Condition for the Future

In the second type of conditional sentence, the main clause describes a situation that will or may be true if the situation described in the if-clause actually happens. In other words, both situations only take place or could take place if the stated condition is true.

Note about verbs: To express conditions that may lead to future results, the if-clause takes a simple present tense verb. In the main clause, the verb for the result is accompanied by common modals such as *will, can, may, might, should*. (See Chapter 9 for more about modals.)

> C. **If** I *study* tonight, I *might get* a good score on the final exam tomorrow.
>
> D. **If** Karkovia *invades* Bratlova, the army of Bratlova *will fight* back with nuclear weapons.
>
> O. **If** it *rains* tomorrow, we *might not drive* to the beach.

Do not use *will* in the if-clause.

> *Incorrect:* If it ~~will rain~~ tomorrow, we *might not drive* to the beach.

Exercise 3 For each of the scenarios below, write two sentences that address the conditions presented. The first one has been done for you.

1. You are not doing well in school. What can you do to improve your grades?

1a. If I study more frequently, my grades will improve.

1b. If I spend more time on my homework, my grades will improve.

2. You are not sure what to cook for your dinner guests. What can you serve them?

2a. _____

2b. _____

3. Your family has a picnic planned for tomorrow. What will you do if the weather is not good?

3a. _____

3b. _____

4. You are worried about your exam tomorrow. What will you do if you do not do well on the exam?

4a. _____

4b. _____

Exercise 4 Write six sentences based on a given scenario to complete a story that shows a chain of events. Each event has an effect on the next event. Use the verb in the main clause of one sentence as the verb in the if-clause in the next sentence. Circle the verbs in both clauses. The first one has been done for you.

SCENARIO: I have a choice between going to the library on Saturday and playing football with my friends. I am thinking about playing football.

1. If I (play) football on Saturday, I (will see) my good friends Jacob and Henry.

2. If I (see) my friends Jacob and Henry, I (will show) them my new car.

3. _____

4. _____

5. _____

6. _____

12.4 Conditional 3: Unreal or Imaginary Conditional

In the third type of conditional sentence, the if-clause describes a condition that is not true and the main clause describes a result that is not true. In other words, the information in both the if-clause and the main clause is unreal or imaginary.

Note about verbs: With unreal conditions, the if-clause takes a form that looks like a simple past tense verb. In the main clause, the verb for the unreal result is accompanied by the modals *would* or *could*.

> E. **If** Bolivia *possessed* a seacoast, the country's economy *would be* very different.
> (Bolivia does not possess a seacoast, so the economy is not different.)

F. If cars *were able to run* on water, the world *would have* a better environment.
(Cars cannot run on water, so the world does not have a good environment.)

The verb *be* in the if-clause for unreal conditions is always expressed as *were*. In informal English, which is never good formal writing, you may hear *was* used instead of *were*.

Formal: **If** more money *were* given to education, we *would have* better schools.

Informal: **If** more money *was* given to education, we *would have* better schools.

Exercise 5 Write six sentences based on a given scenario to complete a story that shows a chain of events. Each event has an effect on the next event. Use the verb in the main clause of one sentence as the verb in the if-clause in the next sentence. Circle the verbs in both clauses. The first one has been started for you.

SCENARIO: Imagine that you have just won the lottery. The grand prize is $1,000,000.

1. If I (won) one million dollars in the lottery, I (would) buy a new car. _____

_____

2. If I (bought) _____

_____

3. _____

_____

4. _____

_____

5. _____

_____

6. _____

_____

12.5 Conditional 4: Past Conditional With Hypothetical Results

In the fourth type of conditional sentence, both the if-clause and the main clause describe a past condition and a past result, but neither of them actually happened. In other words, both the condition and the result are hypothetical.

Note about verbs: The verb in the if-clause is past perfect tense (*had* + PAST PARTICIPLE). In the main clause, the verb for the hypothetical result consists of the modal (usually *would*) + *have* + PAST PARTICIPLE.

G. **If** the paparazzi *had not chased* Princess Diana, she *would not have died* in 1997. (The paparazzi chased Princess Diana, and she died.)

H. **If** AIDS *had been cured* early, millions of people *would have survived.* (AIDS was not cured early, and millions of people did not survive.)

If the verb in the if-clause is *have*, then the correct form for the past perfect is *had had*.

P. **If** we *had had* more time, we *would have stayed* in Greece an extra week.

If-clause without *if:* You can write a past conditional if-clause without *if* by moving *had* before the subject. This structure is characteristic of advanced writing, and you should try to include it in your writing when possible.

G. **Had** the paparazzi **not chased** Princess Diana, she **would not have died** in 1997.

H. **Had** AIDS **been cured** early, millions of people **would have survived.**

Exercise 6 For each of the scenarios listed below, answer the question by writing two sentences that address the conditions presented. The first one has been done for you.

1. You did not pass yesterday's exam. What could you have done to avoid this situation?

   1a. <u>If I had studied more, I would have passed yesterday's exam.</u>

   1b. <u>If I had paid attention more in class, I would have passed yesterday's exam.</u>

2. You didn't get the job you wanted. What could you have done differently?

   2a. _____

   2b. _____

3. You had to cancel your trip to Mexico because of a problem. You lost all of your money on the flights and hotels. What could you have done to avoid this situation?

   3a. _____

   3b. _____

4. Write your sentences for 1a, 2a, and 3a again, but this time omit the word *if* and move *had* before the subject.

   4.1a. _____

   4.2a. _____

   4.3a. _____

Exercise 7   Read each set of sentences. In the blanks, write the correct form of the verbs in parentheses. Refer to Sections 12.2 to 12.5 if you need help. The first one has been done for you.

1. (study, do)

1a. If I __study__ for tomorrow's test, surely I __will do__ well.

1b. If I _____ more every day, I _____ better on my class quizzes,

but I just do not have enough time.

1c. If I _____ last week, I _____

better on yesterday's test.

2. (know, translate)

2a. If I _____ that Italian word on the wall, I _____

it for you when you asked me yesterday.

2b. I don't know Italian. If I _____ Italian, I _____

this letter for you now.

2c. I will go with you to your interview at the Italian Embassy tomorrow. If I

_____ what the interviewer is asking in Italian, I _____

_____ it for you.

3. (have, take)

3a. If I _____ a car, I _____ you to the mall right now.

3b. If I _____ my car back from the shop by tomorrow, of course

I _____ you to the mall.

3c. I couldn't take you to the mall yesterday because my car was still at the shop.

If I _____ my car back, I certainly _____

_____ you to the mall.

4. (see, tell)

4a. OK. If I _____ Jim in the next few minutes, I _____

_____ him that you are looking for him.

4b. I didn't see Jim. If I _____ him, of course I

_____ him that you were looking for him.

Exercise 8 Read the paragraph. In the blanks, write the correct form of the verbs in parentheses.

Off to Alaska

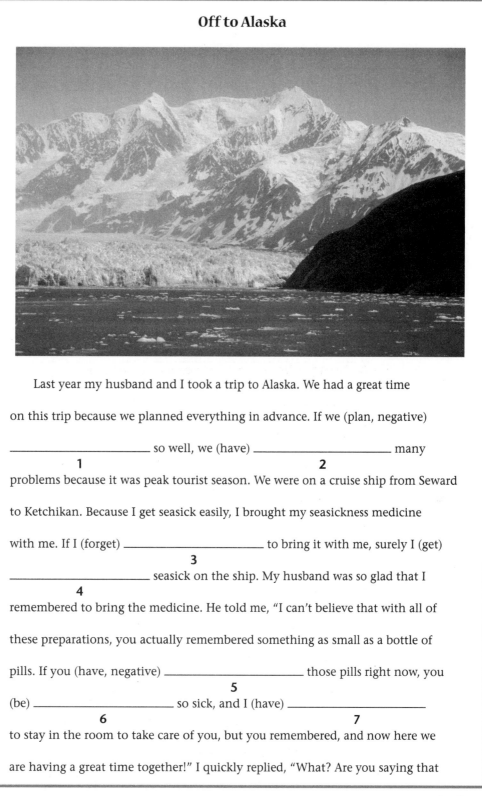

Last year my husband and I took a trip to Alaska. We had a great time

on this trip because we planned everything in advance. If we (plan, negative)

_____ so well, we (have) _____ many
             1   **2**

problems because it was peak tourist season. We were on a cruise ship from Seward

to Ketchikan. Because I get seasick easily, I brought my seasickness medicine

with me. If I (forget) _____ to bring it with me, surely I (get)
                              3

_____ seasick on the ship. My husband was so glad that I
       4

remembered to bring the medicine. He told me, "I can't believe that with all of

these preparations, you actually remembered something as small as a bottle of

pills. If you (have, negative) _____ those pills right now, you
                                5

(be) _____ so sick, and I (have) _____
         6   **7**

to stay in the room to take care of you, but you remembered, and now here we

are having a great time together!" I quickly replied, "What? Are you saying that

(continued)

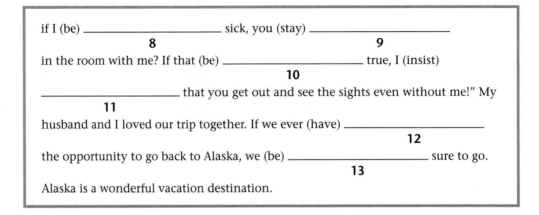

if I (be) _____ sick, you (stay) _____
                    8   **9**

in the room with me? If that (be) _____ true, I (insist)
                                              10

_____ that you get out and see the sights even without me!" My
        11

husband and I loved our trip together. If we ever (have) _____
                                                                    12

the opportunity to go back to Alaska, we (be) _____ sure to go.
                                                          13

Alaska is a wonderful vacation destination.

Exercise 9   Internet Language Search

Choose a topic that you are interested in and find a website related to it. Search the website for sentences that contain the word *if*. Copy four sentences here for your topic. Write your topic on the first line. Circle the main verbs and analyze why the writer has used certain tenses for these verbs. This search is an excellent way of improving your academic English.

Your topic: _____

1. _____

   _____

2. _____

   _____

3. _____

   _____

4. _____

   _____

Exercise 10   Circle the letter of the correct answer. Be prepared to explain your answers.

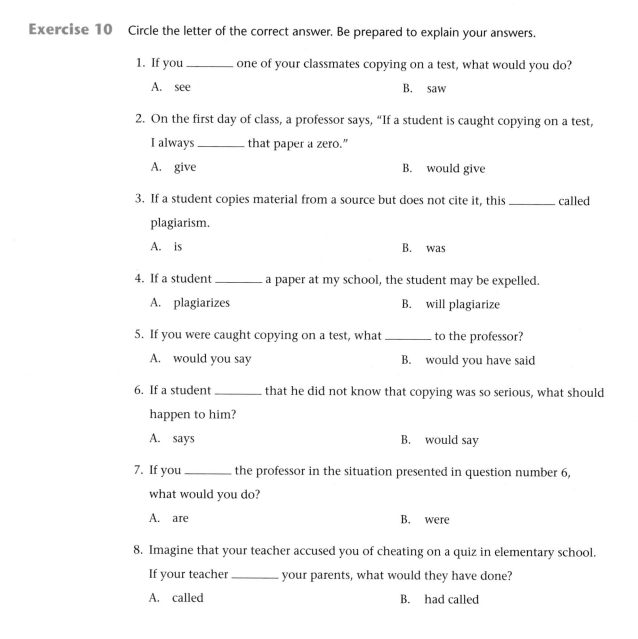

1. If you _____ one of your classmates copying on a test, what would you do?

   A. see   B. saw

2. On the first day of class, a professor says, "If a student is caught copying on a test,

   I always _____ that paper a zero."

   A. give   B. would give

3. If a student copies material from a source but does not cite it, this _____ called

   plagiarism.

   A. is   B. was

4. If a student _____ a paper at my school, the student may be expelled.

   A. plagiarizes   B. will plagiarize

5. If you were caught copying on a test, what _____ to the professor?

   A. would you say   B. would you have said

6. If a student _____ that he did not know that copying was so serious, what should

   happen to him?

   A. says   B. would say

7. If you _____ the professor in the situation presented in question number 6,

   what would you do?

   A. are   B. were

8. Imagine that your teacher accused you of cheating on a quiz in elementary school.

   If your teacher _____ your parents, what would they have done?

   A. called   B. had called

Exercise 11   Write a paragraph about an event that did not have a good ending. Explain how things would have been different if certain conditions had existed or if other events had happened. Use at least three if-clauses in your paragraph. Omit the *if* from one clause. Exchange paragraphs with a partner and check each other's work for correct verb tense.

_____

_____

_____

_____

_____

_____

_____

_____

_____

_____

_____

_____

_____

_____

_____

_____

_____

_____

_____

_____

_____

13 Word Order and Word Combinations

In this chapter, you will review <u>word order</u> in English sentences and common <u>word combinations</u> found in English. Preposition combinations will also be treated extensively.

✔ CHECK YOUR GRAMMAR

Three of the five underlined phrases contain an error related to word order or word combinations. Can you explain why each of these underlined areas is (or is not) wrong? Discuss with a partner.

Bill Gates

In 1974, Bill Gates decided to drop out of Harvard and with high school friend Paul Allen wrote <u>operating software</u> for the <u>newly emerging computers personal</u>. They formed Microsoft and created MS-DOS. <u>Later twelve years</u>, Microsoft dominated the personal market computer, and Gates became the nation's richest billionaire.

From: Berkin et al., *History of the United States*, p. 968.

13.1 Review of Basic Word Order

The basic word order of an English sentence is SUBJECT + VERB + OBJECT. Of course not all sentences contain objects, and some of the rules vary depending on the type of verb that is used in the sentence. In the following section, you will review word order of sentences using the verb *be*.

13.1.1 *Word Order With the Verb* be

The verb *be* is the most commonly used verb in the English language. Sentences have several basic patterns using the verb *be*. Review the following structures.

Subject + BE + Complement (Noun)

Mr. Davison *was* the **college president** for over fifteen years.
SUBJECT   BE   COMPLEMENT

Subject + BE + Adjective

The dogs *were* **thirsty** after spending the day at the dog park.
SUBJECT   BE   ADJECTIVE

Subject + BE + Prepositional Phrase

The check *is* **in the mail**.
SUBJECT   BE PREPOSITIONAL PHRASE

Subject + BE + Present Participle (verb + -*ing*)

All of my classmates **are studying** for the final exam right now.
SUBJECT   BE + PRESENT PARTICIPLE

Subject + BE + Past Participle (Passive Voice) (verb + -*ed*/-*en* [irregular])

The final exam for ENG 107 **was given** on Monday, August 21.
SUBJECT   BE + PAST PARTICIPLE

Exercise 1 Read the following paragraph. Fill in the blanks with an appropriate adjective, complement, prepositional phrase, or present participle. The first one has been done for you.

Attractions of Rome

Rome, Italy, <u>*is a popular tourist destination*</u> (be + complement). It is in the Lazio
                              1
region on the western coast of Italy. Rome _____
                                                        2

_____ (be + adjective) with many museums and parks to visit. For example,

the Sistine Chapel, which was built in the 1470s, _____
                                                                    3

_____ (be + adjective) because of the beautiful images and colors that

Michelangelo painted. Another interesting place to visit is, of course, the 2,000-year-

old Coliseum. The Coliseum _____
                                        4

(be + prepositional phrase), so tourists can easily walk from there to other nearby

ruins like the Circus Maximus. Thousands of people visit this ancient part of the

city every day. Not too far from this area is the Trevi Fountain. This fountain

_____ (be + complement) where
                        5
tourists throw small coins for good luck. All in all, the attractions in Rome

_____ (be + adjective), historic, and
                        6
memorable.

13.2 Word Order of Adverbials

You learned that English sentences generally follow the SUBJECT + VERB + OBJECT pattern. It is common, however, to vary word order so that your writing does not sound too mechanical. One method of doing so is the placement of adverbials. Adverbials can be simple adverbs, adverb clauses or phrases (see Chapter 15), or prepositional phrases (see Chapter 7). Like adverbs themselves, adverbials describe *how*. Study the following groups of sentences, paying close attention to the word order. Notice how the position of the adverbial can change.

adverb:	His view of the world changed **immediately**.
	Immediately, his view of the world changed.
	His view of the world **immediately** changed.
adverb clause:	The experiment succeeded **because the data were collected by hand**.
	Because the data were collected by hand, the experiment succeeded.
prepositional phrase:	The child's cat sat **on the roof** and meowed loudly.
	On the roof, the child's cat sat and meowed loudly.
	Meowing loudly, the child's cat sat **on the roof**.

13.2.1 *Negative Adverbs of Frequency*

The normal position for adverbs of frequency is before the main verb but after *be*, modals, and auxiliary verbs.

> During the fall semester, I **usually** *go* home for the weekend.

> *Correct:* In this area, the noon temperature **never** *drops* below 100 degrees in July.

> *Incorrect:* In this area, the noon temperature ~~*drops* **never**~~ below 100 degrees in July.

When using a negative adverb of frequency (*never, rarely, seldom, barely, hardly ever*), your writing will sound more advanced if you occasionally put the negative adverb in front of the subject. However, this placement means that you must rewrite the verb using "question" order, the same order as if it were a question.

> Businesses with low capital **rarely** survive past their first year.
> SUBJECT + NEGATIVE ADVERB + PRESENT TENSE VERB

> *Change to:* **Rarely do** businesses with low capital survive past their first year.
> NEGATIVE ADVERB + DO + SUBJECT + VERB

> A composition class **should never** have more than twenty students.
> SUBJECT + MODAL + NEGATIVE ADVERB

> *Change to:* **Never should** a composition class have more than twenty students.
> NEGATIVE ADVERB + MODAL + SUBJECT + VERB

13.2.2   Prepositions of Location

Depending on the intransitive verb used, you can sometimes invert the subject and verb after a prepositional phrase of location.

A brightly painted picture hangs **on the wall.**
    SUBJECT   +   VERB + PREPOSITIONAL PHRASE

Change to: **On the wall** hangs a brightly painted picture.
    PREPOSITIONAL PHRASE + VERB   +   SUBJECT

Editing
 **Exercise 2**   As you rewrite each sentence, vary the beginning to add interest or emphasis. Begin your new sentence with the underlined word. Make any other changes as necessary. The first one has been done for you.

1. Carla and Bob moved to the city to be closer to cultural attractions <u>despite</u> the poor housing market and high crime rate in the area.

    Despite the poor housing market and high crime rate in the area, Carla and Bob moved to

    the city to be closer to cultural attractions.

2. They walked around their new neighborhood <u>casually</u> yet purposefully.

    _____

    _____

3. Residents have formed a neighborhood watch group <u>in</u> an all-out effort to discourage crime.

    _____

    _____

4. Carla and Bob sat and drank lemonade <u>under</u> a slowly spinning fan on their porch.

    _____

    _____

5. With so much time spent organizing their new home, they <u>rarely</u> have the time to do this.

    _____

    _____

Exercise 3 Read the following paragraph. Circle the five errors and write the corrections on the lines. The first one has been done for you.

1. did I imagine   3. _____   5. _____

2. _____   4. _____

A New Job

Never in my life (I imagined) that I would get a job at a TV studio. I'd always wanted to be a doctor, and now I'm a television producer. I work in a local studio, and it is a building extremely modern. My office behind the main lobby, so I can be the first one to see who is visiting the station. My schedule is general flexible, so I'm able to take care of outside business fairly easily. While I didn't study to become a producer, I find it a very rewarding job. I've worked on news shows, variety programs, and even telethons! Rarely I get bored with my job duties.

13.3 Word Combinations With Prepositions

You reviewed the use of prepositions in Chapter 7. In this section, you will be given a more comprehensive list of word combinations with prepositions.

13.3.1 *Noun + Preposition Combinations*

Nouns + *about*	Noun + *between*	Nouns + *on*	Nouns + *to**
confusion	difference	advice	alternative
question		tax	connection
			damage
			invitation
			reaction
			reply
			solution

(continued)

---

*Although some of these nouns can be followed by infinitives, this combination involves a different structure. Here we are referring to the need for the preposition *to* between the noun and any following noun. Compare:

The scientists found a **solution** *to stop* the problem. (NOUN + infinitive)
The scientists found a **solution** *to* the *problem*. (NOUN + PREP + NOUN)

Nouns + *of*	Nouns + *for*	Nouns + *in*	Nouns + *with*
advantage	answer	background	agreement
benefit	application	change	connection
cause	check	decrease	contact
cost	concern	experience	contract
decrease	demand	fall	experience
diagram	excuse	increase	the matter
example	fondness	interest	negotiations
experience	interview	rise	trouble
fall	need		
group	order		
illustration	payment		
increase	question		
lack	reason		
map	request		
opinion	something		
payment			
photograph			
picture			
price			
rise			
understanding			

Exercise 4   Fill in the correct preposition according to the noun. Then complete the sentence with the wording of your choice. The first one has been done for you.

1. I've always had an understanding *of technical machinery.* _____

2. I have a question _____.

3. Lately, I've developed a special interest _____.

4. To be a better student, I need to take advantage _____.

5. There is no excuse _____.

6. I have little experience _____.

7. I may need advice _____.

8. What was your reaction _____?

Verb + Preposition Combinations

As with preposition + noun combinations, prepositions that are combined with verbs must be learned as a unit. Below are some of the most common combinations, grouped by preposition.

Verbs + *about*	Verbs + *at*	Verbs + *for*	Verbs + *of*	Verbs + *off*
ask	guess	apologize	complain	break
complain	laugh	ask	die (also *die from*)	call
dream	look	buy		cut
forget	smile	do	dream	fall
talk	stare	look	get rid	jump
think	yell	make	think	keep
worry		pay		live
		study		take
		thank		turn

Verbs + *on*	Verbs + *to**	Verbs + *toward*	Verbs + *with*	Verbs + *in*
count	agree	head	agree	excel
disagree	apologize	turn	argue	succeed
have	be used	walk	break up	
keep	belong	work	compete	
pick	complain		cooperate	
put	contribute		disagree	
rely	explain		fill	
take	introduce		get along	
wait	listen		help	
work	object		finish	
	pay attention		work	
	relate			
	reply			
	say			
	speak			
	talk			

---

*Although some of these verbs can be followed by infinitives, this combination involves a different structure. Here we are referring to the need for the preposition *to* between the verb and any following noun. Compare:

The scientists **listened** carefully **to understand** our report. (VERB + infinitive)

The scientists **listened** carefully **to** our ***report***. (VERB + PREP + NOUN)

Exercise 5 Read the following paragraphs with underlined VERB + PREPOSITION combinations. Find and correct the five mistakes in the combinations.

The Perfect Employee

One of the most sought-after qualities in an employee is the ability to <u>get along</u>
                                                                                    1
<u>with</u> others. In today's world, and especially in the world of business, employees are

seen as team members. They are expected to <u>relate with</u> all other members of the team
                                                        2
and to <u>work toward</u> a common goal, company success.
          3

Similarly, employees are also expected to <u>think about</u> and <u>contribute toward</u>
                                                      4   **5**
achieving the company's mission. Although at times employees may not <u>agree about</u>
                                                                                6
a specific company policy, they are expected to support and follow it. At times they

may even have to temporarily <u>forget about</u> their personal goals and desires in order
                                        7
to accomplish the goals of the company.

Employees who cannot or will not <u>cooperate with</u> others on the team often find
                                                8
they no longer <u>belong at</u> the "inner circle" and begin to <u>worry for</u> keeping their jobs.
                      9   **10**
In many cases, they leave the company in search of another that better suits their

work style and personality.

Exercise 6 Read the verbs in the list below. Fill in the blanks with an appropriate preposition. Then choose five of the VERB + PREPOSITION combinations and write an original sentence for each one. The sentences should be related to your academic studies.

guess _____   listen _____   study _____   work _____

apologize _____   dream _____   rely _____   pay attention _____

disagree _____   complain _____   think _____   talk _____

1. _____

   _____

2. _____

   _____

3. _____

   _____

4. _____

_____

5. _____

_____

13.3.3 Adjective + Preposition Combinations

Certain adjectives can be combined with prepositions. These, too, function as one unit and must be learned together. Listed below are some of the most common combinations.

Adjectives + *about, at, for, with*	Adjectives + *by, with*	Adjectives + *for*	Adjectives + *from*
angry about / at / with	bored by / with	accountable	different
concerned about/ with	embarrassed by	bad	divorced
excited about	frustrated by / with	good	isolated
happy about / with		ready	
sorry about / for		necessary	
think about			
unhappy about / with			
worried about			

Adjectives + *in, with*	Adjectives + *of*	Adjectives + *to**	Adjectives + *with*
disappointed in / with	afraid	boring	familiar
interested in	fond	committed	impressed
	guilty	confusing	pleased
	in favor	important	satisfied
	proud	married	
	sure	opposed	
	tired	pleasing	
	unsure	related	
		similar	
		unimportant	

(For a review of adjective + prepositions used with gerunds, see Chapter 10, Section 10.2.1).

---

*Although some of these adjectives can be followed by infinitives, this combination involves a different structure. Here we are referring to the need for the preposition *to* between the adjective and any following noun. Compare:

The scientists were **pleased** *to receive* the final report. (ADJ + INFINITIVE)

The scientists were **pleased** *with* the final *report*. (ADJ + PREP + NOUN)

Editing

⌃ Exercise 7   Find the seven errors in ADJECTIVE + PREPOSITION usage and correct them.

Adolescence

Young people are often unsure with themselves in social situations. During adolescence, teens are especially concerned in what others think of them. It's important to them that their peers like them. Surprisingly, some teens often act as if they don't care what others think on them. Although this conflict is normal, many adolescents are often frustrated at these feelings they experience.

As they mature, adolescents are ready for more responsibility, and yet oftentimes they are angry for their parents for making them accountable of their actions. Some teens are afraid of their growing independence while others are proud for it.

Editing

⌃ Exercise 8   In each sentence one of the four underlined words or phrases is not correct. Circle the letter of the error and write a correction above the error.

1. I know you want to come over <u>this weekend</u>, but I'm not <u>interested with</u> your plan
                                        A   **B**

   right now. I <u>have plans</u> of my own that <u>need attention</u>.
                C   **D**

2. Perhaps <u>next week</u>, if you <u>agree about</u> me, we can go <u>to a restaurant</u> that's
              A   **B**   **C**

   <u>different from</u> our regular café.
       D

3. There has been a lot of <u>confusion of</u> our weekend schedule; <u>why don't we</u> make
                         A   **B**

   <u>some time to</u> coordinate our plans and reach some kind <u>of agreement</u>?
       C   **D**

4. <u>Seldom we have</u> these types of arguments, but if we're <u>concerned about</u> our friendship,
      A   **B**

   we need to <u>talk about</u> it more and try to <u>cooperate with</u> each other.
             C   **D**

5. Right now I have to <u>work on</u> my studies. My exam is <u>two days</u>, so I really need to
                     A   **B**

   <u>get back to</u> the library. Let's talk <u>in a few days</u>.
      C   **D**

Exercise 9   Circle the letter of the correct answer. Be prepared to explain your answers.

1. For weeks prior to graduation, the students at my school were so excited _____ graduation that they could not contribute anything of substance _____ class discussions unless the discussion involved graduation.

   A. for ... to

   B. for ... with

   C. about ... to

   D. about ... with

2. Because attending graduation was so important _____ me, I did not object _____ how much renting the gown and getting the invitations actually cost.

   A. to ... to

   B. to ... about

   C. by ... to

   D. by ... about

3. My mother wanted everyone in my family, including distant cousins that I had not seen in years, to attend my graduation, but I disagreed _____ her opinion. In the end, however, I gave in because I did not want to be the cause _____ any family problems.

   A. about ... of

   B. about ... for

   C. with ... of

   D. with ... for

4. The graduation event was amazing. The auditorium was packed. Never _____ so many people at one event!

   A. I saw

   B. did I see

   C. I had seen

   D. had I seen

5. The speaker chosen for our graduation ceremony clearly had a passionate interest _____ education, which was at least partially due to the fact that she is married _____ a former high school teacher.

   A. for ... to

   B. in ... to

   C. for ... with

   D. in ... with

6. I had to laugh _____ my little brothers. They were so frustrated _____ the length of graduation that they were falling asleep during the ceremony. At least they sat still for once.

   A. for ... at

   B. at ... at

   C. for ... by

   D. at ... by

7. Now that graduation is behind me, I cannot wait for my first interview _____ a real

job. I am certainly tired _____ working as a graduate assistant.

A. for ... for

B. in ... for

C. for ... of

D. in ... in

8. I hope to excel _____ my new job so that my parents will continue to be _____

of me.

A. in ... happy

B. with ... happy

C. in ... proud

D. with ... proud

Exercise 10   Write a paragraph about a special place that you would like to visit. Identify the place and describe it. Tell why you want to visit that particular place. Underline at least five examples of the grammar points regarding word order and word combinations that you have studied in this chapter. Exchange paragraphs with a partner and check each other's work for correct word order and word combinations.

_____

_____

_____

_____

_____

_____

_____

_____

_____

_____

_____

_____

_____

_____

_____

_____

_____

_____

_____

_____

14 Adjective Clauses and Reductions

This chapter reviews everything you need to know about <u>adjective clauses and reductions</u>.

✔ CHECK YOUR GRAMMAR

One of the three underlined phrases contains an error related to adjective clauses and reductions. Can you explain why each of these underlined areas is (or is not) wrong? Discuss with a partner.

Thomas Edison

What are some of the important inventions <u>for which Edison was responsible</u>? Born in 1847, Thomas A. Edison secured the first of his thousand-plus patents in 1869. In 1876, Edison, who was not even thirty years old, set up the first modern research laboratory, <u>where could work he and his staff</u>. In 1887, he opened a new facility <u>that quickly became the world leader</u> in research and development, especially for electricity.

Adapted from: Berkin et. al., *Making America*, p. 533.

14.1 Adjective Clauses and Relative Pronouns

An adjective clause is a group of words with a subject and a verb that modifies or describes a noun or a pronoun. An adjective clause functions just like an adjective.

> The firefighters tried to save the **old** house. (The adjective describes *house*.)

> The firefighters tried to save the old house **that was burning.** (The adjective clause describes *house*.)

You will recognize adjective clauses by the following relative pronouns: *who, which, that, whom, whose.*

Relative pronoun	Original sentence	Sentence with adjective clause
who	The boy is my friend. He lives down the street.	The boy **who lives down the street** is my friend.
which	Two news articles were written by my science professor. They appeared in the latest edition of *Nova*.	Two news articles **which appeared in the latest edition of *Nova*** were written by my science professor.
that	The Japanese food is sashimi. Keith likes it best.	The Japanese food **that Keith likes best** is sashimi.
whom	The people are very interesting. Beverly works for them.	The people **whom Beverly works for** are very interesting.
whose	The TV newscaster is on channel 7. I trust her opinions most.	The TV newscaster **whose opinions I trust most** is on channel 7.

Who and *whom* are used only for people. *Which* is used only for things. *That* is used for both people and things (less formal than *who(m)* and *which*). *Whose* is the possessive and is used for both people and things. Note that *what* is not used as a relative pronoun.

Exercise 1 Read the paragraph and underline the six adjective clauses. The first one has been done for you.

SUVs

One of the most common types of cars is the SUV (Sport Utility Vehicle). SUVs are machines <u>that were originally used in the military or in rugged terrain</u>. These cars, which normally have four-wheel drive, are better able to maneuver in rough road conditions. Jeeps, which have been popular around the world for many years, originated with the U.S. military. Similarly, Land Rovers are vehicles that the British military has utilized extensively. SUVs are vehicles that have many advantages, but the amount of gas that they use is extremely high.

⚠ Exercise 2 Read the following sentences. If the sentence is correct, put a C in the blank. If it is incorrect, put an X in the blank and make the correction.

_____ 1. I wish I had pictures of all the places that I have visited.

_____ 2. Perhaps the best memories of my trips are of the people which I have met.

_____ 3. Of all the wonderful places I have been, the one that I remember the most is Cape Breton, Canada.

_____ 4. Even though they will probably never have the chance to visit me, I keep in contact with many foreign friends which I have made over the years.

_____ 5. Nowadays, however, it is the Internet who helps me maintain my contacts.

_____ 6. Without this tool, I would be unable to keep up with my friends, whose lives change as much as mine does.

Exercise 3 Read the paragraph and add appropriate adjective clauses where indicated.

Interview Tips

A successful job interview is one that results in a job offer. Interviewers who are

skilled in interviewing techniques are good listeners who get the information they

need to make a wise hiring decision. Most job interviews follow a question-and-answer

format that may or may not be predictable. To increase your chances of getting the job

_____,

1

you will need to prepare for the interview. You should anticipate questions _____

_____

2

and formulate your answers ahead of time. You also need to form your own list of

questions to ask the interviewer. By asking questions, you show interest in the job that

you have applied for. On the day of the interview, dress appropriately for the position

_____.

3

Be on time. Introduce yourself and shake hands with the interviewer. During the

interview, listen carefully to the questions that you are being asked. Remember that

you are speaking to the person _____

_____

4

(continued)

the job that you want. Close the interview with a statement that emphasizes your

interest in the job and thank the interviewer for his/her time. Later, send a thank-you

letter to the interviewer _____

_____ .

5

14.2   Non-restrictive and Restrictive Adjective Clauses

Adjective clauses come in two types: non-restrictive and restrictive. Non-restrictive clauses are separated from the rest of the sentence by a comma. Restrictive clauses are not.

14.2.1   *Non-restrictive Adjective Clauses*

When the information in the adjective clause is not essential to the meaning of the sentence, set it off with a comma or commas.

> My only sister, **who lives in California,** is a doctor.

> (The adjective clause gives extra information. You can take out the information between the commas and not change the meaning of the sentence.)

> The Eiffel Tower has an elevator, **which I rode to the top.**

Non-restrictive clauses always use a comma. Do not use *that* with non-restrictive adjective clauses.

> *Incorrect:*   My only sister, ~~that~~ **lives in California,** is a doctor.

> The Eiffel Tower has an elevator, ~~that~~ **I rode to the top.**

14.2.2   *Restrictive Adjective Clauses*

When the information in the adjective clause is essential to the meaning of the sentence, do not set it off with a comma or commas. If you take a restrictive clause out of the sentence, either the sentence will not make sense or the meaning will not be correct.

> My sister **who lives in California** is a doctor.

> (If you have more than one sister, then the adjective clause gives essential information. If you take out the information, it is not clear which sister you mean.)

> The car **that has a broken headlight** belongs to Mrs. Williams.

> (The adjective clause specifies a particular car. Without this descriptive information, you would not know which car belongs to Mrs. Williams.)

Exercise 4 Use the extra information in the second sentence to create a non-restrictive adjective clause that you add to the first sentence. To begin the clause, use the relative pronoun in parentheses. Be sure to use commas to set off the clause. The first one has been done for you.

1. Tashkent is experiencing economic growth these days. Tashkent is the capital of Uzbekistan. (which)

   <u>Tashkent, which is the capital of Uzbekistan,</u>

   <u>is experiencing economic growth these days.</u>

2. My boss is planning to transfer to Uzbekistan.

   My boss has been working for the company for ten years. (who)

   _____

   _____

3. His consulting firm is opening a new Central Asian office.

   The firm is one of the most successful in the country. (which)

   _____

   _____

4. The consulting firm's financial advisers were happy with the expansion.

   The advisers routinely analyze economic trends abroad. (who)

   _____

   _____

5. My boss will leave for Uzbekistan at the end of the year.

   His family will be accompanying him. (whose)

   _____

   _____

Editing

Exercise 5 Read the following sentences and underline the adjective clause. If the sentence is punctuated correctly, put a C in the blank. If it is not punctuated correctly, put an X in the blank and make the correction. The first two have been done for you.

___C___ 1. My parents, <u>who are now retired</u>, live in a suburb of London.

___X___ 2. Their son, <u>who is a student at London's School of Economics</u>, lives with them.

_____ 3. This university which is one of the most prestigious in all of Europe caters to some of the brightest young minds of today.

_____ 4. The students who study there can be assured that they will get a quality education.

_____ 5. High-paying jobs will certainly be available for the students who graduate from the London School of Economics.

_____ 6. A recent graduate who has landed a job at the United Bank of Europe has already begun making a name for herself.

14.3 | Subject and Object Relative Pronouns

Relative pronouns can function as subjects or objects in adjective clauses.

Subject pronouns:	who	which	that	whose
Object pronouns:	whom	which	that	whose

14.3.1 | *Subject Relative Pronouns:* who, which, that, whose

Many people **who work in customer service** experience stress. (*Who* describes *people* in the main clause and is the subject of the adjective clause.)

The tennis match, **which had been scheduled for noon,** was canceled. (*Which* describes *tennis match* in the main clause and is the subject of the adjective clause.)

14.3.2 | *Object Relative Pronouns:* whom, which, that, whose

Many people **whom I know** work in customer service. (*Whom* describes *people* in the main clause and is the object of the verb *know* in the adjective clause: *I know whom.*)

Because *whom* is considered formal language, you will see it more often in written English than you will hear it in spoken English.

The book **that I read** was very interesting. (*That* describes *book* in the main clause and is the object of the verb *read* in the adjective clause: *I read that.*)

who and whom: To know when to use *who* or *whom*, read the adjective clause. After *whom*, you should always have a subject:

The people **whom** *my brother and I* <u>saw</u> are friends of his.
             SUBJECT   VERB

After *who*, you should always have a verb:

The presidential candidate **who** *won* the party's nomination doesn't have much experience.   VERB

Exercise 6   Read the paragraph and insert the correct relative pronouns in the blanks. Sometimes more than one answer is possible. The first one has been done for you.

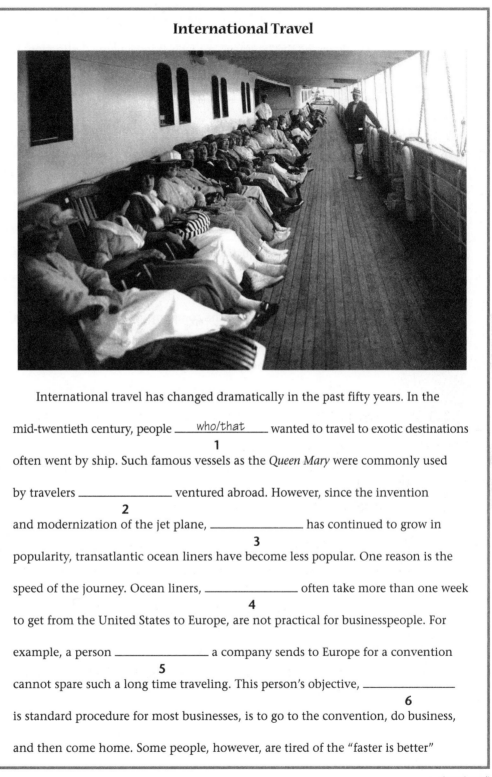

International Travel

International travel has changed dramatically in the past fifty years. In the

mid-twentieth century, people ___*who/that*___ wanted to travel to exotic destinations

1

often went by ship. Such famous vessels as the *Queen Mary* were commonly used

by travelers _____ ventured abroad. However, since the invention

2

and modernization of the jet plane, _____ has continued to grow in

3

popularity, transatlantic ocean liners have become less popular. One reason is the

speed of the journey. Ocean liners, _____ often take more than one week

4

to get from the United States to Europe, are not practical for businesspeople. For

example, a person _____ a company sends to Europe for a convention

5

cannot spare such a long time traveling. This person's objective, _____

6

is standard procedure for most businesses, is to go to the convention, do business,

and then come home. Some people, however, are tired of the "faster is better"

(continued)

mentality _____ modern airlines are advertising. They are now looking
            7

for alternative, more exotic modes of travel. For these people, _____ are
                                                                        8

anticipating the "journey" as much as visiting the destination, high-priced ocean

liner trips are just the ticket!

14.3.3 Omitting the Object Relative Pronoun

When the relative pronoun is the object of the adjective clause, native English speakers
often omit the relative pronoun. (See also Section 14.7 about adjective clause reductions.)

> The women **whom *I regularly see on Sundays*** are my mother's friends.

> The women **I regularly see on Sundays** are my mother's friends.

> The job advertisement **that *the company provided to the newspaper*** appeared
> last week.

> The job advertisement **the company provided to the newspaper** appeared last week.

It is incorrect to omit the relative pronoun when it is the subject of the adjective clause.

> *Incorrect:*   The girl is sitting in the park looks nervous.

> *Correct:*   The girl **who *is sitting in the park*** looks nervous.
>   SUBJECT

Editing
Exercise 7   Read the diary entry and circle the six relative pronouns. If a relative pronoun can be
eliminated, draw a line through it. The first one has been done for you.

Dear Diary,

Today was a very exciting day for me. It was my first day in high school, and I was

extremely excited. I signed up for the Spanish class (which) I had wanted for a long

time. Surprise! I got into the class! The teacher, who is from Malaga, Spain, is very

nice. I also got into a chemistry class. The lab, which is filled with all sorts of scientific

equipment, is a bit scary, but I think it will be interesting. Lunchtime was great

because I got to see all the friends that I hadn't seen all summer long. Overall, I think

this will be a wonderful year. There are so many interesting extracurricular activities

that I want to participate in, as well. Overall, I think this is a year that will keep me

busy and happy!

14.4 Relative Pronouns as Objects of Prepositions in Adjective Clauses

In addition to functioning as subjects or as objects, relative pronouns can also begin adjective clauses that function as objects of prepositions. Here are some examples with the prepositions *to* and *for*:

The fitness club **to *which I belong*** is coed. (Common in formal language, including writing: *which* is the object of the preposition *to* and refers to *club* in the main clause.)

Other variations are possible when there is a preposition in the adjective clause:

The fitness club **which *I belong*** to is coed.

The fitness club **that *I belong*** to is coed.

Incorrect:	The fitness club **that *I belong*** is coed. (Be careful not to forget the preposition if it is necessary.)
Incorrect:	The fitness club **to that *I belong*** is coed. (Don't put a preposition before the relative pronoun *that*.)
Correct:	The fitness club *I belong* to is coed. (relative pronoun omitted; very common in spoken English, especially informal language)
Incorrect:	The woman **for ~~who~~ you bought the flowers** was very happy. (Don't put a preposition before the relative pronoun *who*.)
Correct:	The woman **for whom you bought the flowers** was very happy to receive them.

Remember: Of all of these options, the preferred way to construct a relative clause with a preposition in writing is using PREPOSITION + *which* or *whom* at the beginning of the clause.

Formal	Informal
• The period in American history to which you are referring is called the Depression.	• The period in American history that you are referring to is called the Depression.
	• The period in American history you are referring to is called the Depression.
• The candidate about whom we were talking is a Democrat.	• The candidate that we were talking about is a Democrat.
• The candidate whom we were talking about is a Democrat.	• The candidate who we were talking about is a Democrat.
	• The candidate we were talking about is a Democrat.

Exercise 8   In each pair of sentences, change the second sentence to an adjective clause. Add a relative pronoun and commas where they are needed. The first one has been done for you.

1. The college has a professional development office.

   George just graduated from the college.

   The college from which George just graduated has a professional development office.

2. The woman works in the university's professional development office.

   George spoke to the woman.

   _____

   _____

3. The Student Services Building is near the center of campus.

   This office is located in the Student Services Building.

   _____

   _____

4. The university students are recent graduates.

   These services are most beneficial for university students.

   _____

   _____

5. Some of the employment tests took two hours to complete.

   George paid a small fee for some of these tests.

   _____

   _____

6. A private employment agency would be his last resort.

   George has heard good things about this agency.

   _____

   _____

14.5   Adjective Clauses With the Possessive *whose*

Sometimes when you combine two sentences using an adjective clause, the second sentence contains a possessive. In this case, use the relative pronoun *whose*.

Irene doesn't know the family **whose** *car was stolen.*

Main sentence: Irene doesn't know the Smiths.

Second sentence: **Their** car was stolen.

The possessive adjective *their* becomes *whose* when the sentence is made into an adjective clause.

The author **whose** *book was published posthumously* won the Nobel Prize for Literature.

Main sentence: The author won the Nobel Prize for Literature.

Second sentence: **His** book was published posthumously.

The possessive adjective *his* becomes *whose* in the adjective clause.

Exercise 9   Study the picture and write an original sentence about each student. Use an adjective clause with the relative pronoun *whose*. The first one has been done for you.

1. The boy whose glasses are on his head is Charles.

2. _____

   _____

3. _____

   _____

4. _____

   _____

5. _____

   _____

14.6 Adjective Clauses That Describe Place, Time, and Reason

An adjective clause can describe a place, a time, or a reason. These clauses begin with the relative adverbs *where, when,* and *why.*

14.6.1 Adjective Clauses That Express Place: where

Use the relative adverb *where* to describe a place.

> The city **where** *I was born* is an ancient Roman site.

> The rooms **where** *George Washington slept* are now famous landmarks.

When we talk about places, we often use the prepositions *in* and *at.*

> **in** Singapore   **at** the beach

In adjective clauses, the relative adverb *where* often replaces the phrase *in which* or *at which.*

> the city **where** *I was born* = the city **in which** *I was born*

> the room **where** *George Washington slept* = the room **which** *George Washington slept* **in**

14.6.2 Adjective Clauses That Express Time: when

Use the relative adverb *when* to express time and time relationships.

> The exact moment **when** *I won the Spanish poetry contest* was last Friday afternoon at 3:15 p.m.

> Do you recall the day **when** *we got married*?

In adjective clauses, *when* can replace *in which* or *on which.*

> The exact moment **when** *I won the Spanish poetry contest* = The exact moment **in which** *I won the Spanish poetry contest*

> The day **when** *we got married* = The day **on which** *we got married*

14.6.3 Adjective Clauses That Give Reasons: why

To give reasons and answer *why,* you can use *for which* or *that* to begin the adjective clause.

> The reason **for which** *Dr. Hughes won the hospital award* was his hard work.

> The reason **that** *Dr. Hughes won the hospital award* was his hard work.

Do not use WHY to introduce adjective clauses.

> *Incorrect:*   The reason ~~why~~ he bought that car is its good fuel efficiency.

> *Correct:*   The reason **that** he bought that car is its good fuel efficiency.

Exercise 10 Complete the dialogue using the answers from the box. You may use some of the answers more than once.

> who(m)   which   that   whose   where   when   Ø

John: Hey, Pablo! What's new?

Pablo: Not much. My professor just returned the exams _____ we took last week.
1

John: Oh yeah? How'd you do?

Pablo: Not as well as I had hoped, unfortunately. I misunderstood two questions _____
2
were in part 2 of the test, and they were worth twenty points each!

John: That's a bummer. Maybe you can do some extra work. Is the professor _____
3
teaches the class flexible?

Pablo: I think so. I just can't believe that the reason _____ I missed those questions was
4
because I read the directions too quickly.

John: Hey, that happens. I remember one time _____ I thought I had done so well on a
5
test, and later I found out that all my answers were supposed to be the opposite! You

know how sometimes questions ask for the negative? So, I understand.

Pablo: I don't know. Maybe I *should* talk to my professor. This exam grade _____ I got
6
will ruin my grade point average.

John: Look, it's noon. Why don't you go to the place _____ your professor has lunch and
7
talk to him? It can't hurt.

Pablo: You're right, John. I'm going to go right now. And I'll let you know what happens.

If nothing else, I've learned that this is a professor _____ directions are tricky!
8

John: Good luck.

Pablo: Thanks . . .

14.7   Adjective Clause Reductions

Sometimes a clause, which contains a subject and a verb, can be reduced or shortened to a phrase. Here are two rules about adjective clause reductions.

1. If the adjective clause contains the verb *be* (in any form), you can omit the relative pronoun and the verb *be*.

> The man **who is** *next to me* must be a diplomat of some kind.
>
> ⇩
>
> The man next to me must be a diplomat of some kind.

> People **who** *were born before 1960 in the United States* are called "Baby Boomers."
>
> ⇩
>
> People born before 1960 in the United States are called "Baby Boomers."

> Shakespeare, **who is** *the most well-known British author of all time,* continues to fascinate readers today.
>
> ⇩
>
> Shakespeare, the most well-known British author of all time, continues to fascinate readers today.

This particular reduction is called an *appositive*. It is a noun phrase that gives a definition or explanation of the previously mentioned noun.

2. You can sometimes reduce adjective clauses without the verb *be*. In this case, omit the relative pronoun and change the verb to the *-ing* or present participle form.

> We study in a university **which consists of** *six separate colleges.*
>
> ⇩
>
> We study in a university **consisting of** six separate colleges.

> People **who live** *in cities* generally do not exercise as often as those **who live** *in rural areas.*
>
> ⇩
>
> People **living** in cities generally do not exercise as often as those **living** in rural areas.

Exercise 11   Underline the nine adjective clauses in the paragraph. If an adjective clause can be reduced to a phrase, make those changes above the clause.

Mother of Miami

Mrs. Julia Sturtevant Tuttle is known as the "Mother of Miami." In 1873, she

brought her two small children to see the land that her father had purchased, land

which was located on the Miami River. She fell in love with the wilderness that she

saw, and formed a vision that included beautiful homes and lush gardens. In 1891,

---

(continued)

after the deaths of both her father and her husband, Julia brought her two children, who were now grown, to live on her father's land, which she had inherited. Julia continued to acquire land, bringing in workers and constructing business and residential buildings in order to see her vision become a reality. At last, in 1896, the city of Miami was incorporated. Julia continued to plan for the growth of the city, plans which included a school, a church, and a hospital. However, the country fell into an economic depression, and the influx of people to Miami lessened. In addition, a fire, which destroyed twenty-eight of the town's buildings, caused a setback in the town's growth and seriously affected Julia's health. Mrs. Tuttle, whose land remained largely vacant, died in 1898. Although she did not live to see her vision completed, she never doubted that Miami would have a great future.

Editing
⚠ Exercise 12

In each sentence, one of the four underlined words or phrases is not correct. Circle the letter of the error and write the correction above the error.

1. The <u>music in which</u> you were used to <u>listening</u> to when you <u>were younger</u> is no
         A   **B**   **C**

   longer in <u>fashion</u>.
          D

2. Can someone <u>who</u> works here <u>help me</u> find the <u>line in where</u> I get a refund, <u>please</u> ?
             A   **B**   **C**   **D**

3. Nashville, <u>where</u> this CD <u>was recorded</u>, is well known in the country music industry, and
            A   **B**

   thousands of people visit <u>Nashville, that is</u> a small town Tennessee, <u>every year</u>.
                           C   **D**

4. People <u>trying</u> to advance their careers in the music business too quickly often lose
          A

   <u>their sense</u> of self; this can lead to problems for <u>which</u> there are no solutions <u>for</u>.
     B   **C**   **D**

Exercise 13 Circle the letter of the correct answer. Watch out for punctuation! Be prepared to explain your answers.

1. Last night the car _____ I own broke down for the eighth time.

   A. what

   B. in which

   C. that

   D. where

2. How many people _____ a car like mine have the same problem?

   A. who are owning

   B. owning

   C. whose are owning

   D. whose own

3. We can build a space shuttle _____ carry a man into space, but we can't build a car that runs regularly!

   A. that

   B. that can

   C. , that

   D. , that can

4. The mechanic _____ garage the car was towed to said he could not get to it for at least three days.

   A. that

   B. which

   C. whose

   D. of whom

5. Can you tell me how I'm supposed to get to a job _____ fifteen miles from my home?

   A. that located

   B. in which is located

   C. located

   D. whose located

6. My car, _____ engine is falling apart, is not worth anything anymore!

   A. whose

   B. that

   C. of which

   D. for which

7. Perhaps the best solution _____ for my problem is to buy a bus pass.

   A. can find

   B. find can

   C. that can I find

   D. that I can find

8. I do not know why, but a _____ perpetually has problems _____ called a lemon.

   A. car ... that is

   B. car that ... is

   C. car ... is

   D. car that ... that is

Exercise 14 Write a paragraph or short essay about your school. Give descriptions of some of your classmates, the classrooms, your instructors, or the textbooks. Use at least five adjective clauses in your writing. Try to use some restrictive clauses (no commas) and non-restrictive clauses (commas). Use as many of the following relative pronouns as you can: *who(m)*, *where*, *which*, *when*, *that*, *why*, and *whose*. Include some adjective clauses with prepositions. Exchange your writing with a partner. Review your partner's paragraph, underlining all the adjective clauses and checking for their correct use.

_____

_____

_____

_____

_____

_____

_____

_____

_____

_____

_____

_____

_____

_____

_____

_____

_____

_____

_____

_____

15 Adverb Clauses and Reductions

This chapter reviews everything you need to know about adverb clauses and their reduced forms.

✔ CHECK YOUR GRAMMAR

Two of the three underlined phrases contain an error related to adverb clauses and reductions. Can you explain why each of these underlined areas is (or is not) wrong? Discuss with a partner.

Culture

If the humanities are concerned with culture in an individual sense, they are also concerned with it in an anthropological sense. Think of the comparison between a child's mind and a farmer's field. The child's mind is cultivated, it develops and an individual acquires habits, beliefs, and values. When use the word *culture* in this sense, it often helps to compare it to the cultivating that takes place in biology.

From: Witt et al., *The Humanities*, p. xxvii.

15.1 Adverb Clauses and Subordinating Conjunctions

An adverb clause is a group of words with a subject and a verb that modifies a verb, an adjective, or another adverb. An adverb clause functions similarly to an adverb.

> My roommate *will go* home to visit her parents **when she finishes her research paper.** (The adverb clause modifies, or tells more about, the verb *will go*.)

You will recognize adverb clauses by the following subordinating conjunctions, most of which come at the beginning of the clause. (Subordinating conjunctions connect elements that are not equal, such as a dependent clause with an independent clause. See Chapter 17, Section 17.1, and Appendix 4, p. 299)

Reason/Cause:	because	since			
Condition:	if*	even if	unless	when	in case	in the event that
	provided that				
Contrast:	while	although	whereas		
Concession:	although	though	even though		
Result:	so *(not used to begin sentences)*				
Purpose:	so that	so			
Time relationship:	after	as soon as	before	when	while	until
	whenever	as	once			

15.2   Punctuating Adverb Clauses

Here is the rule for punctuating an adverb clause: Put a comma after the clause if the clause begins the sentence. If the adverb clause comes after the main clause, no punctuation is needed.

> Hee-Jon went to the park **because the weather was fine.**

> **Because the weather was fine,** Hee-Jon went to the park.

Therefore, whenever an adverb clause begins a sentence (i.e., it comes before the main clause), you need a comma.

> **Although the movie was well advertised,** it did not make a lot of money at the box office.

> **Until we get money to buy a car,** we are going to take the bus to work.

It is easy to make a mistake with *because*. Do not put a comma before the subordinating conjunction *because*.

> *Incorrect:*   The British eventually won the war, because they had superior troops and supplies.

> *Correct:*   The British eventually won the war because they had superior troops and supplies.

When the conjunction *so* introduces an adverb clause of purpose, we do not need a comma. In this case, *so* can also be replaced with *so that*. When the conjunction *so* introduces a result, we use a comma.

> I went to the library so I could print my paper on a laser printer. (purpose)

> I went to the library, so I was able to print a copy of my paper on the laser printer. (result)

---

* Hypothetical if-clauses are covered at length in Chapter 12.

Exercise 1   In each sentence, underline the subordinating conjunction and write its function on the line. Refer to the chart on page 206. Add or correct the punctuation if necessary. The first one has been done for you.

1. <u>Whenever</u> Irene looks for a new job ,she gets nervous. ___time___

2. This happens, because she doesn't have a lot of experience in interviewing. _____

3. If she took a course in job hunting she would probably be more confident. _____

4. She will appear more motivated and ready to start a new career, after doing this. _____

5. While the course is not free the benefits will help her in the long run. _____

Editing
▲Exercise 2   Read the following sentences. Some contain errors in punctuation or syntax (function in the sentence). If the sentence is correct, put a C in the blank. If the sentence is incorrect, put an X in the blank and make the correction. The first one has been done for you.

___X___ 1. While they are theoretically beneficial ,global trade agreements do not always work to the benefit of everyone. An example of this is the international steel industry.

_____ 2. As the U.S. steel industry began losing more and more money, its steelworkers worried about losing their jobs.

_____ 3. The domestic situation deteriorated steadily as cheaper steel imports began to flood the U.S. market.

_____ 4. Because the president wanted to protect the domestic steel industry he decided to levy a heavy tax on steel imports.

_____ 5. Importers of steel from abroad began to question the lawfulness of this action, after it was decided upon.

_____ 6. So that it could prevent this from happening again the European Union called on the World Trade Organization (WTO) to investigate.

_____ 7. While this situation can be remedied by using external forces such as the WTO, it is unlikely that the import/export battles between the United States and the rest of the world will end soon.

Exercise 3 Some clauses in this paragraph are incomplete. Read the paragraph once. Then go back and fill in the missing information.

A Productive Day

After I _____

_____
1

_____

_____, I immediately went to my

room. It was extremely dirty, so _____

_____
2

_____.

My family hates it when _____

_____
3

_____. This

process took about two hours,

but it was not unpleasant. I

listened to my favorite CD while

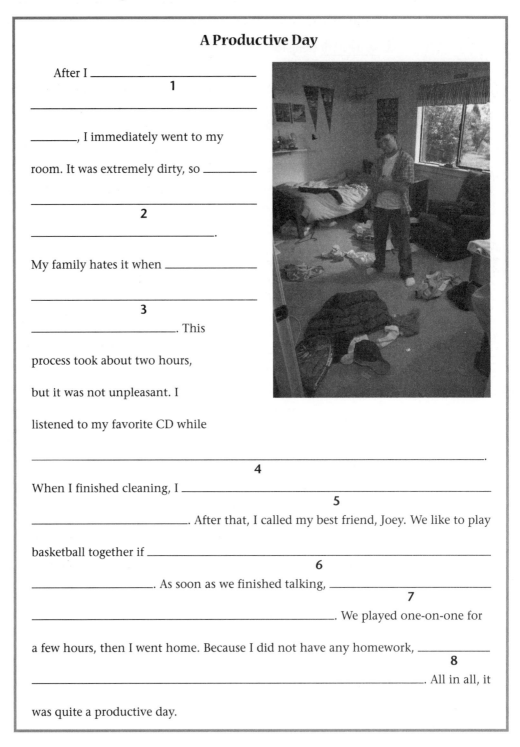

_____.
4

When I finished cleaning, I _____
5

_____. After that, I called my best friend, Joey. We like to play

basketball together if _____
6

_____. As soon as we finished talking, _____
7

_____. We played one-on-one for

a few hours, then I went home. Because I did not have any homework, _____
8

_____. All in all, it

was quite a productive day.

15.3 Adverb Clauses and Verb Tense

In sentences with adverb clauses, use the same verb tense in both parts of the sentence—the main clause and the adverb clause.

> Whenever the manager **calls** a meeting, the employees **get** nervous. (present tense)

> Because the manager **called** a meeting, the employees **got** nervous. (past tense)

Do not use future tense in an adverb clause even if the time of the action is clearly a future event. Instead, use the simple present tense.

> *Incorrect:*   When the world's population ~~will reach~~ 10,000,000,000, there might not be enough food.

> *Correct:*   When the world's population **reaches** 10,000,000,000, there might not be enough food.

Exercise 4   Complete each sentence with information that makes sense. Be sure to pay attention to the verb tense in both clauses.

1. When dot.com companies first appeared, many business people _____

   _____

2. This economic boom began to drop as _____

   _____

3. Many investors lost money after _____

   _____

4. While dot.coms struggle to hold on to their profits, other respectable companies _____

   _____

5. Because investors often show less interest in risky ventures, they _____

   _____

Exercise 5   Use the introductory information in column 1 and the subordinating conjunctions in column 2 to create sentences with adverb clauses. Draw a line from each main sentence to a subordinating conjunction that makes sense and then complete the adverb clause. Remember that an adverb clause takes the form: SUBORDINATING CONJUNCTION + S + V. More than one match is correct. The first one has been done for you.

Main Sentence	Adverb Clause
1. The students were exhausted	although _____
2. My classmate is crying	because _they finally finished their projects._
3. We start a new semester tomorrow	after _____
	if _____
4. My final grade in biology was only 79	before _____
5. I did not get along with my math professor	since _____
	so that _____
6. I started to go to the library more	, so _____
7. Students could not survive a day at school	once _____
8. I did not like math class	provided that _____

Exercise 6   Rewrite sentences from Exercise 5 with the adverb clause beginning the sentence. Add the appropriate punctuation. The first one is done for you. Write three more.

1. _Because they finally finished their projects, the students were exhausted._

2. _____

   _____

3. _____

   _____

4. _____

   _____

15. 4   Adverb Clause Reductions—Forming Adverb Phrases

Sometimes a clause, which contains a subject and a verb, can be reduced or shortened to a phrase. To reduce an adverb clause to an adverb phrase, you usually omit the subject and sometimes alter or omit the verb. The following subordinating conjunctions begin adverb clauses that can be reduced.

if	even if	unless	when	while	although
though	after	before	until	whenever	even though

There are two ways to form an adverb phrase from an adverb clause.

1. Delete the subject and the *be* verb.

    When John is tired, *he* usually goes home to take a nap.

    When tired, *John* usually goes home to take a nap.

Sometimes you need to change the pronoun in the main clause to the specific noun. *John* replaces the pronoun *he* in the main clause.

2. If the adverb clause contains a verb that is not a *be* verb, you can sometimes delete the subject and change the verb to the progressive form.

    While Karen ate the pizza, *she* watched a horror movie on TV.

    While eating the pizza, *Karen* watched a horror movie on TV.

15.4.1   *Dangling Modifiers*

If you are not careful when you reduce adverb clauses, it is easy to create a dangling modifier. First, make sure that the subject of the adverb clause is the same as the subject of the independent clause. If the subjects are different, reducing the adverb clause to an adverb phrase creates a dangling modifier.

Correct: While Irene was studying, the dog began to bark.

Incorrect: While studying, the dog began to bark. (The dog was not studying, so *studying* is a dangling modifier. It does not have anything to modify that makes sense.)

Another way to check that your adverb phrase is correct is to take the subject of the main clause, put it in front of the adverb clause, and see if it makes sense:

The dog, while studying … (You can stop there because the dog can't study in the sense Irene studies.)

▲ Exercise 7 Underline the four adverb clauses in the following paragraph. If an adverb clause can be reduced to an adverb phrase, make the changes above the clause. The first one is done for you.

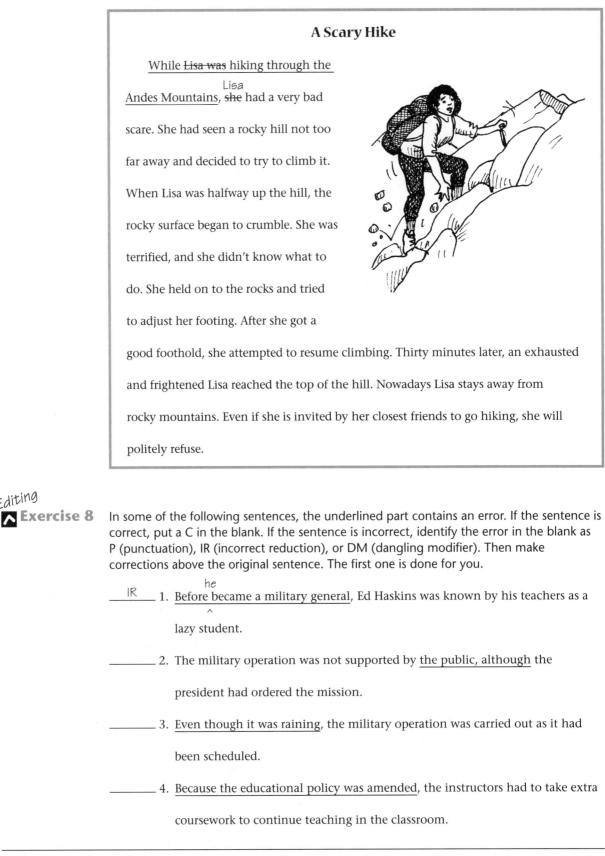

A Scary Hike

While ~~Lisa was~~ hiking through the

Lisa
Andes Mountains, ~~she~~ had a very bad

scare. She had seen a rocky hill not too

far away and decided to try to climb it.

When Lisa was halfway up the hill, the

rocky surface began to crumble. She was

terrified, and she didn't know what to

do. She held on to the rocks and tried

to adjust her footing. After she got a

good foothold, she attempted to resume climbing. Thirty minutes later, an exhausted

and frightened Lisa reached the top of the hill. Nowadays Lisa stays away from

rocky mountains. Even if she is invited by her closest friends to go hiking, she will

politely refuse.

▲ Exercise 8 In some of the following sentences, the underlined part contains an error. If the sentence is correct, put a C in the blank. If the sentence is incorrect, identify the error in the blank as P (punctuation), IR (incorrect reduction), or DM (dangling modifier). Then make corrections above the original sentence. The first one is done for you.

he
_IR_ 1. Before <u>became a military general</u>, Ed Haskins was known by his teachers as a
ʌ

lazy student.

_____ 2. The military operation was not supported by <u>the public, although</u> the

president had ordered the mission.

_____ 3. <u>Even though it was raining</u>, the military operation was carried out as it had

been scheduled.

_____ 4. <u>Because the educational policy was amended</u>, the instructors had to take extra

coursework to continue teaching in the classroom.

_____ 5. The states' political delegates returned to their <u>hotel after the presentations</u> <u>ended</u>.

_____ 6. <u>While preparing for his presidential address to Congress</u>, a serious car accident occurred outside the White House.

_____ 7. <u>Unless the workers unite</u>, the company will not prosper in the global marketplace.

_____ 8. <u>After hearing the government's latest pollution statistics</u> many scientific experts commented on the validity of the numbers.

| 15.5 | # Reason and Concession: Clauses Versus Phrases |

Both adverb clauses and adverb phrases can show reason and concession.

| 15.5.1 | ## _Showing Reason:_ Because _versus_ Because of |

Because and _because of_ show reason and take different grammatical structures. It's important to know the difference. Adverb clauses can begin with _because:_

> **Because _it was raining,_** we decided to cancel our trip to the mountains.

Adverb phrases can begin with _because of:_

> **Because of** the rain, we decided to cancel our trip to the mountains.

The two sentences have the same meaning, but note that in the second sentence, _because of_ must be followed by a noun.

| 15.5.2 | ## _Showing Concession:_ Although _Versus_ In spite of / Despite |

Although and _in spite of_ or _despite_ show concession and take different grammatical structures. It is important to know the difference. Adverb clauses can also begin with _although:_

> **Although** it did not rain, the crops did not die.

Adverb phrases can also begin with _in spite of_ or _despite:_

> **Despite** the lack of rain, the crops did not die.

Use _of_ with _in spite of_ but not with _despite._

> _Incorrect:_   **Despite ~~of~~** the lack of rain, the crops did not die.

Exercise 9   In each sentence, change the adverb clause to an adverb phrase or change the adverb phrase to an adverb clause. The first one has been done for you.

1. Because of low production costs, the company exceeded its output of merchandise.

   Because production costs were low, the company exceeded its output of merchandise.

2. Because export taxes increased, prices rose sharply.

   _____

3. Consumers bought more import automobiles although they cost more than domestic models.

   _____

4. In spite of difficult labor relations, the company turned a profit.

   _____

5. Greece's agricultural production increased despite the drought.

   _____

Editing
⌃ Exercise 10   In each sentence, one of the four underlined words or phrases is not correct. Circle the letter of the error and write a correction above the error.

1. Despite <u>it was beautiful</u>, the <u>five-star hotel</u> was <u>too</u> expensive for <u>Ned to enjoy</u>.
             A   **B**   **C**   **D**

2. <u>After Ned</u> returned <u>from the beach</u>, he <u>takes a bath</u> in the beautiful hotel bathtub
       A   **B**   **C**

   <u>to relax</u>.
   D

3. Ned and his wife will certainly <u>enjoy</u> the rest of <u>their vacation</u> when their son <u>and</u>
                              A   **B**   **C**

   daughter <u>will stop arguing</u>.
           D

4. <u>Though boring</u>, Ned's family <u>decided</u> to stay and watch the <u>remaining portion</u> of the
     A   **B**   **C**

   Broadway musical <u>last night</u>.
           D

Exercise 11   Circle the letter of the correct answer. Be prepared to explain your answers.

1. Retirement is viewed differently in different cultures. Although most people around the world look forward to their retirement _____ in some cultures worry about their future health, homes, and lives.

   A. years but people

   B. years but, people

   C. years, people

   D. years people

2. According to information from the United Nations, the world may begin to see new problems by the year 2050 _____ almost 2 billion people, or roughly 22 percent of the world's population, will reach retirement age.

   A. so

   B. that

   C. because

   D. therefore

3. I am nowhere near retirement age. _____ my young age, I am already thinking about what I will do when I retire and how I will pay for everything when I no longer have a weekly paycheck.

   A. So

   B. Despite

   C. Because

   D. Until

4. The only person that I know who has retired is my uncle. After _____ his company for more than thirty-five years in not only the main office but also in three branch locations around the country, Uncle Phil decided to retire.

   A. serve

   B. was served

   C. he serves

   D. serving

5. Uncle Phil is not as worried as many people appear to be; he received a full _____ long service with the company.

   A. pension, because his

   B. pension because his

   C. pension, because of his

   D. pension because of his

6. After Uncle Phil _____ his final bonus, he took his family out to celebrate.

   A. received

   B. is receiving

   C. was received

   D. receives

7. One of my biggest fears is that I will be bored when I retire because I can't find something specific to occupy my time. Uncle Phil will not have this problem. Whenever Uncle Phil _____ tries a new hobby.

   A. gets bored he   C. was bored he

   B. gets bored, he   D. was bored, he

8. _____ and a much lower cost of living can be factors that sway some retirees to move from the United States to spend their retirement years in countries such as Mexico and Costa Rica.

   A. Lower taxes   C. Because of lower taxes

   B. If lower taxes   D. Because the taxes are lower

Exercise 12 Write a paragraph or short essay about something that you did as a child that you were punished for or something that you were praised for. Include some of the following information.

- What you did

- Whom you were with

- How it happened

- Why you did it

- How you got caught or how someone found out

- What kind of punishment or praise you received

- If you ever did it again

Use at least five adverb clauses or adverb phrases in your writing. Refer to the list of subordinating conjunctions on page 206 to help you. Exchange your writing with a partner. Review your partner's paragraph, underlining all the adverb clauses or adverb phrases and checking for their correct use.

_____

_____

_____

_____

_____

_____

_____

_____

_____

_____

_____

_____

_____

_____

Hurricane Katrina **could have** *hit* New Orleans directly, but it affected areas to the east of the city more.

She **might have** *left* her keys on the table, but she is not sure.

It **may have** *rained* last night. Look, the grass looks wet.

You **would have** *gotten* the job for sure if you had applied for it.

With past modal constructions, you must always use the past participle of the verb after MODAL + *have.*

Incorrect:	She **must have** ~~*take*~~ the 7 p.m. flight to New York.
Correct:	She **must have** *taken* the 7 p.m. flight to New York.

With past modal constructions, never use *had*; always use *have:*

Incorrect:	She **must** ~~**had**~~ **taken** the 7 p.m. flight to New York.
Correct:	She **must have** *taken* the 7 p.m. flight to New York.

9.5   The Modal *should* in the Past

Use *should* + *have* + PAST PARTICIPLE to form the past modal.

1. We use *should have* + PAST PARTICIPLE when the action (of the verb) did not happen and someone is sorry (regrets) that the action did not happen.

   I failed the test. I **should have** *studied* last night. (The speaker did not study. The speaker regrets not studying last night.)

2. We use the negative form, *should not have* + PAST PARTICIPLE, when the action (of the verb) happened and someone is sorry (regrets) that the action happened.

   My stomach hurts! I **shouldn't have** *eaten* those four doughnuts. (The speaker ate four doughnuts. The speaker regrets eating them.)

Exercise 1   Underline the *should have* + PAST PARTICIPLE construction in each sentence. Then put a check mark (✔) beside all of the sentences underneath that are true. The first one has been done for you.

1. She <u>should have cooked</u> the beans and the rice in separate pots.

   _____✔_____ a. She cooked the beans and rice in the same pot.

   _____ b. She cooked the beans and rice in two pots.

2. Tom is sure that he shouldn't have traveled to Taiwan in the summer.

   _____ a. Tom traveled to Taiwan.

   _____ b. Tom regrets traveling to Taiwan.

3. You should have told me this news sooner.

_____ a. The speaker now knows the news.

_____ b. The speaker still doesn't know the news.

4. I'm sorry for not inviting you to my party. I should have sent you an invitation.

_____ a. The speaker invited the person to the party.

_____ b. The speaker did not invite the person to the party.

5. Many people think that the U.S. shouldn't have dropped atomic bombs on Japan.

_____ a. Many people agree with the use of atomic bombs in World War II.

_____ b. Many people disagree with the use of atomic bombs in World War II.

6. That shirt shouldn't have faded after just one washing.

_____ a. The shirt lost some color when it was washed.

_____ b. The shirt looked better after it was washed.

Exercise 2   Write a sentence that uses *should have* or *should not have* + PAST PARTICIPLE to express the same idea. The first one has been done for you.

1. Joe bought a used car. He regrets buying it.

   _Joe should not have bought a used car._____

2. You did not get a new umbrella. You are sorry about this.

   _____

   _____

3. Instead of taking a taxi, we took a bus from the airport. Taking a bus took much longer

   and was not as good as taking a taxi.

   _____

   _____

4. Toshio regrets quitting his job today.

   _____

   _____

5. Last night I went to bed after midnight. I regret doing this.

_____

_____

9.6 The Modal *must* in the Past

Use *must + have +* PAST PARTICIPLE to form the past modal.

1. Use *must have +* PAST PARTICIPLE when you are almost certain that the action happened. Based on the facts or current situation, you conclude that the action happened.

    Joe looks really tired today. He **must have** *gone* to bed late last night. (The speaker thinks that Joe went to bed late last night.)

2. Use the negative form, *must not have +* PAST PARTICIPLE, when you are almost certain that the action did not happen.

    Irene failed her spelling test. She **must not have** *studied* very much. (The speaker thinks that Irene did not study very much.)

Exercise 3 To complete these sentences, write the correct construction using *must (not) have +* PAST PARTICIPLE with the verb in parentheses. The first one has been done for you.

1. No one ordered any dessert after dinner. Everyone (be) _____ *must have been* _____

    full.

2. When I saw Ben this morning, he didn't know who had won the football match last

    night. He (watch) _____ it on TV.

3. Paula's French is outstanding. I know she's a good language learner, but she (have)

    _____ a great French teacher, too.

4. Ellen returned four of the five dresses that she bought yesterday. They (fit)

    _____ her very well.

5. Rick didn't follow the teacher's directions for this assignment. He (understand)

    _____ the directions clearly.

6. Look at the decorations on these cakes! They're so elaborate! It (take)

    _____ a long time to make them!

9.7   The Modal *could* in the Past

Use *could have* + PAST PARTICIPLE to form the past modal.

1. Use *could have* + PAST PARTICIPLE when the speaker had the opportunity to do something, but you are not sure he did it. You can also use it when the action was possible, but you are not sure if it really happened.

> After dinner, I felt really sick. It **could have** *been* the fish. It tasted a little strange. (The speaker thinks that one possible reason for being sick was the fish.)

2. Use the negative form *could not have* + PAST PARTICIPLE, when you are almost positive that the action did not happen. This form implies that it was impossible for the action to have occurred.

> The evidence proves that the woman **couldn't have** *killed* her husband because she was traveling in a different country when he was killed. (According to the evidence, it was impossible for the woman to have killed the man.)

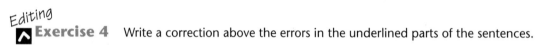 Editing
Exercise 4   Write a correction above the errors in the underlined parts of the sentences.

1. If you missed eight of the ten questions on the test, you <u>could have passed</u> it.

2. No one believes that the man <u>could have kill</u> his boss.

3. My late grandfather was extremely rich. He didn't own a BMW, but he <u>couldn't have easily bought</u> one or more of them.

4. I <u>could visit</u> many more places in Paris if I had had more time.

5. I <u>could have lent</u> you my car yesterday because I needed it all day.

6. I could have lent you my car because I <u>needed</u> it all day yesterday.

7. When we went to France last year, we <u>could have fly</u> on the Concorde.

8. It <u>couldn't rain</u> this morning. I would have noticed if the ground had been wet!

9.8   The Modal *might* in the Past

Use *might have* + PAST PARTICIPLE to form the past modal.

1. Use *might have* + PAST PARTICIPLE when the action was possible, but you are not sure if it happened. (This is the same meaning as *may have* or *could have* + PAST PARTICIPLE.)

> After dinner, I felt really sick. It **might have** *been* the fish. It tasted a little strange. (The speaker thinks that one possible reason for being sick was the fish.)

2. *Might have* + PAST PARTICIPLE has a second meaning. It can be a suggestion about a past event, like *could have*. Sometimes it is a form of complaint.

> Mother: The train trip took us several hours. I don't know why we came by train.
>
> Ana: We **might have** *flown.* It would have been so much faster.

3. The negative form, *might not have* + PAST PARTICIPLE is used when the negative situation was possible, but you are not sure if it happened. (This is the same meaning as *may not have* + PAST PARTICIPLE.)

> The teacher believes that Joe **might not have** *written* his paper by himself. (The teacher believes it is possible that someone helped Joe write his paper.)

Exercise 5   Read each sentence. Then write a sentence that means the same as the first sentence. Use *might have* or *might not have* + PAST PARTICIPLE. The first one has been done for you.

1. It is possible that it rained last night. I'm not sure.

   It might have rained last night.

2. When you called last night, maybe David wasn't home then.

   _____

3. Why did Hector leave the party? Maybe he didn't feel well.

   _____

4. The student's answers are all wrong. Maybe he didn't understand the directions.

   _____

   _____

5. Perhaps the doctor prescribed the wrong medicine.

   _____

6. Why did the accident happen? Maybe the pilot turned onto the wrong runway.

   _____

   _____

The Modal *may* in the Past

Use *may have* + PAST PARTICIPLE to form the past modal.

1. Use *may have* + PAST PARTICIPLE when the action was possible, but you are not sure if it happened.

> After dinner, I felt really sick. It **may have** *been* the fish. It tasted a little strange.
> (The speaker thinks that one possible reason for being sick was the fish.)

2. The negative form *may not have* + PAST PARTICIPLE is used when the negative situation was possible, but you are not sure if it happened.

> The teacher believes that Joe **may not have** *written* his paper by himself.
> (The teacher believes it is possible that someone helped Joe write his paper.)

Exercise 6   Read each sentence. Then write a sentence that means the same as the first sentence. Use *may have* or *may not have* + PAST PARTICIPLE. The first one has been done for you.

1. Perhaps Jennifer went to her cousin's house.

   *Jennifer may have gone to her cousin's house.*_____

2. It's possible that Ned didn't like the gift that Linda gave him.

   _____

   _____

3. Maybe some passengers survived the plane crash.

   _____

   _____

4. Maybe he didn't hear the announcement.

   _____

   _____

5. It's possible that the secretary has already received the documents.

   _____

   _____

6. Perhaps it was too late for Alan to buy a cheap ticket for the flight.

   _____

   _____

The Modal *would* in the Past

Use *would have* + PAST PARTICIPLE to form the past modal.

1. Use *would have* + PAST PARTICIPLE when the action did not happen. This meaning is for the main clause in conditional sentences: another condition was missing, and that's why the second action did not happen.

    The young couple **would have** *purchased* the house if it had had two bathrooms. (The house did not have two bathrooms, so the young couple didn't purchase it.)

2. The negative form *would not have* + PAST PARTICIPLE is used when the action actually happened, but it would not have happened if something else had occurred first.

    The pie **wouldn't have** *tasted* so sweet if I had added the correct amount of sugar. (The pie tasted too sweet because the speaker added the wrong amount of sugar.)

NOTE: Sometimes the *if*-clause is not stated; it is understood. You can find more information about *if*-clauses in Chapter 12.

Exercise 7 Fill in the blanks with *would have* + PAST PARTICIPLE of the verbs in parentheses. The first one has been done for you.

1. (start, [negative]) Perhaps if Lincoln had not become the 16th president, the Civil War

    would not have started in 1861.

2. (like) People _____ the party better if you had had good

    music.

3. (be, [negative]) The spaghetti _____ crunchy if you had

    cooked it a little longer.

4. (win) If Kostov had done better in the second set, perhaps he _____

    _____ the match.

5. (be) The outcome of the election _____ the same if people

    had voted on computers instead of using the old methods.

6. (have, [negative]) If you had taken the medicine correctly, you _____

    _____ any problems with your stomach.

Exercise 8   Underline the six past modal forms in this paragraph and explain their meanings to a partner.

My Oldest Memory

My oldest memory is of a time when I was a very young child. I couldn't have been more than five years old. In fact, I might have been as young as three. I remember that I was with a woman who was our neighbor. It must have been around 6 or 7 o'clock because it was getting a little dark. The woman told me that we were going to walk to the store on the corner to get an ice cream cone. Just as we left the front steps of our house, the light above the store went out. It had just closed. We should have left earlier. If we had left the house a few minutes earlier, then we might have gotten to the store in time. If we had done that, then I could have had some ice cream. To this day, I cannot remember exactly who the woman was, but I certainly remember the day that I didn't get any ice cream.

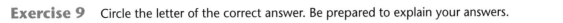

Exercise 9   Circle the letter of the correct answer. Be prepared to explain your answers.

1. As I sat waiting for my flight to take off, I read this statement on the information card:

   "In an emergency, all passengers _____ the directions of the crew."

   A.   must follow   C.   might follow

   B.   must have followed   D.   might have followed

2. I overheard a mother tell her son, "If you need to use your cell phone, you _____ do

   it now because you _____ make a call during the flight."

   A.   had better … cannot   C.   must … do not able to

   B.   had better to … cannot   D.   must to … do not able to

3. A passenger seated next to me told me about a problem on her previous flight. As the

   passengers were boarding the plane, an alarm went off. She thought that one of the

   passengers may _____ an emergency door by mistake.

   A.   open   C.   have opened

   B.   have open   D.   to open

4. About an hour after takeoff, the flight attendant gave each of us a small sandwich, but

   I could not eat mine because the cooks had put spicy mustard on all of them. They

   really _____ such spicy mustard.

   A.   should have added   C.   shouldn't have added

   B.   should add   D.   shouldn't add

5. One passenger said that his worst flight was aboard a 747 with Southwest Airlines,

   but a flight attendant who was standing nearby corrected him. She said, "Are you sure

   it was a 747 with Southwest? Actually, if it was a Southwest jet, it _____ been a 747

   because that airline does not have any jumbo jets."

   A.   might not have   C.   might not had

   B.   could not have   D.   could not had

6. The pilot announced, "Ladies and gentlemen, we are very near the Salt Lake City

   Airport. We _____ shortly, so please follow the flight attendants' instructions at this

   point."

   A.   land   C.   could land

   B.   must land   D.   will land

7. A man next to me remarked, "I hate having to wait for my luggage. I wish they could just take my luggage directly to my car. That _____ great!"

   A. would be

   B. should be

   C. would have been

   D. should have been

8. As we were exiting the airplane, an agent told us that we _____.

   A. should pick up our baggage at carousel 7

   B. might have waited ten minutes for our baggage

   C. must to have our baggage claim tickets in our hands

   D. were able ask for assistance at the baggage claim area

Exercise 10 Write a paragraph about an important event in history or in your life. Tell what happened and why it happened. Tell how it could have been different. Consider what should have been done to make it different (if it was something negative). Use at least five of the past modals from this chapter. Use both affirmative and negative forms. Exchange paragraphs with a partner. Circle all the past modals on your partner's paper and check for their correct use.

_____

_____

_____

_____

_____

_____

_____

_____

_____

_____

_____

_____

_____

_____

_____

_____

_____

_____

_____

_____

_____

_____

10 Gerunds and Infinitives

verb ⊕ ing. (noun) *serves as a (noun)*

Two verb forms in English are used as nouns: <u>gerunds</u> and <u>infinitives</u>. Gerunds are verbs ending in *-ing*. Infinitives are *to* + VERB. How do you know when to use an infinitive and when to use a gerund? This chapter will answer that question.

✔ CHECK YOUR GRAMMAR

Four of the eight underlined words contain an error related to gerunds and infinitives. Can you explain why each of these underlined areas is (or is not) wrong? Discuss with a partner.

Reading Skills

<u>To read</u> is much more than <u>run</u> your eyes across the page and <u>recognizing</u> words. It involves <u>grasping</u> the meaning of what is written, <u>understanding</u> the relationship of each sentence and paragraph to all the others. <u>Getting</u> more from your reading, you will need <u>skim</u>, reflect, <u>read</u>, and review each chapter.

From: V. Ruggiero. (2002). *Becoming a Critical Thinker*, 4th ed. Boston: Houghton Mifflin, p. xvi.

10.1 Forming Gerunds and Gerund Phrases and Infinitives and Infinitive Phrases

Here are the basic forms of gerunds and infinitives:

Gerund	Infinitive
VERB + -ing	*to + VERB*
swimming	to swim
laughing	to laugh

A gerund phrase includes the gerund and its related information.

Taking *good class notes* makes it easier to review for exams.

An infinitive phrase includes the infinitive and its related information.

To take *good class notes,* you should read about the subject in advance.

Exercise 1 Read the following paragraph on stress. Underline all the gerunds and infinitives. The first one has been done for you. There are ten more.

> ### Handling Stress
>
> To relieve stress, you must first understand which brain hemisphere is stressed. Feeling depressed or emotionally overwrought means your stress is in the right hemisphere. This is the creative, emotional, holistic side of your brain. To cut stress, switch to your matter-of-fact left hemisphere. How? Doing math or writing factual prose calms down the emotional right brain. Another option is to organize something; it has the same calming effect. Feeling time-stressed and overburdened means the left hemisphere of your brain is stressed. Singing or playing a sport will allow you to switch to your right brain and to reduce your stress.

From: Berko et al., *Communicating,* p. 188.

10.2 Gerunds and Gerund Phrases

Although gerunds, like infinitives, are formed with verb stems, they function like nouns. A gerund phrase is a gerund followed by a noun or pronoun.

1. Gerunds and gerund phrases as **subjects**

    Eating *vegetables* is a good way to stay healthy.

A gerund as the subject of a sentence takes a singular verb. When multiple gerunds are used as the subject, they take a plural verb.

    Eating *vegetables* and **exercising** are excellent ways to stay healthy.

When a gerund has multiple objects, the subject is singular.

    Eating *broccoli, carrots, and tomatoes* is an excellent way to stay healthy.

2. Gerunds and gerund phrases as **direct objects** (see Section 10.2.1)

    However, many people dislike **preparing** *vegetables.*

3. Gerunds and gerund phrases as **subject complements** (after the verb *be*)

    One easy preparation method is **eating** *them raw with a simple sauce.*

In this case, the gerund is often inverted to the subject position without changing the meaning of the sentence.

    Eating *vegetables raw with a simple sauce* is one easy preparation method.

4. Gerunds and gerund phrases as **objects of prepositions** (see Chapter 7)

Another method of **preparing** *vegetables* is stir-frying.

5. To form the negative of a gerund, simply place *not* immediately before the gerund.

Not cooking *vegetables* allows you to prepare a meal faster.

Exercise 2   Complete the following sentences with a gerund or gerund phrase using some of the words below or your own words. In the parentheses, write the function of the gerund in the sentence. The gerund can serve as the subject, direct object, subject complement (after the verb *be*), or object of a preposition. The first one has been done for you.

Verbs			Nouns		
clean	fry	slice	counter	new recipes	salt
cook	mop	taste	dishes	olive oil	seafood
cut	peel	try	fruit	praise	tomatoes
eat	receive	use	meat	salad	vegetables

1. I'm tired of _____cooking_____ meals every day of the week. (*object of preposition*)

2. Lisa's favorite hobby is __eating__. (sbj complement)

3. __tasting__ is one of the benefits all cooks enjoy! (sbj)

4. It's almost impossible to make a meal without __cutting__. (obj. prep)

5. While some people enjoy __cleaning__, I think it's a boring activity. (direct obj).

6. My mother is great at __cooking__, but I'm not so good at it. (obj. prep)

7. I don't mind __moping__, but I am tired of __cleaning__ every week! (direct obj) (obj. preposition)

10.2.1   *Verbs Commonly Followed by Gerunds*

1. These verbs frequently have a gerund or a gerund phrase following them:

appreciate	delay	dislike	involve	practice	risk
avoid	detest	enjoy	miss	quit	stop
consider	discuss	finish	postpone	recommend	suggest

My mother *appreciated* **getting a puppy** for her birthday.

2. Whenever a verb follows a preposition, the verb takes the gerund form. The common expressions in the following chart have a gerund or gerund phrase following them. (For a longer list of prepositions after certain verbs and adjectives, see Sections 13.3.2 and 13.3.3 in Chapter 13.)

be afraid of	be interested in	be worried about	dream about	thank (someone) for
be good at	be responsible for	argue about	excel at	think about
be used to	be accustomed to	believe in	talk about	think of

Common error: We **are interested in take** summer classes.

Correct: We *are interested in* **taking** summer classes.

Common error: Did she **thank you for drive** her to work this morning?

Correct: Did she *thank you for* **driving** her to work this morning?

3. Other common expressions include:

- *by + gerund* to explain how something is done

  You can pass this class **by reading** the text and **keeping up** with assignments.

- *go + gerund* to describe activities

  Would you rather ***go* bowling** or ***go* swimming** this afternoon?

Exercise 3   Complete each sentence with the verb or expression in parentheses and add an appropriate gerund or gerund phrase. The first one has been done for you.

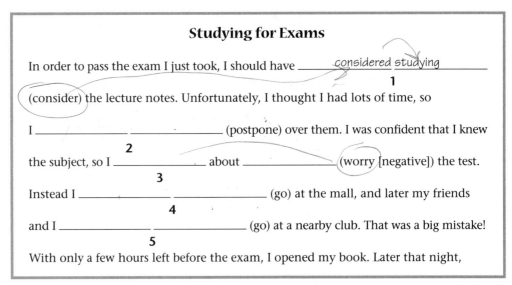

Studying for Exams

In order to pass the exam I just took, I should have _____considered studying_____

1

(consider) the lecture notes. Unfortunately, I thought I had lots of time, so

I _____ _____ (postpone) over them. I was confident that I knew

2

the subject, so I _____ about _____ (worry [negative]) the test.

3

Instead I _____ _____ (go) at the mall, and later my friends

4

and I _____ _____ (go) at a nearby club. That was a big mistake!

5

With only a few hours left before the exam, I opened my book. Later that night,

(continued)

while sleeping, I _____ about _____ (dream) the
6

test. I woke up from that nightmare and _____ _____ (finish)
7

the rest of the chapter. Then I went to school and took the exam. I learned my

lesson the hard way. What do I recommend? I _____ not _____
8

(recommend) what I did. Instead, I _____ _____ (suggest)
9

your notes regularly. By reviewing them every day, you won't _____

about _____ (worry) any exam!
10

10.3 Infinitives and Infinitive Phrases

Infinitives consist of two words: *to* + VERB. An infinitive phrase is the infinitive followed by any noun or pronoun and modifying words.

1. Infinitives and infinitive phrases as a reduction of the phrase *in order to* (showing purpose)

   To build its international business, the company spent millions on advertising in sixteen different languages. = [In order] **to build** its international business, the company spent …

2. Infinitives and infinitive phrases as subjects

   To live *in a large city* requires a lot of patience and nerve. (less common)

Compare with the gerund as the subject paired with the same verb. (Infinitives can be subjects, but gerunds are much more common as subjects.)

   Living *in a large city* requires a lot of patience and nerve. (more common)

Remember: When an infinitive phrase begins a sentence, it is probably a "purpose" phrase, not the subject:

   To live *in a large city*, you need a lot of patience. ([in order] to + verb = purpose)

3. Infinitives and infinitive phrases as direct objects

   Mario wanted **to stay** *at the beach*, but it began **to rain.**

4. Infinitives and infinitive phrases after phrases beginning with *it* (*it* + *be* + ADJECTIVE or NOUN + INFINITIVE)

   It is impossible **to get** *a cheap apartment* in a large city.
   ADJECTIVE   INFINITIVE

   Many people say that *it is a good idea* **to save** *money for the future.*
   NOUN   INFINITIVE

Here are some common adjectives and nouns that are preceded by *it + be* and followed by an infinitive:

bad	dangerous	difficult	easy
fun	hard	important	impossible
interesting	necessary	relaxing	a good idea
a bad idea	a pity	a shame	a waste

5. Infinitives and infinitive phrases with the verb *take* (*it + take* + NOUN + INFINITIVE)

   It takes a lot of **energy to find** *the perfect job.*

6. Infinitives and infinitive phrases after certain adjectives

   Habiba was **happy to learn** *that she'd been accepted to graduate school.*

Here are some common adjectives followed by infinitives.

afraid	glad	relieved	sorry
ashamed	happy	reluctant	surprised
bound	lucky	sad	sure
careful	proud	shocked	willing

Note that *accustomed to* always takes a gerund.

   I am **accustomed to waking up** at 5 a.m. every day.

7. To form the negative of an infinitive, simply place *not* immediately before the infinitive.

   You should be **careful not to strain** *your eyes* in front of the computer.

Exercise 4   Complete the sentences with an infinitive phrase. In the parentheses, write the function of the infinitive in the sentence. Choose from one of the four following options: *direct object, after a phrase with* it + ADJECTIVE, *to show purpose*, or *after certain adjectives*. The first one has been done for you.

1. Margaret and her sister Jenna went to college <u>to become their family's first college</u>

   <u>graduates. (to show purpose)</u>

2. They were afraid _____

   _____, but their family encouraged them. (_____

   _____)

3. Margaret and Jenna wanted _____

   _____ at a prestigious university in

   California, but it was too expensive. (_____

   _____)

2. (Shorten) This recipe is easy to understand, and it's easy to prepare.

_____

_____

3. (Use an appositive) Anna Svenson is the creator of the *Heavenly Taste* recipe books, and she was interviewed on *Food for Families,* which is a television cooking show that is extremely popular with women between the ages of twenty-five and thirty-nine.

_____

_____

4. (Convert compound sentence to complex type; use *although* or *even though*) Baking is a fairly easy task, but some people are not comfortable using an oven.

_____

_____

5. (Convert compound sentence to complex type; use *because*) We did not have enough eggs, and we had to go to the supermarket yet again!

_____

_____

Editing

▲ **Exercise 3** Using the directions in parentheses, rewrite these sentences as a paragraph in the space provided. Remember to indent your paragraph.

1. (Combine into one sentence) The city was on the Atlantic Ocean. The city was hit by a hurricane. The city was almost entirely destroyed.

2. (Separate into two or more sentences) Electrical power to the city was cut off, and the water was contaminated, and many trees were uprooted after the hurricane, and people were very worried about their homes.

3. (Combine into one sentence) Mrs. Heldon was the mayor of the city. She appealed to the citizens. She asked them to remain calm, and she asked them to wait for rescue teams.

4. (Separate into two or more sentences) The Red Cross is an international relief organization, and it set up tents for homeless people, and it delivered food and clothing to the residents, and it fed the workers who rescued people from their homes.

_____

_____

_____

_____

_____

_____

_____

_____

_____

_____

_____

17.3   Common Sentence Problems and Challenges

If your writing contains errors in sentence structure, it is difficult for readers to understand your ideas clearly. This section addresses the most common types of sentence-structure errors: run-on sentences, comma splices, fragments, and punctuation.

17.3.1   *Run-on (Fused) Sentences and Comma Splices*

Run-on Sentence

It is easy to mistakenly connect two sentences when you add sentence variety to your paragraphs, especially in the form of compound and complex sentences. If you don't add a connector or punctuation correctly, the result can be a run-on, or fused, sentence. Here are two simple ways to fix run-ons:

1. Separate the two independent clauses with a period. Do this if the sentence is too long or if the clauses are not closely related.

Incorrect:	We need to make a decision soon our choices are to either refinance our mortgage or take out a home equity loan. (sentence too long)
Correction:	We need to make a decision soon. Our choices are to either refinance our mortgage or take out a home equity loan.
Incorrect:	We need to make a decision soon the Stones have decided to refinance their mortgage. (clauses unrelated)
Correction:	We need to make a decision soon. The Stones have decided to refinance their mortgage.

2. Separate the two independent clauses with a semicolon. Do this if the sentences are not too long or if they are closely related.

> Incorrect: A fifteen-year mortgage will mean high monthly rates a thirty-year mortgage will lower the monthly mortgage payment.

> Correction: A fifteen-year mortgage will mean high monthly rates; a thirty-year mortgage will lower the monthly mortgage payment.

3. Connect the two independent clauses with a coordinating conjunction.

> Incorrect: A fifteen-year mortgage will mean high monthly rates a thirty-year mortgage will lower the monthly mortgage payment

> Correction: A fifteen-year mortgage will mean high monthly rates, **but** a thirty-year mortgage will lower the monthly mortgage payment.

Comma Splice

Another problem is connecting two sentences with only a comma. This type of error is called a comma splice.

> Incorrect: An adjustable rate mortgage is one option, a fixed rate mortgage is another.

To fix a comma splice, connect the two sentences with some type of connector. Common connectors include coordinating conjunctions (such as *and, but, or, so*), subordinating conjunctions (such as *because, although, when*), and adverbial conjunctions, or transitions, (such as *however, therefore, consequently*). (See Appendix 4, p. 299.)

> An adjustable rate mortgage is one option, **and** a fixed rate mortgage is another. (coordinating conjunction)

> An adjustable rate mortgage is one option **while** a fixed rate mortgage is another. (subordinating conjunction)

> An adjustable rate mortgage is one option; **however,** a fixed rate mortgage is another. (adverbial conjunction/transition)

The punctuation in the examples changes, depending on the kind of connector.

Editing
Exercise 4   Read each sentence. Put a C in the blank if the sentence is correct and an X if it is incorrect. On a separate sheet of paper, correct each sentence that is incorrect.

_____ 1. Taking a course online has some disadvantages, for example if you have a question, you can't get an immediate answer.

_____ 2. Discussion boards are forums for posting thoughts and opinions; however, as in a classroom, you must monitor what you say in order not to offend your classmates.

_____ 3. Students in some online courses participate from countries all over the world and it's interesting to exchange ideas and information with them.

_____ 4. Online courses require students to be self-disciplined it's easy to put off doing assignments.

_____ 5. In some respects, online classes are similar to those held in a classroom in other respects they are very dissimilar.

_____ 6. Assignments are graded in an online course; therefore, it is important to allow yourself enough time to do them well.

⚠ Exercise 5 Correct run-on sentences and comma splices in the following paragraphs.

Benefits of Baking

There are many ways to reduce stress in your life, one of the best ways I have found is through baking. It takes your mind off your everyday problems and redirects your energy, and you become creative and productive.

The benefits of baking include the pleasure you derive from being creative and the gratitude you receive from the people who are the recipients of your efforts. Like cookies, praise is never hard to swallow.

Baking also has a down side. It often happens that once people discover that stress for you equals baked goods for them, they begin to find ways to increase your stress, for example you are assigned to many committees suddenly. The solution? I have not had time to figure it out yet, I am too busy baking.

17.3.2   *Fragments*

Have you ever tried to be concise and put end punctuation after a phrase or dependent clause, creating an incomplete sentence? These incomplete sentences, known as fragments, may have a subject and a verb, but they cannot stand alone as complete thoughts or sentences.

Important: Fragments are considered one of the worst writing errors. Learn what fragments are and how to avoid them.

You can correct sentence fragments in two ways:

1. Connect the fragment to an independent clause.

Incorrect:	I had a hard time getting up this morning. ~~Although I slept well last night.~~
Correction:	I had a hard time getting up this morning **although I slept well last night.**

2. Change the fragment to an independent clause.

Incorrect:	She was born in Northwoods. ~~A small town with no stoplights on Main Street.~~
Correction:	She was born in Northwoods. **It is a small town with no stoplights on Main Street.**

Read the following short essay and underline the nine fragments. The first one has been done for you.

My "To Do" List

I start off every weekend with a long "To Do" list. <u>And lots of energy.</u> On Friday night, I reward myself by relaxing. I might watch a movie or go out with my friends. <u>Or even stay home and read a book.</u>

When Saturday morning rolls around, I take advantage of the opportunity to sleep in. By noon I'm up and ready to tackle the items on my list. I do a load of laundry and then head for the grocery store. <u>Where I spend time looking at all the luscious tropical fruits and choosing some for my Sunday breakfast.</u>

<u>During the late afternoon.</u> I finish the laundry and usually discover my energy level has dropped. I'm going out later, so I take a quick nap. <u>Although I haven't finished my chores.</u> Suddenly, it's Sunday. <u>Before I know it.</u> I read the paper and enjoy a leisurely breakfast. I check my "To Do" list to see what else I can accomplish. <u>But I'm always shocked.</u> Here it is, <u>mid-afternoon on a Sunday. Too late to start a new project.</u> I might as well finish reading the paper. <u>And think about writing a new list again next week.</u> Where does weekend time go?

17.3.3 *Sentence Punctuation*

Sentence punctuation helps you create the meaning you want. It also tells readers how to read a sentence, so learning how to use punctuation correctly is essential. Listed here are six of the major punctuation marks that you will need to write correct sentences—period, comma, semicolon, colon, apostrophe, and quotation marks. If you want more detailed information than you find here, it is a good idea to consult an in-depth style and writing guide or grammar reference.

1. Period

   • Indicates a full stop at the end of a sentence

     I am thinking about going to graduate school next year.

   • Used at the end of an abbreviation

     Dr. Ballard has a Ph.D. in linguistics.

2. Comma

   • Separates items in a series

     We have meat, cheese, and bread for lunch.

   • Separates independent clauses connected by a coordinating conjunction

     The car needs gas, but it does not need any windshield wiper fluid.

- Separates phrases or dependent clauses before independent clauses

  Even though they have two biological daughters, they are adopting another daughter.

- Sets off non-restrictive elements

  Mr. Lantern, owner of the corner bakery, just sold his shop and retired.

- Sets off direct quotations

  "Dan," she said, "please don't forget to mail these letters."

3. Semicolon

- Separates two independent clauses with related information

  Joey came on Saturday; Bobby will come tomorrow.

- Separates two independent clauses connected by an adverbial conjunction or transition

  Last week they bought a plane ticket to Los Angeles; however, today they changed their minds and decided to drive there instead.

- Separates items in a list whose items contain commas

  Please be sure to bring your passport, if it is current; your inoculation card, which must be certified; and your admission letter, which needs to be stamped and signed by the school official.

4. Colon

- Introduces information in a list

  The cost of the trip includes the following: round trip airfare, hotel accommodations, transportation charges, and all meals.

- Introduces an explanation of the first clause

  Most of the students share a common goal: they want to improve their writing.

5. Apostrophe

- Indicates omissions in contracted forms

  He's coming, but we've heard that before, haven't we?

- Shows possession

  Would you please return Juan's book to him?

6. Quotation Marks

- Indicate the beginning and end of a direct quote

  An important leader in the American Revolution, Patrick Henry said, "Give me liberty or give me death."

- Indicate the title of a short work

  Have you ever read Franz Kafka's short story "Metamorphosis"?

Editing

Exercise 7 Insert correct punctuation in the sentences below and change the incorrect punctuation. When you insert a period, be sure to capitalize the first word of the next sentence. There may be more than one way to punctuate some sentences.

Dream Analysis

I have just finished reading an article called "Living in a Dream World" by Dr. Carl Young in *Psychology: It's All in Your Mind* magazine. This article explains a great deal about dreams. For example, it explains that all dreams are not equal in importance. Dreams that have importance will remain in a person's memory for years, dreams that have little or no importance are easily forgotten.

In order to analyze one's dreams, it helps to recall the following the people, animals, or objects in the dream; the mood; the atmosphere; and any color in the dream. It was surprising to discover that not all people dream in color.

Dreams and their meanings differ from person to person; however, there are common themes. A dream about a bird may represent freedom; a dream about insects may represent the dreamers' hard work; a dream about floating down a river may refer to the passage of time in the dreamer's life.

After I finished reading the article, I realized that a person's dreams are an emotional barometer of sorts that should be explored in order to learn what messages the unconscious mind is sending the conscious one.

Exercise 8   For each item, read the first sentence and determine whether it contains any errors. Then read the three choices and circle the letters of all the correct revisions. Be prepared to explain your answers.

1. Whenever I see an ATM, I am tempted to withdraw funds.

    A. I see an ATM, I am tempted to withdraw funds.

    B. Whenever I see an ATM; I am tempted to withdraw funds.

    C. No changes

2. Harrison Loechler is a felon, he is also an identity theft specialist.

    A. Harrison Loechler, a felon, is also an identity theft specialist.

    B. Harrison Loechler is a felon and an identify theft specialist.

    C. No changes

3. People need to safeguard their ATM cards and Social Security numbers. Because identity theft is becoming more widespread.

    A. Because identity theft is becoming more widespread, people need to safeguard their ATM cards and Social Security numbers.

    B. Because identity theft is becoming more widespread people need to safeguard their ATM cards and Social Security numbers.

    C. No changes

4. I get nervous. Every time I buy something online.

    A. I get nervous every time I buy something online.

    B. Every time I buy something online; I get nervous.

    C. No changes

5. You are the perfect person for this security job you have all the qualifications.

    A. You are the perfect person for this security job; you have all the qualifications.

    B. You are the perfect person for this security job, you have all the qualifications.

    C. No changes

6. The U.S. government publishes a pamphlet to help consumers learn about the crime of identity theft. It provides detailed information to help deter, detect, and defend against identify theft.

    A. The U.S. government publishes a pamphlet to help consumers learn about the crime of identity theft, it provides detailed information to help deter, detect, and defend against identify theft.

B. The U.S. government publishes a pamphlet to help consumers learn about the crime of identity theft, provides detailed information to help deter, detect, and defend against identify theft.

C. No changes

7. A common method of identity theft is called phishing. Thieves phish. When they do this. They pretend to be financial companies. They send spam. The purpose of this spam is to get you to reveal your personal information.

A. A common method of identity theft, is called phishing. When phishing, thieves pretend to be financial companies, They send spam to get you to reveal your personal information.

B. A common method of identity theft is called phishing. When phishing, thieves pretend to be financial companies and send spam to get you to reveal your personal information.

C. No changes

8. Another method that identity thieves use is referred to as skimming, a process in which thieves steal credit or debit card numbers by using a special storage device, when they are processing your card for a legitimate business transaction.

A. Another method that identity thieves use is referred to as skimming, a process in which thieves steal credit or debit card numbers by using a special storage device when they are processing your card for a legitimate business transaction.

B. Identity thieves use another method. It is referred to as skimming. In this process, thieves steal credit or debit card numbers. They do this by using a special storage device. When they are processing your card for a legitimate business transaction.

C. No changes

Exercise 9   Write a paragraph describing one of your dreams. (If you can't remember one, dream one up!) Before you begin writing, review the sentence types and the ways you can add variety to your writing. Try to use all three sentence types. When you finish, edit your writing for correct grammar and punctuation. Exchange paragraphs with a partner and check each other's work for correct sentence types and sentence variety.

_____

_____

_____

_____

_____

_____

_____

_____

_____

_____

_____

_____

_____

_____

_____

_____

_____

_____

_____

_____

_____

18 *Parallel Structure*

In this chapter, you will review and practice using grammatical structures to make your writing balanced. Balancing the grammatical structures of words, phrases, clauses, or sentences in your writing is called parallel structure. It gives coherence to your writing, and you can use it to link ideas. Structures that are connected with coordinating conjunctions or correlative (paired) conjunctions are written in parallel form, and writers often emphasize parallel structure through comparisons and repetition. This chapter offers practice that will improve your writing through the use of parallelism.

✔ CHECK YOUR GRAMMAR

Two of the five underlined phrases contain an error related to parallel structure. Can you explain why each of these underlined areas is (or is not) wrong? Discuss with a partner.

Left-Hemisphere Dominance

Generally speaking, the left hemisphere in most people appears to be dominant for language abilities: <u>speaking, reading, and written</u>. The <u>hemisphere of the left</u> also appears to be dominant for tasks requiring <u>logical analysis</u>, <u>problem solving</u>, and <u>mathematical computations</u>.

From: Jeffrey S. Nevid (2007). *Psychology Concepts and Applications.* Boston: Houghton Mifflin, p. 71.

18.1 Parallel Words

Good English writers make the following elements parallel:

- Words that are paired (*tall* and *slim:* <u>both are adjectives</u>)

- Items of equal rank (*animal, vegetable,* and *mineral:* <u>all three are nouns</u>)

- Items in a series (*bike, swim,* and *run:* <u>all three are verbs</u>)

Using multiple items that are grammatically parallel makes writing sound better by providing a better balance for the sentence. Consider the difference that one extra adjective makes in the following two sentences:

Students returning to school on Monday were greeted by **clogged** *streets and garages* as the roughly 8,000 parking spaces quickly filled up.

Students returning to school on Monday were greeted by **clogged** *streets and* **packed** *garages* as the roughly 8,000 parking spaces quickly filled up.

In the second example the adjectives *clogged* and *packed* are synonyms, but they are not redundant. Together, they are balanced. Each adds a special "flavor" to the sentence that makes the writing sound better. We see the parallel structure in the prepositional phrase: preposition + adjective + object + *and* + adjective + object.

In parallel structure, you balance nouns with nouns, verbs with verbs, adjectives with adjectives, and so forth. Here are some examples.

1. Words connected with coordinating conjunctions: *for, and, nor, but, or, yet, so.* (See Appendix 4, p. 299.)

   My favorite subjects are **history, psychology, and math.** (3 nouns)

   The dentist did not let me **eat** *or* **drink** anything for at least an hour. (2 verbs)

   Their wedding day was **beautiful, bright, and festive.** (3 adjectives)

   The ambassador spoke **quietly** *yet* **forcefully.** (2 adverbs)

2. Words connected with correlative conjunctions. (These conjunctions work only in pairs, such as *both/and, neither/nor.*)

   I like *neither* **Vivaldi** *nor* **Mozart.** (2 nouns)

   To succeed in this job, you must *both* **learn fast** *and* **work hard.** (2 verb phrases)

   The morning dawned *not* **foggy** *but* **clear,** *not* **humid** *but* **dry.** (4 adjectives)

Two subjects connected by *both … and* take a plural verb.

   Both <u>my plane ticket</u> *and* <u>my passport</u> **were** lost. (2 subjects)

Exercise 1   As you read the paragraph, circle and identify the seven examples of parallel structure: adjectives (3), adverbs (1), noun/pronoun (1), and verbs (2). The first one has been done for you.

1. _adjectives_   3. _____   5. _____   7. _____

2. _____   4. _____   6. _____

Choosing a Career

Choosing a career is at the same time both (exciting and frightening). On one

hand, it is exciting because there are so many professions and fields from which you

can choose. On the other hand, it is frightening because if you make a mistake, decide

on the wrong career, and find yourself with a lousy job, you may be unhappy or

frustrated for your entire working life. Clearly, it is important to consider your options

(continued)

---

completely and thoroughly before making the final decision. To find the perfect job, you should both research your field of interest and talk to a career counselor to help make the correct choice. However, your ultimate career choice must be based on personal, professional, and financial reasons that make sense to you. This life-altering decision matters so much because it will affect not only you but also your family.

18.2 Parallel Phrases

Phrases, as well as words, must be balanced in your writing. Be sure to balance like elements: prepositional phrases with prepositional phrases, infinitive phrases with infinitive phrases, and gerund phrases with gerund phrases. Phrases may be joined with coordinating conjunctions or correlative conjunctions. Here are some examples.

1. Phrases connected with coordinating conjunctions:

    The cat climbed **over the fence, up the tree,** *and* **onto the roof** of the house next door. (3 prepositional phrases)

    The judge told her **to take the stand** *and* **to tell the truth.** (2 infinitive phrases)

    They usually spend their weekends **entertaining their friends** *or* **fixing up their house.** (2 gerund phrases)

2. Phrases connected with correlative conjunctions:

    His satisfaction lies *not* **in his title** *but* **in his daily work.** (2 prepositional phrases)

    They can't decide *whether* **to take a cruise** *or* **to go on a safari.** (2 infinitive phrases)

    His idea of a relaxing evening is *either* **biking around the island** *or* **watching the sun set over the lake.** (2 gerund phrases)

⚠ Exercise 2 As you read the paragraph, underline the seven parallel words and phrases. Then locate and correct the three errors.

Cloud Types

How much do you know about the clouds you see in the sky every day? Clouds

are defined by their general appearance and by their altitude in the atmosphere.

Cloud types include cirrus, stratus, and cumulus. There are three basic cloud levels:

under 10,000 feet, between 10,000 and 20,000 feet, and higher than 20,000 feet.

Nimbus clouds produce precipitation and can tower up to 60,000 feet. Learning these

few terms and to gaze at the sky are all that you will need to begin impressing your
                    gazing

friends and family. Once you have learned the cloud classification system and the

weather associated with specific cloud types, you can begin to predict the weather
              to match

and matching skills with your local TV meteorologist!

| 18.3 | **Parallel Clauses** |

In your writing, be sure to balance noun, adjective, and adverb clauses to give them equal weight. Use coordinating and correlative conjunctions to join your clauses. Study the examples below.

1. Clauses connected with coordinating conjunctions:

    Unfortunately for all of us, **what she says *and* what she does** are very often two different things! (2 noun clauses)

    I am a person **who works hard *and* who gets along well with others.** (2 adjective clauses)

    Are you staying home **because you are tired *or* because it is a school night?** (2 adverb clauses)

2. Clauses connected with correlative conjunctions:

    He appreciated *neither* **what she said** *nor* **how she said it.** (2 noun clauses)

    She's asking *not* **where he went** *but* **when he went.** (2 noun clauses)

    They won the contract *either* **because they bid low** *or* **because they knew someone on the committee.** (2 adverb clauses)

For the following paired correlative conjunctions, the subject closer to the verb determines whether the verb is singular or plural.

Not only my parents *but also* my brother **visits** Colorado every winter.

Either my brother *or* my parents **are coming** to Colorado to visit this winter.

Neither my sister *nor* her son **has ever been** to Colorado.

Editing
Exercise 3 As you read the paragraph, study the underlined words, phrases, and clauses. Then locate and correct the five errors in parallel structure.

Diet and Exercise

exercise

What people eat and how much they are exercising are two factors that determine

their overall health. Eating a diet of foods that supply inadequate nutrients and that

contain high amounts of refined carbohydrates leads to weight gain and increased

risk of heart disease, diabetes, and getting cancer. Thus, it is important to eat not

only a wide variety of fresh fruit and vegetables every day but also grains, proteins,

and so-called healthy fats. Many people also suffer poor health because they fail to

exercise or to be active. Failing to exercise because they do not have enough time

because
or that they find it boring is probably the biggest problem they face. However, time

and being bored are not reasons to give up but hurdles that they have to overcome.

18.4	**Parallel Sentences**

Finally, balancing sentences with sentences adds parallelism to your writing. Just like words, phrases, and clauses, sentences can be joined with coordinating or correlative conjunctions. (See Chapter 17 for information about sentence types.)

1. Connected with coordinating conjunctions:

    One day he was there, *and* **the next day he was gone.** (simple)

    He was tired, and he looked ill, *so* **I urged him to see a doctor**, *and* **he saw one the next day.** (compound)

    If you leave now, you can still catch a bus, *but* **if you stay, you'll have to take a cab home.** (complex)

2. Connected with correlative conjunctions (often sounds formal):

    Not only **does she hold a full-time job Monday through Friday**, *but* **she** *also* **volunteers at a hospice on weekends.**

    Either **he turns in his report tomorrow** *or* **he starts looking for a new job.**

Nor is most commonly used with *neither* as a correlative conjunction.

    Neither he **nor** I can come to the party.

For as a coordinating conjunction means *because* and is considered formal usage.

> We decided to abandon the idea of buying a house, **for** the prices had risen dramatically and were now out of our range.

Exercise 4 Add a clause to each of the incomplete structures below in order to make each structure parallel. The first one has been done for you.

1. The first exercise in the unit was easy, but _the rest were hard._

2. The idea of parallel structure makes sense, and it's almost formulaic, _____

   _____.

3. Either the grammatical structures are balanced or _____

   _____.

4. Not only do instructors mark down for errors in parallelism, but _____

   _____.

5. If you proofread your work, you'll catch your mistakes, but _____

   _____.

Editing
⚠ Exercise 5 Rewrite these sentences to make their elements parallel.

1. The Great Plains is a vast, relatively flat region, and the region has no trees that stretches from north to south across the center of the nation.

   _____

   _____

2. The buffalo provided most essentials: meat, clothing and shelter, bones and horns were made into implements, and even fuel for fires.

   _____

   _____

3. Women raised corn and squash and gathered wild fruit and vegetables, and men did the hunting and went fishing near their village and cultivated tobacco.

   _____

   _____

4. A Plains Indian lesson on sharing is "When you see a boy barefooted and lame, take off your moccasins and give them to him. If you see a boy hungry, you should bring him to your home and give him food."

_____

_____

5. Most white Americans believed that land was a commodity to be bought and sold and that land was to be used but not individually owned was a tradition believed by Native Americans.

_____

_____

Editing
⋀ Exercise 6   Edit and then rewrite the following sentences. Use correlative conjunctions (paired) to make the grammatical structures in each sentence parallel.

1. Almost half of the students in Section 003 of Freshman Composition neither showed up for the final nor did they turn in their five required essays.

_____

_____

2. The composition instructor was not only a knowledgeable teacher but also fair.

_____

_____

3. It would be best if you included sources for your topic both from the Internet and used the university library.

_____

_____

4. The student received a zero for plagiarizing not an essay but for plagiarizing a research paper.

_____

_____

5. The students need to either choose a research topic or they should ask the instructor to assign one.

_____

_____

6. Both the type ~~of test~~ and ~~how long it is~~ are important considerations when studying for an exam.

length of test

_____

_____

18.5   Parallel Comparisons

When you make comparisons using parallel structures, use these expressions:

    er / more / less … than   as … as   the same as   similar to

Remember that the items you are comparing must have the same grammatical structure.

Incorrect:	Going to a movie is more expensive than ~~to rent~~ a video.
Correct:	**Going to a movie** is *more* expensive *than* **renting a video.**
Incorrect:	Investing in his company is the same as ~~to throw~~ your money away.
Correct:	**Investing in his company** is *the same as* **throwing your money away.**

When you use parallelism in comparisons, the comparisons must follow these rules.

1. Comparisons should be complete. Repeat the whole parallel structure in each item and include all the comparison words.

Incorrect:	I am happier at my new job.
Correct:	I am happier **at my new job** *than* **at my old one.**
Correct:	**I am happier at my new job** *than* **I was at my old one.**
Incorrect:	I can't believe you lost. You played as well, if not better than your opponent.
Correct:	I can't believe you lost. **You** played *as* well *as*, if not better *than* **your opponent.**
Incorrect:	Stan Johnson is taller than anyone on the team. (He is on the team, so he can't be taller than anyone on the team.)
Correct:	**Stan Johnson** is taller *than* **anyone else** on the team.
Correct:	**Stan Johnson** is taller *than* **any other player** on the team.

2. Comparisons should be clear. Make sure the meaning of your comparison is obvious.

Incorrect:	I think your boss likes Angela more than you. (Does this mean more than you like Angela or more than your boss likes you? The meaning is unclear.)
Correct:	I think **your boss likes Angela** *more than* **you like Angela.**
Correct:	I think **your boss likes Angela** *more than* **your boss likes you.**

3. Comparisons should be between similar items. The comparison must make sense.

Incorrect:	The cost of a house in Mississippi is less than Texas. (*House* and *Texas* are not similar.)
Correct:	The cost of **a house in Mississippi** is *less than* **one in Texas.**

Incorrect: Popular music in the United States is similar to your country. (*Music* and *your country* are not similar.)

Correct: **Popular music in the United States** is *similar to* **music in your country.**

Editing

⚠ **Exercise 7**   Edit and then rewrite the comparisons in the following sentences to make each sentence parallel. The first one has been done for you.

1. Some students are better at learning languages.

   Some students are better at learning languages than are other students.

2. Writing in a second language is usually more difficult than to speak.

   _____

   _____

3. The book that you used in your grammar class is similar to my class.

   _____

   _____

4. The writing homework was as difficult today as yesterday.

   _____

   _____

5. I think I prefer listening to language CDs more than you.

   _____

   _____

6. The rules for using semicolons in English are almost the same as Spanish.

   _____

   _____

Exercise 8   Use the phrases below to write sentences containing comparisons. Have a partner check your sentences for parallel form. The first one has been done for you.

1. my strengths / my weaknesses

   I think my public speaking strengths are more obvious to people than my weaknesses are.

2. feeling calm / feeling nervous

_____

_____

3. informative speeches / persuasive speeches

_____

_____

4. community college speech courses / community college writing courses

_____

_____

5. planning a speech / presenting a speech

_____

_____

6. good public speakers / poor public speakers

_____

_____

18.6   Parallel Repetition

Parallel repetition means repeating articles, prepositions, *to* before a verb, or other words to emphasize parallel structure. This repetition can help make the parallel items clear and eliminate omissions or potential awkwardness from your writing. When you repeat articles or prepositions, you add clarity to a series of items. The repeated word must appear with each item, not just with two of three items.

At the same time, parallel structure makes repeating some words unnecessary. In general, avoid repetition when it makes your writing too wordy. Compare the examples below.

Articles

Possible: For the first time in his life he had *a* **good job,** *a* **home,** and *a* **family.**

Possible: For the first time in his life he had *a* **good job, home,** and **family.**

Incorrect: For the first time in his life he had *a* **good job,** *a* **home,** and **family.**

to before a verb

Possible: Now is the time *to* organize, *to* plan, and *to* act.

Possible: Now is the time *to* **organize**, **plan**, and **act**.

Incorrect: Now is the time *to* **organize**, **plan**, and *to* **act**.

Prepositions

Possible: She told her son to play ball not *in* **the living room** but *in* **the yard**.

Relative Pronouns

Possible: The candidate believes *that* **this country is ready for change,** *that* **the people are willing to sacrifice,** and *that* **there can be no change without sacrifice.** (Repeated *that* makes the grammar clear.)

Weak: The candidate believes *that* **this country is ready for change, the people are willing to sacrifice,** and **there can be no change without sacrifice.** (Long sentence may increase confusion.)

Subjects

Possible: In her mind, *life* **was an adventure** or **simply wasn't worth living.**

Better: In her mind, *life* **was an adventure** or *life* **simply wasn't worth living.** (Repeated subject improves clarity.)

Wordiness

Weak: My editor is good at **researching** background facts, **researching** hard-to-find material, and **researching** information just published. (Repeating *researching* causes wordiness.)

Better: My editor is good at **researching** background facts, hard-to-find material, and information just published. (Statement is more concise and still clear.)

When you write a paragraph, especially one of comparison/contrast, repeating parallel structures can help you develop the main idea. You may use parallel structure in all or in only some sentences of your paragraph. Study the examples of parallel structure in the following paragraph.

There are several differences between **living in an** apartment *and* **living in a** house. One **difference is** privacy. **Living in a** house offers a person more privacy than **living in an** apartment does. Another **difference is** maintenance. **Living in a** house

(continued)

requires the tenant to make all repairs and upkeep, *but* **living in an** apartment puts responsibility for upkeep on the landlord. A third **difference is** cost. *Not only* is **living in a** house usually more expensive than **living in an** apartment in terms of rent, *but* it *also* costs more **to furnish** *and* **to keep up** a house than it does an apartment.

⚠ Exercise 9   Edit the following sentences, adding or eliminating repetition, to improve the parallel structure.

1. The lawyers were relieved to learn that Mr. Owens, the former executive director, had come, that he had signed the agreement, and had left without incident.

   _____

   _____

2. They had presented a list of issues, possible resolution, and deadline which were all acceptable to their client.

   _____

   _____

3. Mr. Owens went to his attorney's office, and Mr. Owens made an appointment for both himself and his wife.

   _____

   _____

4. His wife is amazing—look at the way she handles the responsibility of home, the responsibility of work, and the responsibility of volunteering amid all this turmoil.

   _____

   _____

5. Mr. Owens told us that he couldn't come to next week's board meeting and he had reasons he couldn't come to next week's board meeting.

   _____

   _____

6. Mr. Owens lost the respect of the board, not because he wasn't working hard but his employees weren't.

   _____

   _____

⚠ Exercise 10 Read the following excerpts from famous speeches, noting the underlined structures. Locate the nine errors in parallelism and correct them by rewriting the structures, adding or deleting words as necessary.

1. **Patrick Henry to the Second Virginia Convention on March 23, 1775:**

   "… Sir, we have done everything that could be done to avert the storm that is now coming on. <u>We have petitioned</u>; <u>we remonstrated</u>; <u>we have supplicated</u>; we <u>have prostrated</u> ourselves before the throne and <u>have implored</u> its interposition to arrest the tyrannical hands of the Ministry and Parliament.

   … The battle, sir, is not to <u>the strong</u> alone; it is to <u>the vigilant</u>, <u>the active</u>, <u>the brave</u>. I know not what course others may take, but as for me—<u>give me liberty</u> or <u>you can give me death!</u>"

2. **Abraham Lincoln at the dedication of a cemetery in Gettysburg, Pennsylvania, on November 19, 1863:**

   "… We have come to dedicate a portion of that field as a final resting-place for those who here gave their lives that that nation might live.… But in a larger sense, <u>we cannot dedicate</u>, <u>we cannot consecrate</u>, this ground <u>cannot be hallowed by us</u>.… It is rather for us to be here dedicated to the great task remaining before us … that we here highly resolve <u>that these dead</u> shall not have died in vain, <u>that this nation</u> under God will have a new birth of freedom, and <u>government of the people</u>, <u>by the people</u>, and <u>for people</u> shall not perish from the earth."

3. **John F. Kennedy at his inauguration in Washington, D.C., on January 20, 1961:**

   "We observe today not a victory of party but a celebration of freedom.… <u>Let us</u> never negotiate out of fear, but <u>let us</u> never fear to negotiate.

   <u>Let both sides</u> explore what problems unite us instead of belaboring those problems which divide us. <u>Let both sides</u> seek to invoke the wonders of science instead of its terrors.… <u>The energy</u>, <u>the faith</u>, <u>devotion</u> which we bring to this endeavor will light our country and all who serve it, and <u>the glow</u> from that fire can truly light the world.

   And so, my fellow Americans, <u>ask not what your country can do for you</u>; <u>ask what you are able to do for the country</u>."

4. **Robert F. Kennedy at a rally informing the audience that Martin Luther King, Jr., had been assassinated on April 4, 1968:**

   "… <u>What we need in the United States is not division</u>; <u>what we need in the United States is not hatred</u>; <u>what the United States needs is not violence or lawlessness</u>; but <u>love</u> and <u>wisdom</u>, and <u>compassion</u> toward one another, and a feeling of justice toward those who still suffer within our country, whether <u>they be white</u> or <u>they are black</u>."

Exercise 11   Circle the letter of the correct answer. Be prepared to explain your answers.

1. I tried to get in touch with Jessica by calling her home telephone number on Monday and _____, but I was not able to reach her on either day.

   A. again on Tuesday   C. I called again on Tuesday

   B. Tuesday again   D. I called again Tuesday

2. _____ her cell phone _____ her e-mail were out of service.

   A. Not only ... but also   C. Both ... and

   B. Not ... but   D. When ... and

3. _____ Erica's parents' number _____ her last apartment telephone number was programmed into any of the three cell phones that I own.

   A. Either ... nor   C. Both ... and

   B. Neither ... nor   D. Perhaps ... and

4. When I sent her an e-mail, a message came to me saying that her e-mail inbox had more messages _____.

   A. than it would allow   C. would allow than it

   B. than would allow it   D. would it allow than

5. She has _____ time, _____ money, and _____ technology to keep in touch with everyone, but she chooses not to do this.

   A. the ... the ... the   C. the ... ø ... the

   B. ø ... ø ... the   D. ø ... the ... ø

6. In order to speak with her today, I am willing to drive to her place of employment. Unfortunately, I have no idea where she _____.

   A. both works   C. but works

   B. or works   D. works

7. My communication preferences may be different from most people's, but my three favorite ways to communicate are _____.

   A. meeting face-to-face, sending e-mail, and to use voicemail   C. to meet face-to-face, to send e-mail, and using voicemail

   B. to meet face-to-face, to send e-mail, and to use voicemail   D. meeting face-to-face, sending e-mail, or using voicemail

8. Without a doubt, everyone understands that staying in touch with family and

_____ is important.

A. friends

B. touch with friends

C. staying in touch with friends

D. to stay in touch with friends

Exercise 12   Imagine you are running for a school office such as class president. Write a speech presenting your view of an issue or offering solutions to an issue important in your school. Examples of issues are increased tuition, large class sizes, or limited parking. Before you begin, make a list of some parallel structures you want to include in the speech. In your speech, underline the parallel structures you were able to use from your list. Exchange paragraphs with a partner and check each other's work for correct parallel structure.

_____

_____

_____

_____

_____

_____

_____

_____

_____

_____

_____

_____

_____

_____

_____

_____

_____

_____

_____

_____

19 Confusing Words and Structures

In this chapter, you will review and practice words that can confuse writers and speakers of English.

✔ CHECK YOUR GRAMMAR

Two of the five underlined phrases contain an error related to <u>confusing words and structures</u>. Can you explain why each of these underlined areas is (or is not) wrong? Discuss with a partner.

> ### Time
>
> Each of us has an idea of what <u>time</u> is, but most of us have never really learned a proper definition. We cannot <u>look</u> time; however, we certainly know that it exists. We may know that events are affected by <u>times</u>, but a clear definition may elude us. We <u>feel</u> that we know what <u>time</u> is, but defining it is difficult.

Adapted from: J. T. Shipman, Wilson, J. D., and Todd, A. W. (2003). *An Introduction to Physical Science,* 10th ed. Boston: Houghton Mifflin, p. 6.

19.1 Verb Pairs

Verb pairs can be confusing. Take some time to study and review these pairs. Then do the exercises that follow.

(fall) **fell** / **fallen** = to collapse, drop, or go down

> She **fell** off a ladder while she was trimming the trees in her yard.

> Before the leaves had **fallen,** it snowed.

Prepositions link nouns or pronouns to other words in the sentence in order to express relationships. Examples of relationships include time, location, and direction. (See Chapter 7 for more about prepositions.)

Many prepositions are confusing because they are used idiomatically. Study the uses and examples in this section.

> **between:** used for two persons or things
>
>> The inheritance was split **between** the two brothers.
>
> **among:** used for three or more persons or things
>
>> **Among** the seven children, only three were able to attend college.
>
> **in, after:** to indicate time (*in*+length of time; *after*+name of the time or event)
> Remember that *in* for the future is the opposite of *ago* for the past:
> in six weeks ≠ six weeks ago.
>
>> I'll see you **in** a week **after** final exams.
>
> **since:** from a time in the past (*since*+name of the time or event)
>
>> I've known him **since** 1999.
>
> **for:** amount or duration of time (*for*+length of time)
>
>> I've known him **for** three years.

Editing
⋀ Exercise 8   Read each sentence and mark C for correct or X for incorrect. Then correct the sentences that contain errors. The first one has been done for you.

Among

___X___ 1. ~~Between~~ all the instructors in the Anthropology Department, Dr. Harris has taught the longest.

_____ 2. Dr. Harris is going to meet with her dean after three days.

_____ 3. Between you and me, I think the anthropology final exam will be very tough.

_____ 4. We've been waiting for our test results from Dr. Harris since a week.

_____ 5. Besides teaching, Dr. Harris has been the chair of the Anthropology Department since four years ago.

_____ 6. Dr. Harris has been publishing her research studies for years.

_____ 7. We're taking our anthropology midterm exam after spring break.

_____ 8. Since 2005, the Anthropology Department has grown threefold!

(feel) felt / felt = to sense or touch; to believe; to be affected by

> She **felt** a sharp pain in her ankle when she hit the ground.

> They **feel** they are learning a lot in that class.

borrow = to ask for temporary use of something from someone; to take

> Can I **borrow** your car this weekend?

> I **borrowed** twenty dollars from him until next Tuesday.

lend = to allow temporary use of something by someone; to give

> She **lent** me her car for the entire weekend.

> Could you **lend** me twenty dollars until next Tuesday?

(lie) lay / lain (intransitive verb—does not take an object) = to recline

> He **lay** on the ground after being hit by an opposing team member.

> I'm tired. I'm going to **lie** down and take a short nap.

(lay) laid / laid (transitive verb—takes an object) = to place or put

> Every night he **lays** his clothes out for the next day.

> I know I **laid** my keys on the counter when I came in. Where are they?

make = to build or construct; to create or produce; to change something

> To **make** you happy, I **made** you a sandwich.

> We need to **make** plans for our new business if we intend to **make** any money.

do = to perform or accomplish something; to talk about actions or work

> Could you **do** me a favor and **do** the shopping for me this weekend?

> What does he **do** for a living? I think he **does** interior decorating.

must not = to prohibit

> You **must not** let your passport expire.

do not have to = to be optional or unnecessary

> You **don't have to** live on campus when you study, but dorms are available.

(NOTE: *Must* and *have to* are very similar in meaning in the affirmative)

(raise) raised / raised (transitive verb—takes an object) = to increase; to lift or move something to a higher position

> Gas station owners **raised** the price of gas by fifty cents almost overnight.

> They play the national anthem whenever they **raise** the flag.

(rise) rose / risen (intransitive verb—does not take an object) = to increase; indicates that something moves to a higher position

Gas prices **rose** by fifty cents almost overnight.

The sun **rises** a few minutes earlier every day until the summer solstice.

say = to speak (used without an indirect object); does not indicate who the listener was

They **said** that they were going to come over about 6:30 tonight.

tell = to speak (used with an indirect object); indicates who was listening; expressions include *tell a lie, tell the truth, tell the time, tell a story*

They **told** me that they were going to come over about 6:30 tonight.

see = to use one's eyes (involuntary action)

I **saw** the accident while I was waiting for the light to change.

look = to use one's eyes (voluntary action); focus is on the object; shorter duration than *watch*

We **looked** at six new houses that were on the market.

Could you **look** at my paper and correct the errors?

watch = to use one's eyes (voluntary action); focus is on what the object is doing; longer duration than *look*

We **watched** that new TV program last night.

I don't want the soup to boil over. Could you **watch** it while I answer the phone?

used to (+ VERB) = to no longer occur or happen (indicates change)

We **used to** watch the news on ABC, but now we watch CBS.

He didn't **use to** come to work so early. It's 7:15, and he starts at 8:00.

be/get used to (+ NOUN or NOUN equivalent) = to become accustomed to or familiar with something

After living in Alabama for ten years, I'm **used to** hot, humid weather.

They arrived here only two weeks ago. They still need to **get used to** hearing English all the time.

waste = to use something unwisely or foolishly

Please turn off the lights when you're not in the room. You're **wasting** energy by leaving them on.

He sat in my office and **wasted** half an hour of my time chatting about his dog.

lose = to be unable to find or locate; to not win

It's easy to **lose** money if you don't invest wisely.

They **lost** the game by two points in the last ten seconds of the final quarter.

Exercise 1 As you read the essay, underline the correct verbs in parentheses. The first one has been done for you.

Colorado Trip

Last summer we (did, <u>made</u>) plans for a trip out west to Colorado. We stopped

1

along the way to enjoy all the outdoors had to offer. From our camper in Denver,

for example, we could (watch, see) the Rocky Mountains. They were absolutely

2

majestic—(rising, raising) mightily from the land, standing tall and stately, looking

3

powerful against the piercing blue Colorado sky. Looking at them (did, made) me

4

(feel, fell) as though I were experiencing nature for the first time.

5

It was only then that we discovered we had forgotten our camera. I don't know

why we forgot—we (were used to traveling, used to travel) more than we have

6

lately, so maybe we just got out of the habit of packing the camera. I thought I had

(said, told) my husband, Dennis, to pack it, but he (said, told) he hadn't heard me

7   8

(say, tell) anything about it.

9

I (felt, fell) awful, but we decided not to (lose, waste) time worrying about it. If we

10   11

couldn't (borrow, lend) a camera from my sister, who lived in nearby Westminster, then

12

we would simply buy a new one. After all, our purpose in traveling to Denver was to

capture the natural beauty of one of America's western states.

Our vacation was wonderful and we (watched, saw) many beautiful places

13

besides Colorado. We (looked, watched) the sun set over rivers, valleys, and

14

mountains all across the West and (saw, looked) it (raise, rise) in the early morning

15   16

stillness that (lay, laid) at the edge of forests and woods. We sat in silence, listening

17

to the sounds of nature: water flowing over rocks in a stream, birds calling, and

small animals scurrying about unseen, in search of food.

(continued)

If you ever get the chance to go camping, you (must not, don't have to) pass

18

it up. Don't (lose, waste) time trying to decide whether it will be a worthwhile

19

opportunity—it will! Camping taught us a great deal. What we brought back with

us, along with our pictures and memories, was a renewed interest in nature. We're

not (losing, wasting) any time planning our next trip. In fact, once we returned

20

home, we got out the atlas right away!

Exercise 2 Put the following list of words, phrases, and expressions in the correct columns below. Then, on separate paper, use three words or phrases from each column in sentences. *Suggestion:* This is not an easy exercise. Consult a dictionary, an English speaker, or a web source for help.

the laundry	for a living	plans for tonight	money	homework
coffee	a living	a good job	one sick	so much noise
a term paper	the shopping	dinner	a key word search	new friends
a phone call	some yard work	trouble	well on an exam	the dishes
a mistake	good time	bread	up an exam	an enemy
fun of	a face	a favor	angry	something over
a salad	housework	time in jail	math	someone happy

DO	MAKE
the laundry	

19.2   The Verb *get*

It is very easy to confuse some verbs because they are used in idiomatic expressions and thus have multiple meanings. One of the most problematic of all verbs in English is *get*.

> *get* meaning *arrive* (*get* + TO + PLACE; *get* + HOME)

> > What time does your plane **get** to Atlanta?

> > When did you **get** home?

> *get* meaning *become* (*get* + ADJECTIVE)

> > Are you **getting** hungry?

> > She **got** excited about the party.

(ALSO: *get sick, get sleepy, get angry, get upset, get engaged, get married, get divorced, get busy, get tired, get well*)

> *get* meaning *receive* (*get* + NOUN)

> > He's **getting** a raise.

> > I **got** a letter from Mom today.

(ALSO: *get a ticket* (meaning: a citation from the police), *get a job, get a new car, get some news, get a call*)

> *get* meaning *to cause something to happen* (*get* + PRONOUN + INFINITIVE)

> > I **got** them to reduce my taxes.

> > We **got** her to reconsider taking the job.

> **Special expressions:**

> > I **got up** late today.

> > He **got off** the plane at 6:00.

(ALSO: *get on the bus, get over an illness, get out of the car, get in trouble, get with something, get behind in work, get off work*)

Although the word *get* is extremely common, avoid using this word in formal writing. Instead, use one of its more specific synonyms. For example, write *become weak* instead of *get weak*.

Exercise 3   Answer the questions, using the verb *get* as defined in Section 19.2. Use the pronoun *I* to begin each sentence. The first one is done for you.

1. When did you arrive?

   I got here late last night.
   _____

2. When did you receive your degree?

   _____

3. When did you become ill?

_____

4. What time did you finish work last night?

_____

5. When did you have Alex paint your house?

_____

19.3	# Verb + Object + Base Verb

A confusing English structure for some writers is two consecutive verbs. If two verbs are near each other in a sentence, the most common pattern uses an infinitive for the second verb: verb + infinitive.

If you **want** *to succeed* in business, you must have a solid plan and be ready to work.

If you **want** me *to assist* you with any of the work, call me on my cell phone.

However, three verbs—*make, have, let*—are followed by only the base form of the verb:

make:	The boss **made** us all *work* late.
have:	Mike **had** Nancy *complete* the final inspection forms because everyone else was busy.
let:	I **let** the children *stay* up late tonight.

In addition, verbs of perception—*see, hear, watch, feel*—are often followed by the base form of the verb:

see:	I **saw** Josh *leave* the party.
hear:	The flight attendant **heard** the young passenger *scream*.
watch:	The police officers **watched** the man *break* into the house.
feel:	During the earthquake, we **felt** the building *move* violently.

Verbs of perception may be followed by a gerund (*-ing* form) to emphasize the length or repetition of the action:

| *hear:* | The flight attendant **heard** the young passenger *screaming*. |
| *feel:* | During the earthquake, we **felt** the building *moving*. |

Exercise 4 Use the words given to write sentences telling what mothers usually do for their children. Include the words *mothers* and *their children* in each sentence. The first one is done for you.

1. make / eat / spinach Mothers make their children eat spinach.

2. sometimes let / watch / scary movies on TV

_____

3. have / clean up / their own rooms

_____

4. make / do / all of their homework

_____

5. have / call / if they are going to be late

_____

6. never / let / play outside in bad weather

_____

19.4 Nouns

When nouns have similar forms or similar meanings, it is easy to get them confused. Understanding the difference between *count* nouns and *noncount* nouns will help you use nouns correctly in your writing.

As we saw in Chapter 1, count nouns can be counted. They have two forms: singular and plural.

> Could you give me **an example** of a past tense verb?

> Could you give me **three examples** of confusing verbs?

Noncount nouns *cannot* be counted. They have only one form. We don't use noncount nouns with words that indicate singular or plural.

> *Correct:*   The **sand** on this beach is unusually dark.

> *Incorrect:*   The many ~~sands~~ on this beach are unusually dark.

Here is a list of frequently used count nouns and noncount nouns, with their definitions and examples of how they are used.

> **history** (noncount) = events that happened in the past

> They say that **history** repeats itself.

> **story** (count) = literature; retelling of something

> Did you read the **story** on the front page?

> **time** (noncount) = quantity, period, or duration of minutes, hours, months, etc.

> There isn't enough **time** to accomplish all the tasks on my list.

> **time(s)** (count) = separate occasions, experiences

> We had a good **time** at the party last night.

> I've asked him for his e-mail address at least three **times**.

news (noncount) = information about events

I saw the **news** about the war on TV.

information (noncount) = knowledge, facts

Could you give us some **information** about your new restaurant?

work (noncount) = occupation

I love my **work** and the people I work with.

works (count) = product, creation

They have two **works** of art from Picasso displayed.

homework (noncount) = assignment to be completed at home

There's too much **homework** to do in an hour!

number (count) = numeral

Big bold **numbers** on their hats identified the team players.

a number (+ plural; noncount) = several, many (unspecified number)

You have **a number** of options to consider.

the number (+ singular; noncount) = the total, unspecified

The number of people coming is small.

Exercise 5   Complete the sentences using nouns from Section 19.4. The first one has been done for you.

Gifted Education Program

I read an interesting ____*story*____ in the newspaper this morning. It was
                          1

about a person who spends most of her _____ working with children
                                         2

from a local elementary school.

It seems _____ of children in the school are gifted and, thus, are way
          3

ahead of their classmates. For example, one gifted child was known for finishing his

_____ so quickly that his teachers couldn't find any _____ to
   4   **5**

challenge him.

(continued)

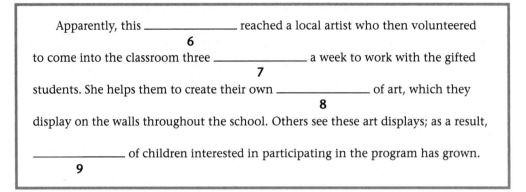

Apparently, this _____ reached a local artist who then volunteered
                     6
to come into the classroom three _____ a week to work with the gifted
                                        7
students. She helps them to create their own _____ of art, which they
                                                    8
display on the walls throughout the school. Others see these art displays; as a result,

_____ of children interested in participating in the program has grown.
      9

19.5 Pronouns and Contractions

Pronouns that have similar spellings can be easily confused. Study the meanings and examples of the following pronouns.

its = possessive form of *it*; indicates belonging to the thing mentioned

The dog wagged **its** tail as I approached.

it's = contracted form of *it is* or *it has*

It's true (it is). **It's** (it has) been years since I visited Chicago.

IMPORTANT: *its'* is NOT a word in English!

their = possessive form of *they*

Have you seen **their** new car?

they're = contracted form of *they are*

They're coming over for dinner tonight.

there = used as subject of *be* verb in a clause or sentence

There is another new car dealer in town. **There** are now at least seven dealers to choose from when buying a car.

whose = possessive for *who* or *which*

Whose car keys are these?

The dog **whose** collar is missing belongs to my neighbor.

who's = contracted form of *who is* or *who has*

Who's (who is) going with me? **Who's** (who has) made the list of what we need to get?

your = possessive for *you*

Please spell **your** last name for me.

you're = contracted form of *you are*

You're the new secretary, aren't you?

Exercise 6   Circle the correct form of the word in parentheses.

1. The public relations and advertising people in every campaign are vital to a campaign's success. (There, They're) is no doubt that (they're, their) the ones ultimately responsible for winning an election.

2. In a televised debate, some questions are spontaneous; others are planted. I do not think that this is a fair practice; however, (its, it's) not my decision to make.

3. (Who's, Whose) questions will be asked during the debate? (Who's, Whose) in charge of this important step in a public debate?

4. After the debate, experts attempt to predict which candidate did better in the debate. (There, Their, They're) opinions may not matter so much. What really counts is what the voters think. On election day, the voters will speak, and only then can we find out (they're, their) preferences.

5. In large campaigns, the area will be divided into smaller zones or districts to be more efficient with the campaign's people and money resources. By the way, do you know (whose, who's) the leader for (you're, your) district?

6. I am pretty sure (its, it's) Randall Kelly.

7. (You're, Your) lucky that (it's, its) not Pat Goodman. Not one of the campaign volunteers wants to deal with him. The volunteers literally run away when he heads in (there, their) direction!

19.6   Quantifiers, Intensifiers, and Emphasizers

Writers use the adjectives in this section to indicate how many or to intensify or emphasize something.

many: used with count nouns

There are rules, but there are **many** exceptions as well.

much: used with noncount nouns; usually used in negative sentences

We haven't had **much** time to practice this season.

quite: intensifier; not as strong as *very*

I got home **quite** late last night.

The test was **quite** hard.

very: intensifier

> I got home **very** late last night.

> The test was **very** hard.

too: emphasizer; implies excessiveness and often requires additional information to complete the meaning; used with a negative meaning (that is, something was not possible)

> I got home **too** late to watch the news last night.

 In formal writing, do not use the word *too* with a positive adjective or adverb.

> *Incorrect:*   The food was ~~too~~ delicious. (What is the negative meaning?)

> *Correct:*   The food was **very** delicious. (OR: The food was **extremely** delicious.)

so (+ ADJECTIVE / ADVERB *that*): emphasizer; if an explanation is not given, the assumption is that the listener knows the result

> I got home **so** late last night that I couldn't function at the office today.

> The test was **so** hard. (This would usually mean that I'm sure I failed it. It is not necessary to say the second part. It is understood.)

such (+ *a / an* + ADJECTIVE + NOUN *that*): emphasizer; if an explanation is not given, the assumption is that the listener knows the result

> I got home at **such** a late hour last night (that I'm tired today).

> It was **such** a difficult test (that I'm sure I failed it).

Editing
▲ **Exercise 7**   Read the following paragraph. Find and correct the four errors in quantifiers, intensifiers, or emphasizers.

Stress and Vacation Time

In the past, not very many research had been conducted on the topic of stress

and its effects on the body. Today, however, there has been so an increased interest

in the subject that government grants are available for continued study on the

topic, especially the effect of vacation time on an individual. In the United States,

unfortunately, few employers offer their employees more than two weeks of vacation

time each year. A few U.S. companies offer three to four weeks of vacation, but

employees usually have to have already worked at least ten years for the company to

qualify for that many time off. In many cultures, a two-week vacation is little short

to "recharge a person's batteries." More research still needs to be done to evaluate the

effects of vacation time on workers.

19.8 Confusing Adjectives and Adverbs

Many adjectives and adverbs in English can be difficult to use correctly. Study the following meanings and examples. (Note that some pronouns can be confused with adjectives or adverbs that are spelled the same way.)

ago = in the past; used with amount of time; reference point is the present time

I worked with him three years **ago**.

before (+ NOUN or clause) = in the past; used with or without amount of time; reference point is past time

I've worked with him **before**.

all = total amount

All of the students worried about the exam.

almost = nearly; not quite

Almost all of the students passed the exam.

most = the largest number or amount

Most students had studied for the exam.

bad = substandard, poor; not good; incorrect; not in good health; sorry

The movie we watched last night was **bad**.

I feel **bad** for her—she just had her car stolen for the third time.

badly = poorly, in a bad way or manner

The team played **badly** in the final quarter and lost the game.

good = positive, not bad; appropriate; high quality

The meal at La Maison was **good** but not too expensive.

well (ADJECTIVE) = in good health

I was sick last week, but I'm **well** now.

well (ADVERB) = successfully; proficiently; in a good way or manner

You handled that awkward situation quite **well**.

ever = at any time

Have you **ever** driven in a stock car race?

She hadn't **ever** planned to open her own business.

never = at no time

No, I have **never** heard of the rock group Boulder Heads.

alike = (ADJECTIVE, used after linking verbs) = similar

People say we look **alike.**

like (PREPOSITION) = having the same characteristics; equivalent

John looks **like** his brother.

Like Bolivia, Austria has no seacoast.

another (ADJECTIVE) = additional

I need **another** cup of coffee.

another (PRONOUN) = an additional one

She drank a cup of coffee and then **another.**

other (ADJECTIVE) = different or distinct from someone / something

Other students took the same exam.

others (PRONOUN) = additional ones

Others took the same exam.

the other(s) one of two; the remaining one or ones

I didn't care much for this video. **The other** one I watched was funnier. (ADJECTIVE)

I didn't care much for this video, but I liked **the other.** (PRONOUN)

this, that singular; near / far

This kind of music hurts my ears.

That problem is one I just can't solve.

these, those plural; near / far

These kinds of exams are hard.

Those stories are wonderful for kids.

Editing

⬆ **Exercise 9** As you read the passage, find and correct the eight errors in word usage.

Retirement Money Tips

How many people each year lose large sums of money through bad investments?

How many others aren't even aware that almost their money has been invested badly?

Whether you're already an investor or are ready to become one, you can benefit from

---

(continued)

these six tips. Be sure all your retirement funds will still be there when you need them!

Know your financial goals and your "risk-comfort level." If high-risk investments make you anxious, then invest in something that will preserve your capital and offer you less risk. This kinds of funds will obviously yield a lower rate of return than other higher-risk investments, but these lower return is your trade-off for feeling comfortable.

Consult a financial planner. Meet with the planner to discuss your personal financial goals and to develop a plan specific to your needs and circumstances. These kinds of meetings should continue to occur with your planner even if your investments are doing well.

Alike most others investment consultants, your financial planner will be paid for his or her services. Know what fees you will pay and how they are calculated. Ask questions if you are unsure how the fees are assessed.

Make sure your investments are diversified. Don't never invest all of your money in the same kinds of asset classes. Find out if there is a fee to transfer from one fund to another.

Monitor both your investments and account statements. Before investing in a new fund, read the prospectus. If you do not understand it well enough, ask the other person to read it as well. If you still have questions, consult other sources.

Finally, be prepared to invest for the long term. If an investment sounds too good to be true, it probably is. Unlike good investments, scams often promise unusually high rates of return. These promises should be investigated thoroughly before you invest in the fund. You don't want to invest bad.

19.9 Other Confusing Words

too, so, either, neither: used to avoid repeating words or phrases

Julie is confused about all of this. I am, **too.**

Julie is confused about all of this. **So am I.**

He didn't turn in his final paper. I didn't **either.**

He didn't turn in his final paper. **Neither** did I.

so, not: used to respond to a question or comment

Is Liz working today? I think **so.** I don't think **so.**

How was your interview? Did it go well? I'm afraid **not.**

Will it rain? I hope **so.** I hope **not.**

Exercise 10 Read the following dialogue. Fill in the blanks using *too, so, either,* or *neither*. The first one has been done for you.

James: I completely forgot to do the assignment!

Kevin: ___So___ did I.
    1

James: Does this mean we're going to get a zero for the day?

Kevin: I'm afraid _____.
        2

James: Hey Kevin, you heard about Sherrie's party tonight? I'm not going.

Kevin: I'm not _____. By the way, didn't you have a job interview last week?
        3

James: Yep.

Kevin: Well? Did you get it? I hope _____.
                4

James: As a matter of fact, I did. I start next week.

Kevin: That's great. Listen, we'll all be at the mall by 7:00 p.m.

James: Oh, okay. I will _____. I'd like to see that new movie while we're there. I haven't
            5

seen any movies recently.

Kevin: _____ have I. Sounds like a plan! See you there.
    6

Exercise 11   Circle the letter of the correct answer. Be prepared to explain your answers.

1. Debbie ran off to join the circus? That makes _____ _____ sense. I don't get it. _____ do I.

   A. such ... little ... So

   B. such ... little ... Neither

   C. so ... few ... Neither

   D. so ... little ... Either

2. I _____ that everyone except you knew that Debbie was leaving.

   A. fell bad

   B. fell badly

   C. feel bad

   D. feel badly

3. _____ me a favor. Don't tell anyone about Debbie's decision. She might actually succeed! Then we'd all _____ bad.

   A. Do ... feel

   B. Make ... feel

   C. Do ... fell

   D. Make ... fell

4. How strange ... We talked to her only three weeks _____. At that time, she said that she would _____ leave her job for _____ one, even if it paid more.

   A. ago ... ever ... another

   B. before ... ever ... the other

   C. before ... never ... another

   D. ago ... never ... another

5. It's an interesting _____. She's always loved the circus. In fact, I _____ to the circus museum three times this year!

   A. history ... saw her to go

   B. story ... saw her to go

   C. story ... saw her go

   D. history ... saw her go

6. As a child, Debbie _____ dream about being a tightrope walker; she _____ me this last summer.

   A. was use to ... told

   B. used to ... told

   C. was used ... said

   D. used to ... said

7. Now don't take this wrong. I think Debbie's _____ time and energy joining the circus. She's _____ old to learn acrobatics!

   A. losing ... very

   B. losing ... too

   C. wasting ... very

   D. wasting ... too

8. One thing is certain: Debbie is following her dream. Not _____ people actually do this. They may _____ that they are going to do this one day, but Debbie actually _____ something to achieve her dream.

A. many ... say ... made   C. much ... tell ... made

B. much ... tell ... did   D. many ... say ... did

Exercise 12   Write a paragraph either (1) giving advice on staying healthy or (2) giving your opinion on an educational issue you are interested in. Before you begin, make a list of the words from this chapter that you will try to include. In your paragraph, underline the ones from the list you were able to use. Exchange paragraphs with a partner, and then check each other's work for correct use of confusing words.

_____

_____

_____

_____

_____

_____

_____

_____

_____

_____

_____

_____

_____

_____

_____

_____

_____

_____

_____

_____

_____

_____

20 Editing It All Together

Each of the four essays in this chapter highlights a particular type of grammatical error. In each case, read the entire essay before you complete the exercises.

20.1 Essay 1

Editing
⚠ Exercise 1 Verb Tense

Read the paragraph and decide whether each of the five underlined phrases is correct. Draw a line through any errors and write the correction above.

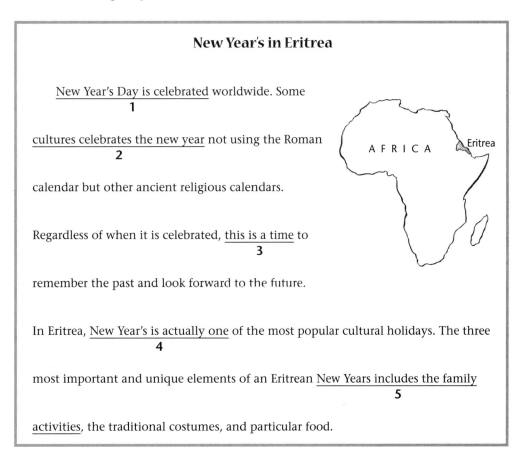

New Year's in Eritrea

New Year's Day is celebrated worldwide. Some
1

cultures celebrates the new year not using the Roman
2

calendar but other ancient religious calendars.

Regardless of when it is celebrated, this is a time to
3

remember the past and look forward to the future.

In Eritrea, New Year's is actually one of the most popular cultural holidays. The three
4

most important and unique elements of an Eritrean New Years includes the family
5

activities, the traditional costumes, and particular food.

AFRICA — Eritrea

Editing

⬆ Exercise 2   Verb Tense

Read the paragraph and decide whether each of the five underlined phrases is correct. Draw a line through any errors and write the correction above.

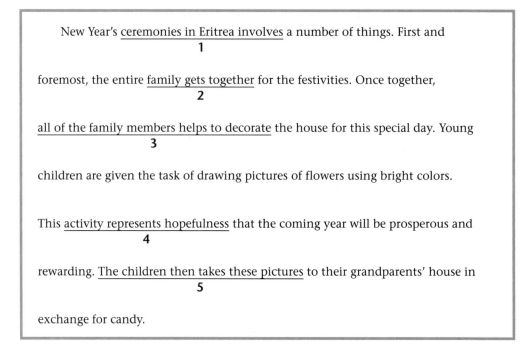

New Year's <u>ceremonies in Eritrea involves</u> a number of things. First and
1

foremost, the entire <u>family gets together</u> for the festivities. Once together,
2

<u>all of the family members helps to decorate</u> the house for this special day. Young
3

children are given the task of drawing pictures of flowers using bright colors.

This <u>activity represents hopefulness</u> that the coming year will be prosperous and
4

rewarding. <u>The children then takes these pictures</u> to their grandparents' house in
5

exchange for candy.

Editing

⬆ Exercise 3   Nouns and Pronouns

Read the paragraph and decide whether each of the five underlined phrases is correct. Draw a line through any errors and write the correction above.

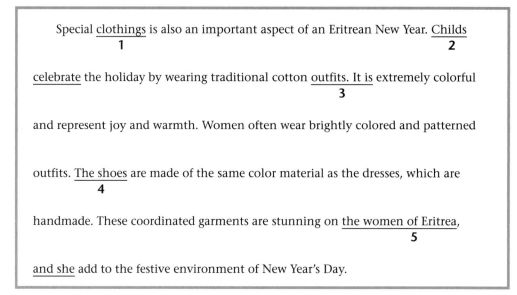

Special <u>clothings</u> is also an important aspect of an Eritrean New Year. <u>Childs</u>
1 2

<u>celebrate</u> the holiday by wearing traditional cotton <u>outfits. It is</u> extremely colorful
3

and represent joy and warmth. Women often wear brightly colored and patterned

outfits. <u>The shoes</u> are made of the same color material as the dresses, which are
4

handmade. These coordinated garments are stunning on <u>the women of Eritrea,</u>
5

<u>and she</u> add to the festive environment of New Year's Day.

Editing
⋀ Exercise 4   Subject-Verb Agreement and Prepositions

Read the paragraph and decide whether each of the five underlined phrases is correct.
Draw a line through any errors and write the correction above.

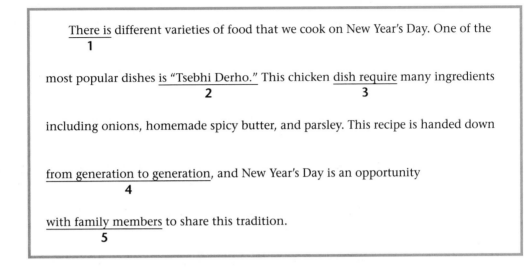

There is different varieties of food that we cook on New Year's Day. One of the
1

most popular dishes is "Tsebhi Derho." This chicken dish require many ingredients
2   3

including onions, homemade spicy butter, and parsley. This recipe is handed down

from generation to generation, and New Year's Day is an opportunity
4

with family members to share this tradition.
5

Editing
⋀ Exercise 5   Review: Subject-Verb Agreement, Prepositions, Nouns, and Pronouns

Read the paragraph and decide whether each of the five underlined phrases is correct.
Draw a line through any errors and write the correction above.

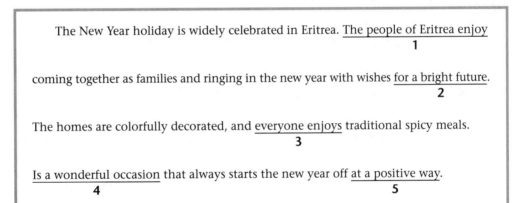

The New Year holiday is widely celebrated in Eritrea. The people of Eritrea enjoy
1

coming together as families and ringing in the new year with wishes for a bright future.
2

The homes are colorfully decorated, and everyone enjoys traditional spicy meals.
3

Is a wonderful occasion that always starts the new year off at a positive way.
4   5

special tutoring and one-on-one academic help. This is not the case at City College.

Without scholarships, many student athletes find little time to concentration on

their studies. They must make the difficulty choice of athletics or academics, and

many of them choice the former. As a result, their grades tend to suffer.

Editing
⚠ Exercise 8   Word Forms and Modals

This paragraph contains seven errors in word forms and/or modals. Find and correct
the errors.

Athletic scholarships may also to help students develop in their personal lives.

Student athletes has to be responsible for always striving to be the best. They have

pay close attention to their physically and mental healthy in order to compete

successfully. With the support of an athletic scholarship program, students could

has put more energy into developing interpersonal skills as well as academic and

athlete skills.

Editing
⚠ Exercise 9   Review: Subject-Verb Agreement, Prepositions, and Modals

This paragraph contains six errors in subject-verb agreement, prepositions, and/or modals.
Find and correct the errors.

Finally and most importantly, athletic scholarships can may help ease

the financial burden of attending college. With financially support, these

students wouldn't have to worry in finding the funds for tuition and books.

As a result, they could focus more on athletics and gain a competitive edge. The

benefits of completing a two-year degree is numerous, and if students not able to

receive the funding to complete this education, they will likely not be successful on

the future.

⚠ Exercise 10   Gerunds and Infinitives

This paragraph contains four errors in gerunds and infinitives. Find and correct the errors.

> Be a college student and athlete takes a lot of effort. There are many pressures overcoming. If community college athletes had access to scholarships, they would certainly excel. They would feel less academic, personal, and financial pressure. To succeeding in sports and education is a difficult task, but it can be done. College athletes love represent their school. They should have access to the same type of support systems that other college students receive. Above all, they should be treated with the same respect as other student athletes.

20.3   Essay 3

⚠ Exercise 11   Parallel Structure

This paragraph contains four errors in parallel structure. Find and correct the errors.

> **Teaching Today**
>
> Children spend the majority of their time in school. Children learn not only their ABCs in school, but also they learn their social and development skills. To this end, we need to ensure that our schools are doing the best they can to support the instructors and teaching our children. Unfortunately, some of our local schools are in need of improvement, specifically in recruiting new teachers, raise the academic standards, and improve facilities.

⚠Exercise 12 Passive Voice and Participial Adjectives

This paragraph contains five errors in passive voice and participial adjectives.
Find and correct the errors.

> A recent survey that was distribute by a local newspaper showed that our
> county's teachers are not satisfying in their professions. The single biggest lament
> was the issue of overcrowded classrooms. Obviously, the most logical way of
> handling this problem is to recruit more teachers. This objective needs to expand
> beyond the local level, however. From the Department of Education to state
> education offices and local universities, recruitment efforts need to be double in
> order to handle the issue of overcrowded. Recruits need to know that they will
> treated professionally and respectfully if they decide to enter the world of teaching.

⚠Exercise 13 Passive Voice and Word Order

This paragraph contains five errors in passive voice and/or word order. Find and correct the
errors.

> By reducing class size, teacher-student ratio will improve. The individual
> attention that given to students, particularly those in the elementary school, is led
> to better learning and achievement. In addition, students will be less likely to be
> distracting by their classmates. Rarely students say that they prefer larger classrooms
> with more classmates. To sum up, lower class size is mutually beneficial. Teachers
> feel more in control of the class and the content, and students are giving more one-
> on-one attention.

Exercise 14   Word Combinations

There are four blanks in this paragraph. Read the paragraph and write the correct preposition to complete each prepositional phrase. Use *in, with, to,* and *on*.

Finally, classroom facilities must be modern and accessible. For instance,

computers and up-to-date textbooks are integral in ensuring a quality school

environment and curriculum. Even those with limited experience _____ education
                                                                        1

can understand that. Students appreciate clean and well-stocked areas. We should

listen _____ them and take better care of our libraries and other common areas.
         2

Students rely _____ these resources, which in turn improve the general school
                  3

environment. A fully functional school environment increases students' pride in

the school and helps keep them motivated. By cooperating _____ each other,
                                                                4

upgrading our school resources shouldn't be so difficult.

**Exercise 15   Review: Subject-Verb Agreement, Verb Tense,
Pronoun, Parallel Structure, and Modals**

This paragraph contains six errors: one error in subject-verb agreement, one error in verb tense, two in pronoun usage, one in parallel structure, and one in the use of a modal. Find and correct the errors.

Our local schools need constant care and attention if it is going to succeed in

their mission of teaching our children. By focusing on teacher quality, how many

students are in the class, and the integrity of the classroom, we could have begin

to increase the success rates of our schools. To achieve our goal, however, we as a

community need to work together and never lose sight of the mission. It was the

least I can do for our children's future.

Editing
⌃ Exercise 16   Adjective Clauses

The following paragraph contains four errors with adjective clauses or adjective clause reductions. Find and correct the errors.

Why I Became a Social Worker

Although a variety of career choices is available, it is surprising that so many people manage to find the perfect career. Young adults, that get input from family, friends, professors, and the media, must think carefully about career possibilities. Regardless of how the choice is made, the fact that choosing the right career will have an impact on the rest of one's life places a heavy burden on each person attempts to cross this life hurdle. Therefore, making a  choice truly matches an individual's goals, personality, and skills is critical. I guess I was lucky to find a career what interested me. My personal decision to study social work comes from a combination of a number of different influences.

Editing
⌃ Exercise 17   Adjective and Adverb Clauses

Read the paragraph and decide whether each of the seven underlined phrases is correct. Draw a line through any errors and write the correction above.

It was easy for me to choose to study <u>social work, because</u> I have been passionate
                                              1

about helping people for as long as I can remember. <u>As growing up,</u> I remember
                                                         2

(continued)

helping my little brothers and sisters <u>when had problems</u>. <u>While I in high school</u>,
  3 4

I volunteered at local shelters and felt an especially close bond to those people

<u>who were socially disadvantaged</u>. More recently, I've been working with
  5

dysfunctional families, minority groups, and individuals. There is nothing more

satisfying than providing hope and encouragement to those <u>who need it the most</u>.
  6

<u>Despite the work is difficult</u>, I enjoy every minute of it.
  7

Editing

⚡ Exercise 18   Noun Clauses and Confusing Words

This paragraph contains six errors: two with noun clauses and four with confusing words. Find and correct the errors.

In college, I participated in a service-learning class that was connected to a sociology course. That experience helped me cement my interest in social work. My service area was working with drug-dependent adults who were housed in an institution. In addition to the research that I made in class, I visited the institution weekly. The patients needed so many help, not only to recover from their badly drug addiction but also to learn how to integrate into society. It was necessary that I to help them break the drug habit. I gave them resources to increase their self-esteem and their communication skills, both of which are important for people trying to return to normal life. In return, they shared memories and interesting histories. The most precious reward for me was hearing them say what I was helping them understand their troubles.

⌃Exercise 19   Review: Passive, Articles, Subject-Verb Agreement, and Confusing Words

This paragraph contains seven errors: two in passive voice, two in articles, one in subject-verb agreement, and two with confusing words. Find and correct the errors.

> I have also enjoyed my volunteer work, which included a visits to children's
>
> hospitals. In that hospital, I was exposing to children who had been mistreated,
>
> abused, and neglect. It was the pleasure to share time and activities with them and
>
> to serve them. Just spending this hours with them helped a lot. I had to reteach
>
> them that it was okay to relax and act like children. In the end, I think most of them
>
> was very relaxed with this experience.

⌃Exercise 20   Review: Adjective Clause, Parallel Structure, If-Clauses, and Gerund/Infinitive

This paragraph contains six errors: two in adjective clauses, two in parallel structure, one in if-clauses, and one in gerund/infinitive. Find and correct the errors.

> In conclusion, I think that many of my life experiences have led me to the path
>
> of social work. I attack each challenge who has the potential to drag me down with
>
> enthusiastic and determination. I want to continue to learning about social work
>
> and developing my skills. The salary which is low compared to many other careers
>
> in public health doesn't drive me. It's the feeling of satisfaction and the accomplish
>
> of helping others to improve their quality of life that drives me to become a social
>
> worker. If I did not become a social worker, I don't know what other profession
>
> I would have chosen. I cannot imagine what other profession could have suited my
>
> personality better.

Appendixes

1. Parts of Speech
2. Comparative and Superlative Forms of Adjectives and Adverbs
3. Irregular Verb Forms
4. Logical Connectors: Conjunctions and Transitions

1 Parts of Speech

1. Noun: the name of a person, place, thing, or idea

   - Count nouns: can be counted; can be singular and plural

   - Noncount (mass nouns): cannot be counted; have one singular form

     The **cashier** put the **cans** of **tuna** in a plastic **bag.**
         C   C   NC   C

2. Verb: a word that expresses action or state of being

   - Transitive verbs: have an object

   - Intransitive verbs: do not have an object

     The secretary **called** the travel agency, but the agent **had left.**
                    TV   IV

3. Pronoun: a word that can replace a noun

   - Subject pronouns: *I, you, he, she, it, we, you, they, who*

   - Object pronouns: *me, you, him, her, it, us, you, them, whom*

   - Possessive pronouns: *mine, yours, his, hers, ours, yours, theirs*

     He will not fix this problem. According to **him,** this problem is **mine.**
     SP   OP   POSS PRO

4. Adjective: a word that describes a noun or pronoun

   - Descriptive adjective (an adjective that gives a description or characteristic): *blue, old*

   - Demonstrative adjectives: *this, that, these, those*

   - Possessive adjectives: *my, your, his, her, its, our, your, their, whose*

   - Articles: *a, an, the, some*

     This green notebook belongs to **a** boy in **my** history class.
     DEM DESC   ART   POSS ADJ

5. Adverb: a word that modifies a verb, an adjective, a whole sentence, or another adverb

- Manner: (tells how) *quickly, slowly*

- Place: (tells where) *there, here*

- Time: (tells when) *yesterday, then*

- Frequency: (tells how often) *always, occasionally*

- Degree: (tells to what degree) *very, extremely*

  She **rarely** goes **there** except when it is **very** hot.
     FREQ   PLACE   DEGREE

6. Preposition: a word (or group of words) that connects nouns or pronouns to a sentence

   According to the paper, the wedding was **at** noon **on** March 25th.
     PREP   PREP   PREP

7. Conjunction: a word that links two clauses, two phrases, or two words

- Coordinating conjunction: connects two words, phrases, or independent clauses FANBOYS: *for, and, nor, but, or, yet, so*

- Subordinating conjunction: introduces a dependent clause: *when, if*

- Correlative conjunctions (paired): connect equivalent sentence parts: *both ... and ...*

  When the meeting ended, **neither** Jo **nor** Sue stood up first.
    SUB   CORR   CORR

8. Interjection: a word that expresses strong feelings or emotion

   Wow! Look at how fast that plane is moving!
    INT

2   Comparative and Superlative Forms of Adjectives and Adverbs

Comparative = used for two people or things

Superlative = used when there are three or more people or items to compare

Syllables	Neutral	Comparative	Superlative
one syllable	tall	taller	the tallest
two syllables ending in –*y*	hungry	hungrier	the hungriest
Others	handsome	more handsome	the most handsome
	quickly	more quickly	the most quickly
	cheaply	more cheaply	the most cheaply
Irregular	good	better	the best
	bad	worse	the worst
	far	farther	the farthest
	far	further	the furthest

Editing

⌃ Exercise 6   Articles

There are five blanks in this paragraph. Read the paragraph and write the articles *a, an, the,* or Ø to complete the sentences.

Athletic Scholarships

Many colleges offer _____ full athletic scholarships. However, most community
                     1

colleges do not participate in this type of program. City College is just one of

_____ many schools that do not offer athletic scholarships. As a result, student
2

athletes at _____ City College are forced to abandon _____ training program
             3   **4**

during their college years. Each City College athlete should be given _____
                                                                       5

athletic scholarship to help him or her academically, personally, and financially.

Editing

⌃ Exercise 7   Word Forms

This paragraph contains five errors in word forms. Find and correct the errors.

Athlete scholarships can help students succeed academically. When students

are lucky enough to get athletic scholarships, they can put equal emphasize on their

studies and sports training. At four-year universities, athletes also have access to

---

(continued)

3   Irregular Verb Forms

Present	Past	Past Participle	Present	Past	Past Participle
arise	arose	arisen	fall	fell	fallen
awake	awoke	awoken	feed	fed	fed
be	was/were	been	feel	felt	felt
bear	bore	born/borne	fight	fought	fought
beat	beat	beaten/beat	find	found	found
become	became	become	fit	fit	fit
begin	began	begun	flee	fled	fled
bend	bent	bent	fling	flung	flung
bet	bet	bet	fly	flew	flown
bid	bid	bid	forbid	forbade	forbidden
bind	bound	bound	forecast	forecast	forecast
bite	bit	bitten	foresee	foresaw	foreseen
bleed	bled	bled	foretell	foretold	foretold
blow	blew	blown	forget	forgot	forgotten
break	broke	broken	forgive	forgave	forgiven
bring	brought	brought	freeze	froze	frozen
broadcast	broadcast	broadcast	get	got	gotten
build	built	built	give	gave	given
burn	burned	burned	go	went	gone
burst	burst	burst	grind	ground	ground
buy	bought	bought	grow	grew	grown
cast	cast	cast	hang	hung	hung
catch	caught	caught	have	had	had
choose	chose	chosen	hear	heard	heard
cling	clung	clung	hide	hid	hidden
come	came	come	hit	hit	hit
cost	cost	cost	hold	held	hold
creep	crept	crept	hurt	hurt	hurt
cut	cut	cut	input	input	input
deal	dealt	dealt	keep	kept	kept
dig	dug	dug	kneel	knelt	knelt
dive	dove	dived	know	knew	known
do	did	done	lay	laid	laid
draw	drew	drawn	lead	led	led
dream	dreamed/dreamt	dreamed/dreamt	leave	left	left
drink	drank	drunk	lend	lent	lent
drive	drove	driven	let	let	let
eat	ate	eaten	lie	lay	lain

(continued)

Present	Past	Past Participle	Present	Past	Past Participle
light	lit/lighted	lit/lighted	sling	slung	slung
lose	lost	lost	slit	slit	slit
make	made	made	speak	spoke	spoken
mean	meant	meant	speed	sped	sped
meet	met	met	spend	spent	spent
mislead	misled	misled	spin	spun	spun
mistake	mistook	mistaken	split	split	split
misunderstand	misunderstood	misunderstood	spread	spread	spread
overcome	overcame	overcome	stand	stood	stood
overdo	overdid	overdone	steal	stole	stolen
override	overrode	overridden	stick	stuck	stuck
oversee	oversaw	overseen	stink	stank/stunk	stunk
oversleep	overslept	overslept	strike	struck	struck/stricken
overtake	overtook	overtaken	string	strung	strung
overthrow	overthrew	overthrown	strive	strove	striven
pay	paid	paid	swear	swore	sworn
prove	proved	proven/proved	sweep	swept	swept
put	put	put	swell	swelled	swollen
quit	quit	quit	swim	swam	swum
read	read	read	swing	swung	swung
ride	rode	ridden	take	took	taken
ring	rang	rung	teach	taught	taught
rise	rose	risen	tear	tore	torn
run	ran	run	tell	told	told
say	said	said	think	thought	thought
see	saw	seen	throw	threw	thrown
seek	sought	sought	thrust	thrust	thrust
sell	sold	sold	understand	understood	understood
send	sent	sent	undertake	undertook	undertaken
set	set	set	undo	undid	undone
sew	sewed	sewn/sewed	uphold	upheld	upheld
shake	shook	shaken	upset	upset	upset
shed	shed	shed	wake	woke	woken
shoot	shot	shot	wear	wore	worn
show	showed	shown/showed	weave	wove	woven
shrink	shrank	shrunk	weep	wept	wept
shut	shut	shut	wet	wet	wet
sing	sang	sung	win	won	won
sit	sat	sat	wind	wound	wound
sleep	slept	slept	withdraw	withdrew	withdrawn
slide	slid	slid	write	wrote	written

4 Logical Connectors: Conjunctions and Transitions

Using logical connectors—conjunctions and transitions—will help your ideas flow and develop your writing. Remember that when connectors occur at the beginning of a sentence, they are often followed by a comma.

Purpose	Conjunctions between independent clauses	Conjunctions that begin dependent clauses	Adverbial conjunctions/ Transitions (usually precede independent clauses)
examples			For example, To illustrate, Specifically, In particular,
extra information	, and		In addition, Moreover, Furthermore,
comparison		like	Similarly, Likewise, In the same way,
contrast	, but	while although unlike	In contrast, However, On the other hand, Conversely, Instead,
refutation			On the contrary,
concession	, yet	although though even though it may appear that	Nevertheless, Even so, Admittedly, Despite this,
emphasis			In fact, Actually,
clarification			In other words, In simpler words, More simply,
reason or cause	, for	because since	
result	, so	so so that	As a result, As a consequence, Consequently, Therefore, Thus,

(continued)

Purpose	Conjunctions between independent clauses	Conjunctions that begin dependent clauses	Adverbial conjunctions/ Transitions (usually precede independent clauses)
time relationships		after as soon as before when while until whenever as	Afterward, First, Second, Next, Then Finally, Subsequently, Meanwhile, In the meantime,
condition		if even if unless provided that when	
purpose		so that in order that	
choice	, or , nor		
conclusion			In conclusion, To summarize, As we have seen, In brief, In closing, To sum up, Finally,

Index